WILLIAM LLOYD GARRISON

The Abolitionist

BY

ARCHIBALD H. GRIMKE, M.A.

NEGRO UNIVERSITIES PRESS
NEW YORK

Originally published in 1891
by Funk & Wagnalls, New York

Reprinted 1969 by
Negro Universities Press
A Division of Greenwood Publishing Corp.
New York

SBN 8371-2190-6

PRINTED IN UNITED STATES OF AMERICA

To Mrs. Anna M. Day, who has been a mother to my little girl, and a sister to me, this book is gratefully and affectionately dedicated, by

Thl Author.

PREFACE.

THE author of this volume desires by way of preface to say just two things:—firstly, that it is his earnest hope that this record of a hero may be an aid to brave and true living in the Republic, so that the problems knocking at its door for solution may find the heads, the hands, and the hearts equal to the performance of the duties imposed by them upon the men and women of this generation. William Lloyd Garrison was brave and true. Bravery and truth were the secret of his marvelous career and achievements. May his countrymen and countrywomen imitate his example and be brave and true, not alone in emergent moments, but in everyday things as well.

So much for the author's firstly, now for his secondly, which is to acknowledge his large indebtedness in the preparation of this book to that storehouse of anti-slavery material, the story of the life of William Lloyd Garrison by his children. Out of its garnered riches he has filled his sack.

HYDE PARK, MASS., May 10, 1891.

CONTENTS.

Chapter XIX.

Chapter XX.

Chapter XXI.

WILLIAM LLOYD GARRISON.

CHAPTER I.

THE FATHER OF THE MAN.

WILLIAM LLOYD GARRISON was born in Newburyport, Massachusetts, December 10, 1805. Forty years before, Daniel Palmer, his great-grandfather, emigrated from Massachusetts and settled with three sons and a daughter on the St. John River, in Nova Scotia. The daughter's name was Mary, and it was she who was to be the future grandmother of our hero. One of the neighbors of Daniel Palmer was Joseph Garrison, who was probably an Englishman. He was certainly a bachelor. The Acadian solitude of five hundred acres and Mary Palmer's charms proved too much for the susceptible heart of Joseph Garrison. He wooed and won her, and on his thirtieth birthday she became his wife. The bride herself was but twenty-three, a woman of resources and of presence of mind, as she needed to be in that primitive settlement. Children and cares came apace to the young wife, and we may be sure confined her more and more closely to her house. But in the midst of a fast-increasing family and of multiplying cares a day's outing did occasionally come to the busy housewife, when she would go down the river to spend it at her father's farm. Once, ten years after her marriage, she had a narrow escape on one of those rare days. She had started in a boat with her youngest child, Abijah, and a lad who worked in her household. It was spring and the St. John was not yet clear of ice. Higher up the river the ice broke that morning and came floating down with the current. The boat in which Mary Garrison and her baby rode was overtaken by the fragments and wrecked. The mother with her child sought refuge on a piece of ice and was driven shoreward. Wrapping Abijah in all the clothes she could spare she threw him ashore. She and the lad followed by the aid of an overhanging willow bough. The baby was unharmed, for she had thrown him into a snow-bank. But the perils of the river gave place to the perils of the woods. In them Mary Garrison wandered with her infant, who was no less a personage than the father of William Lloyd Garrison, until at length she found the hut of a friendly Indian, who took her in and "entertained her with his best words and deeds, and the next morning conducted her safely to her father's."

The Palmers were a hardy, liberty-loving race of farmers, and Joseph Garrison was a man of unusual force and independence of character. The life which these early settlers lived was a life lived partly on the land and partly on the river. They were equally at home with scythe or oar. Amid such terraqueous conditions it was natural enough that the children should develop a passion for the sea. Like ducks many of them took to the water and became sailors. Abijah was a sailor. The amphibious habits of boyhood gave to his manhood a restless, roving character. Like the element which he loved he was in constant motion. He was a man of gifts both of mind and body. There was besides a strain of romance and adventure in his blood. By nature and his seafaring life he probably craved strong excitement. This craving was in part appeased no doubt by travel and drink. He took to the sea and he took to the cup. But he was more than a creature of appetites, he was a man of sentiment. Being a man of sentiment what should he do but fall in love. The woman who inspired his love was no ordinary woman, but a genuine Acadian beauty. She was a splendid specimen of womankind. Tall she was, graceful and admirably proportioned. Never before had Abijah in all his wanderings seen a creature of such charms of person. Her face matched the attractions of her form and her mind matched the beauty of her face. She possessed a nature almost Puritanic in its abhorrence of sin, and in the strength of its moral convictions. She feared to do wrong more than she feared any man. With this supremacy of the moral sense there went along singular firmness of purpose and independence of character. When a mere slip of a girl she was called upon to choose between regard for her religious convictions and regard for her family. It happened in this wise. Fanny Lloyd's parents were Episcopalians, who were inclined to view with contempt fellow-Christians of the Baptist persuasion. To have a child of theirs identify herself with this despised sect was one of those crosses which they could not and would not bear. But Fanny had in a fit of girlish frolic entered one of the meetings of these low-caste Christians. What she heard changed the current of her life. She knew thenceforth that God was no respecter of persons, and that the crucified Nazarene looked not upon the splendor of ceremonies but upon the thoughts of the heart of His disciples. Here in a barn, amid vulgar folk, and uncouth, dim surroundings, He had appeared, He, her Lord and Master. He had touched her with that white unspeakable appeal. The laughter died upon the fair girlish face and prayer issued from the beautiful lips. If vulgar folk, the despised Baptists, were good enough for the Christ, were they not good enough for her? Among them she had felt His consecrating touch and among them she determined to devote herself to Him. Her parents commanded and threatened but Fanny Lloyd was bent on obeying the heavenly voice of duty rather than father and mother. They had threatened that if she allowed herself to be baptised they would turn her out of doors. Fanny was baptised and her parents made good the threat. Their home was no longer her home. She had the courage of her conviction—ability to suffer for a belief.

Such was the woman who subsequently became the wife of Abijah Garrison, and the mother of one of the greatest moral heroes of the century. Abijah followed the sea, and she for several years with an increasing family followed Abijah. First from one place and then another she glided after him in her early married life. He loved her and his little ones but the love of travel and change was strong within him. He was ever restless and changeful. During one of his roving fits he emigrated with his family from Nova Scotia to the United States. It was in the spring of 1805 that he and they landed in Newburyport. The following December his wife presented him with a boy, whom they called William Lloyd Garrison. Three years afterward Abijah deserted his wife and children. Of the causes which led to this act nothing is now known. Soon after his arrival in Newburyport he had found employment. He made several voyages as sailing-master in 1805–8 from that port. He was apparently during these years successful after the manner of his craft. But he was not a man to remain long in one place. What was the immediate occasion of his strange behavior we can only conjecture. Possibly an increasing love for liquor had led to domestic differences, which his pleasure-loving nature would not brook. Certain it was that he was not like his wife. He was not a man in whom the moral sense was uppermost. He was governed by impulse and she by fixed moral and religious principles. He drank and she abhorred the habit. She tried first moral suasion to induce him to abandon the habit, and once, in a moment of wifely and motherly indignation, she broke up one of his drinking parties in her house by trying the efficacy of a little physical suasion. She turned the company out of doors and smashed the bottles of liquor. This was not the kind of woman whom Abijah cared to live with as a wife. He was not the sort of man whom the most romantic love could attach to the apron-strings of any woman. And in the matter of his cup he probably saw that this was what he would be obliged to do as the condition of domestic peace. The condition he rejected and, rejecting it, rejected and cast-off his wife and family and the legal and moral responsibilities of husband and father.

Bitter days now followed and Fanny Garrison became acquainted with grief and want. She had the mouths of three children to fill—the youngest an infant at her breast. The battle of this broken-hearted woman for their daily bread was as heroic as it was pathetic. She still lived in the little house on School street where Lloyd was born. The owner, Martha Farnham, proved herself a friend indeed to the poor harassed soul. Now she kept the wolf from the door by going out as a monthly nurse—"Aunt Farnham" looking after the little ones in her absence. She was put to all her possibles during those anxious years of struggle and want. Even Lloyd, wee bit of a boy, was pressed into the service. She would make molasses candies and send him upon the streets to sell them. But with all her industry and resource what could she do with three children weighing her down in the fierce struggle for existence, rendered tenfold fiercer after the industrial crisis preceding and following the War of 1812. Then it was that she was forced to supplement her scant earnings with refuse food from the table of "a certain mansion on State street." It was Lloyd who went for this food, and it was he who had to run the gauntlet of mischievous and inquisitive children whom he met and who longed for a peep into his tin pail. But the future apostle of non-resistance was intensely resistant, we may be sure, on such occasions. For, as his children have said in the story of his life: "Lloyd was a thorough boy, fond of games and of all boyish sport. Barefooted, he trundled his hoop all over Newburyport; he swam in the Merrimac in summer, and skated on it in winter; he was good at sculling a boat; he played at bat and ball and snowball, and sometimes led the 'Southend boys' against the Northenders in the numerous conflicts between the youngsters of the two sections; he was expert with marbles. Once, with a playmate, he swam across the river to 'Great Rock,' a distance of three-fourths of a mile and effected his return against the tide; and once, in winter, he nearly lost his life by breaking through the ice on the river and reached the shore only after a desperate struggle, the ice yielding as often as he attempted to climb upon its surface. It was favorite pastime of the boys of that day to swim from one wharf to another adjacent, where vessels from the West Indies discharged their freight of molasses, and there to indulge in stolen sweetness, extracted by a smooth stick inserted through the bung-hole. When detected and chased, they would plunge into the water and escape to the wharf on which they had left their clothes." Such was the little man with a boy's irrepressible passion for frolic and fun. His passion for music was hardly less pronounced, and this he inherited from his mother, and exercised to his heart's content in the choir of the Baptist Church. These were the bright lines and spots in his strenuous young life. He played and sang the gathering brood of cares out of his own and his mother's heart. He needed to play and he needed to sing to charm away from his spirit the vulture of poverty. That evil bird hovered ever over his childhood. It was able to do many hard things to him, break up his home, sunder him from his mother, force him at a tender age to earn his bread, still there was another bird in the boy's heart, which sang out of it the shadow and into it the sunshine. Whatever was his lot there sang the bird within his breast, and there shone the sun over his head and into his soul. The boy had unconsciously drawn around him a circle of sunbeams, and how could the vulture of poverty strike him with its wings or stab him with its beak. When he was about eight he was parted from his mother, she going to Lynn, and he, wee mite of a man, remaining in Newburyport. It was during the War of 1812, and pinching times, when Fanny Garrison was at her wit's end to keep the wolf from devouring her three little ones and herself into the bargain. With what tearing of the heart-strings she left Lloyd and his little sister Elizabeth behind we can now only imagine. She had no choice, poor soul, for unless she toiled they would starve. So with James, her eldest son, she went forth into the world to better theirs and her own condition. Lloyd went to live in Deacon Ezekiel Bartlett's family. They were good to the little fellow, but they, too, were poor. The Deacon, among other things, sawed wood for a living, and Lloyd hardly turned eight years, followed him in his peregrinations from house to house doing with his tiny hands what he could to help the kind old man. Soon Fanny Lloyd's health, which had supported her as a magic staff in all those bitter years since Abijah's desertion of wife and children, began in the battle for bread in

Lynn, to fail her. And so, in her weakness, and with a great fear in her heart for her babies, when she was gone from them into the dark unknown forever, she bethought her of making them as fast as possible self-supporting. And what better way was there than to have the boys learn some trade. James she had already apprenticed to learn the mystery of shoe-making. And for Lloyd she now sent and apprenticed him, too, to the same trade. Oh! but it was hard for the little man, the heavy lapstone and all this thumping and pounding to make a shoe. Oh! how the stiff waxen threads cut into his soft fingers, how all his body ached with the constrained position and the rough work of shoemaking. But one day the little nine-year-old, who was "not much bigger than a last," was able to produce a real shoe. Then it was probably that a dawning consciousness of power awoke within the child's mind. He himself by patience and industry had created a something where before was nothing. The eye of the boy got for the first time a glimpse of the man, who was still afar off, shadowy in the dim approaches of the hereafter. But the work proved altogether beyond the strength of the boy. The shoemaker's bench was not his place, and the making of shoes for his kind was not the mission for which he was sent into the world. And now again poverty, the great scene-shifter, steps upon the stage, and Fanny Lloyd and her two boys are in Baltimore on that never-ending quest for bread. She had gone to work in a shoe factory established by an enterprising Yankee in that city. The work lasted but a few months, when the proprietor failed and the factory was closed. In a strange city mother and children were left without employment. In her anxiety and distress a new trouble, the greatest and most poignant since Abïjah's desertion, wrung her with a supreme grief. James, the light and pride of her life, had run away from his master and gone to sea. Lloyd, poor little home-sick Lloyd, was the only consolation left the broken heart. And he did not want to live in Baltimore, and longed to return to Newburyport. So, mindful of her child's happiness, and all unmindful of her own, she sent him from her to Newburyport, which he loved inexpressibly. He was now in his eleventh year. Very happy he was to see once more the streets and landmarks of the old town—the river, and the old house where he was born, and the church next door and the school-house across the way and the dear friends whom he loved and who loved him. He went again to live with the Bartletts, doing with his might all that he could to earn his daily bread, and to repay the kindness of the dear old deacon and his family. It was at this time that he received his last scrap of schooling. He was, as we have seen, but eleven, but precious little of that brief and tender time had he been able to spend in a school-house. He had gone to the primary school, where, as his children tell us, he did not show himself "an apt scholar, being slow in mastering the alphabet, and surpassed even by his little sister Elizabeth." During his stay with Deacon Bartlett the first time, he was sent three months to the grammar-school, and now on his return to this good friend, a few more weeks were added to his scant school term. They proved the last of his school-days, and the boy went forth from the little brick building on the Mall to finish his education in the great workaday world, under those stern old masters, poverty and experience. By and by Lloyd was a second time apprenticed to learn a trade. It was to a cabinetmaker in Haverhill, Mass. He made good progress in the craft, but his young heart still turned to Newburyport and yearned for the friends left there. He bore up against the homesickness as best he could, and when he could bear it no longer, resolved to run away from the making of toy bureaus, to be once more with the Bartletts. He had partly executed this resolution, being several miles on the road to his old home, when his master, the cabinet-maker, caught up to him and returned him to Haverhill. But when he heard the little fellow's story of homesickness and yearning for loved places and faces, he was not angry with him, but did presently release him from his apprenticeship. And so the boy to his great joy found himself again in Newburyport and with the good old wood-sawyer. Poverty and experience were teaching the child what he never could have learned in a grammar-school, a certain acquaintance with himself and the world around him. There was growing within his breast a self-care and a self-reliance. It was the autumn of 1818, when, so to speak, the boy's primary education in the school of experience terminated, and he entered on the second stage of his training under the same rough tutelage. At the age of thirteen he entered the office of the Newburyport *Herald* to learn to set types. At last his boy's hands had found work which his boy's heart did joy to have done. He soon mastered the compositor's art, became a remarkably rapid composer. As he set up the thoughts of others, he was not slow in discovering thoughts of his own demanding utterance. The printer's apprentice felt the stirrings of a new life. A passion for self-improvement took possession of him. He began to read the English classics, study American history, follow the currents of party politics. No longer could it be said of him that he was not an apt pupil. He was indeed singularly apt. His intelligence quickened marvelously. The maturing process was sudden and swift. Almost before one knows it the boy in years has become a man in judgment and character. This precipitate development of the intellectual life in him, produced naturally enough an appreciable enlargement of the *ego.* The young eagle had abruptly awakened to the knowledge that he possessed wings; and wings were for use—to soar with. Ambition, the desire to mount aloft, touched and fired the boy's mind. As he read, studied, and observed, while his hands were busy with his work, there was a constant fluttering going on in the eyrie of his thoughts. By an instinct analogous to that which sends a duck to the water, the boy took to the discussion of public questions. It was as if an innate force was directing him toward his mission—the reformation of great public wrongs. At sixteen he made his first contribution to the press. It was a discussion of a quasi-social subject, the relation of the sexes in society. He was at the impressionable age, when the rosy god of love is at his tricks. He was also at a stage of development, when boys are least attractive, when they are disagreeably virile, full of their own importance and the superiority of their sex.

In the "Breach of the Marriage Promise," by "An Old Bachelor," these signs of adolescence are by no means wanting, they are, on the contrary, distinctly present and palpable. But there were other signs besides these, signs that the youth had had his eyes wide open to certain difficulties which beset the matrimonial state and to the conventional steps which lead to it, and that he had thought quite soberly, if not altogether wisely upon them. The writer was verdant, to be sure, and self-conscious, and partial in his view of the relations of the sexes, but there was withal a serious purpose in the writing. He meant to expose and correct what he conceived to be reprehensible conduct on the part of the gentler sex, bad feminine manners. Just now he sees the man's side of the shield, a few years later he will see the woman's side also. He ungallantly concludes "to lead the '*single life*,' and not," as he puts it, "trouble myself about the ladies." A most sapient conclusion, considering that this veteran misogynist was but sixteen years old. During the year following the publication of this article, he plied his pen with no little industry—producing in all fifteen articles on a variety of topics, such as "South American Affairs," "State Politics," "A Glance at Europe," etc., all of which are interesting now chiefly as showing the range of his growing intelligence, and as the earliest steps by which he acquired his later mastery of the pen and powerful style of composition. In a letter addressed to his mother about this time, the boy is full of Lloyd, undisguisedly proud of Lloyd, believes in Lloyd. "When I peruse them over" (*i. e.* those fifteen communications to the press), "I feel absolutely astonished," he naïvely confesses, "at the different subjects which I have discussed, and the style in which they are written. Indeed it is altogether a matter of surprise that I have met with such signal success, seeing I do not understand *one single rule of grammar*, and having a very inferior education." The printer's lad was plainly not lacking in the bump of approbativeness, or the quality of self-assertiveness. The quick mother instinct of Fanny Garrison took alarm at the tone of her boy's letter. Possibly there was something in Lloyd's florid sentences, in his facility of expression, which reminded her of Abijah. He, too, poor fellow, had had gifts in the use of the pen, and what had he done, what had he come to? Had he not forsaken wife and children by first forsaking the path of holiness? So she pricks the boy's bubble, and points him to the one thing needful—God in the soul. But in her closing words she betrays what we all along suspected, her own secret pleasure in her son's success, when she asks, "Will you be so kind as to bring on your pieces that you have written for me to see?" Ah! was she not every inch a mother, and how Lloyd did love her. But she was no longer what she had been. And no wonder, for few women have been called to endure such heavy burdens, fight so hopelessly the battle for bread, all the while her heart was breaking with grief. Disease had made terrible inroads upon her once strong and beautiful person. Not the shadow of the strength and beauty of her young womanhood remained. She was far away from her early home and friends, far away from her darling boy, in Baltimore. James, her pride, was at sea, Elizabeth, a sweet little maiden of twelve, had left her to take that last voyage beyond another sea, and Abijah, without one word of farewell, with the silence of long years unbroken, he, too, also! had hoisted sail and was gone forever. And now in her loneliness and sorrow, knowing that she, too, must shortly follow, a great yearning rose up in her poor wounded heart to see once more her child, the comfort and stay of her bitter life. And as she had written to him her wish and longing, the boy went to her, saw the striking change, saw that the broken spirit of the saintly woman was day by day nearing the margin of the dark hereafter, into whose healing waters it would bathe and be whole again. The unspeakable experience of mother and son, during this last meeting is not for you and me, reader, to look into. Soon after Lloyd's return to Newburyport a cancerous tumor developed on her shoulder, from the effects of which she died September 3, 1823, at the age of forty-five. More than a decade after her death her son wrote: "She has been dead almost eleven years; but my grief at her loss is as fresh and poignant now as it was at that period;" and he breaks out in praise of her personal charms in the following original lines:

"She was the masterpiece of womankind—
In shape and height majestically fine;
Her cheeks the lily and the rose combined;
Her lips—more opulently red than wine;
Her raven locks hung tastefully entwined;
Her aspect fair as Nature could design;
And then her eyes! so eloquently bright!
An eagle would recoil before her light."

The influence of this superb woman was a lasting power for truth and righteousness in the son's stormy life. For a whole year after her death, the grief of the printer's lad over his loss, seemed to have checked the activity of his pen. For during that period nothing of his appeared in the *Herald*. But after the sharp edge of his sorrow had worn off, his pen became active again in the discussion of public men and public questions. It was a period of bitter personal and political feuds and animosities. The ancient Federal party was *in articulo mortis*. The death-bed of a great political organization proves oftentimes the graveyard of lifelong friendships. For it is a scene of crimination and recrimination. And so it happened that the partisans of John Adams, and the partisans of John Adams's old Secretary of State, Timothy Pickering, were in 1824 doing a thriving business in this particular line. Into this funereal performance our printer's apprentice entered with pick and spade. He had thus early a *penchant* for controversy, a soldier's scent for battle. If there was any fighting going on he proceeded directly to have a hand in it. And it cannot be denied that that hand was beginning to deal some manly and sturdy blows, whose resound was heard quite distinctly beyond the limits of his birthplace. His communications appeared now, not only in the *Herald*, but in the Salem *Gazette* as well. Now it was the Adams-Pickering controversy, now the discussion of General Jackson as a presidential candidate, now the state of the country in respect of parties, now the merits of "American Writers," which afforded his 'prentice hand the requisite practice in the use of the pen. He had already acquired a perfect knowledge of typesetting and the mechanical makeup of a newspaper. During his apprenticeship he took his first lesson in the art of thinking on his feet in the presence of an audience. The audience to be sure were the members of a debating club, which he had organized. He was very ambitious and was doubtless looking forward to a political career. He saw the value of extempore speech to the man with a future, and he wisely determined to possess himself of its advantage. He little dreamt, however, to what great use he was to devote it in later years. There were other points worth noting at this time, and which seemed to prophecy for him a future of distinction. He possessed a most attractive personality. His energy and geniality, his keen sense of humor, his social and bouyant disposition, even his positive and opinionated temper, were sources of popular strength to him. People were strongly drawn to him. His friends were devoted to him. He had that quality, which we vaguely term magnetic, the quality of attaching others to us, and maintaining over them the ascendency of our character and ideas.

In the midst of all this progress along so many lines, the days of his apprenticeship in the *Herald* office came to an end. He was just twenty. With true Yankee enterprise and pluck, he proceeded to do for himself what for seven years he had helped to do for another—publish a newspaper. And with a brave heart the boy makes his launch on the uncertain sea of local journalism and becomes editor and publisher of a real, wide-awake sheet, which he calls the *Free Press.* The paper was independent in politics and proved worthy of its name during the six months that Garrison sat in the managerial chair. Here is the tone which the initial number of the paper holds to the public: "As to the political course of the *Free Press,* it shall be, in the widest sense of the term, *independent.* The publisher does not mean by this, to rank amongst those who are of everybody's and of nobody's opinion; . . . nor one of whom the old French proverb says: *Il ne soit sur quel pied danser.* [He knows not on which leg to dance.] Its principles shall be open, magnanimous and free. It shall be subservient to no party or body of men; and neither the craven fear of loss, nor the threats of the disappointed, nor the influence of power, shall ever awe one single opinion into silence. Honest and fair discussion it will court; and its columns will be open to all temperate and intelligent communications emanating from whatever political source. In fine we will say with Cicero: 'Reason shall prevail with him more than popular opinion.' They who like this avowal may extend their encouragement; and if any feel dissatisfied with it, they must act accordingly. The publisher cannot condescend to solicit their support." This was admirable enough in its way, but it was poor journalism some will say. And without doubt when judged by the common commercial standard it *was* poor journalism. In this view it is a remarkable production, but in another aspect it is still more remarkable in that it took with absolute accuracy the measure of the man. As a mental likeness it is simply perfect. At no time during his later life did the picture cease to be an exact moral representation of his character. It seems quite unnecessary, therefore, to record that he proceeded immediately to demonstrate that it was no high sounding and insincere declaration. For in the second number, he mentions with that singular serenity, which ever distinguished him on such occasions, the discontinuance of the paper on account of matter contained in the first issue, by ten indignant subscribers. "Nevertheless," he adds, "our happiness at the loss of such subscribers is not a whit abated. We *beg* no man's patronage, and shall ever erase with the same cheerfulness that we insert the name of any individual. . . . Personal or political offence we shall studiously avoid—truth *never*." Here was plainly a wholly new species of the *genus homo* in the editorial seat. What, expect to make a newspaper pay and not beg for patronage? Why the very idea was enough to make newspaperdom go to pieces with laughter. Begging for patronage, howling for subscribers, cringing, crawling, changing color like the chameleon, howling for Barabbas or bellowing against Jesus, all these things must your newspaper do to prosper. On them verily hang the whole law and all the profits of modern journalism. This is what the devil of competition was doing in that world when William Lloyd Garrison entered it. It took him up into an exceedingly high mountain, we may be certain, and offered him wealth, position, and power, if he would do what all others were doing. And he would not. He went on editing and publishing his paper for six months regardful only of what his reason approved—regardless always of the disapproval of others. Not once did he palter with his convictions or juggle with his self-respect for the sake of pelf or applause. His human horizon was contracted, to be sure. It could hardly be otherwise in one so young. His world was his country, and patriotism imposed limits upon his affections. "Our country, our whole country, and nothing but our country," was the ardent motto of the *Free Press.* The love of family comes, in the order of growth, before the love of country; and the love of country precedes the love of all mankind. "First the blade, then the ear, then the full corn in the ear," is the great law of love in the soul as of corn in the soil. Besides this contraction of the affections, there was also manifest in his first journalistic venture a deficiency in the organ of vision, a failure to see into things and their relations. What he saw he reported faithfully, suppressing nothing, adding nothing. But the objects which passed across the disk of his editoral intelligence were confined almost entirely to the surface of things, to the superficies of national life. He had not the ken at twenty to penetrate beneath the happenings of current politics. Of the existence of slavery as a supreme reality, we do not think that he then had the faintest suspicion. No shadow of its tremendous influence as a political power seemed to have arrested for a brief instant his attention. He could copy into his paper this atrocious sentiment which Edward Everett delivered in Congress, without the slightest comment or allusion. "Sir, I am no soldier. My habits and education are very unmilitary, but there is no cause in which I would sooner buckle a knapsack on my back, and put a musket on my shoulder than that of putting down a servile insurrection at the South."

The reason is plain enough. Slavery was a *terra incognito* to him then, a book of which he had not learned the A B C. Mr. Everett's language made no impression on him, because he had not the key to interpret its significance. What he saw, that he set down for his readers, without fear or favor. He had not seen slavery, knew nothing of the evil. Acquaintance with the deeper things of life, individual or national, comes only with increasing years, they are hardly for him who has not yet reached his majority. Slavery was the very deepest thing in the life of the nation sixty-four years ago. And if Garrison did not then so understand it, neither did his contemporaries, the wisest and greatest of them so understand it. The subject of all others which attracted his attention, and kept his editorial pen busy, was the claim of Massachusetts for indemnity from the general government, for certain disbursements made by her for the defence of her sea-coast during the war of 1812. This matter, which forms but a mere dust point in the perspective of history, his ardent young mind mistook for a principal object, erected into a permanent question in the politics of the times. But the expenditure of enormous energies upon things of secondary and of even tertiary importance, to the neglect of others of prime and lasting interest, is supremely human. He was errant where all men go astray. But the schoolmaster of the nation was abroad, and was training this young man for the work he was born to do. These six months were, therefore, not wasted, for in the university of experience he did ever prove himself an apt scholar. One lesson he had learned, which he never needed to relearn. Just what that lesson was, he tells in his valedictory to the subscribers of the *Free Press*, as follows: "This is a time-serving age; and he who attempts to walk uprightly or speak honestly, cannot rationally calculate upon speedy wealth or preferment." A sad lesson, to be sure, for one so young to learn so thoroughly. Perhaps some reader will say that this was cynical, the result of disappointment. But it was not cynical, neither was it the result of disappointment. It was unvarnished truth, and more's the pity, but truth it was none the less. It was one of those hard facts, which he of all men, needed to know at the threshold of his experience with the world. Such a revelation proves disastrous to the many who go down to do business in that world. Ordinary and weak and neutral moral constitutions are wrecked on this reef set in the human sea. Like a true mariner he had written it boldly on his chart. There at such and such a point in the voyage for the golden fleece, were the rocks and the soul-devouring dragons of the way. Therefore, oh! my soul, beware. What, indeed, would this argonaut of the press take in exchange for his soul? Certainly not speedy wealth nor preferment. Ah! he could not praise where he ought to reprobate; could not reprobate where praise should be the meed. He had no money and little learning, but he had a conscience and he knew that he must be true to that conscience, come to him either weal or woe. Want renders most men vulnerable, but to it, he appeared, at this early age, absolutely invulnerable. Should he and that almost omnipotent inquisitor, public opinion, ever in the future come into collision upon any principle of action, a keen student of human nature might forsee that the young recusant could never be starved into silence or conformity to popular standards. And with this stern, sad lesson treasured up in his heart, Garrison graduated from another room in the school-house of experience. All the discoveries of the young journalist were not of this grim character. He made another discovery altogether different, a real gem of its kind. The drag-net of a newspaper catches all sorts of poets and poetry, good, bad, and indifferent—oftener the bad and indifferent, rarely the good. The drag-net of the *Free Press* was no exception to this rule; but, one day, it fetched up from the depths of the hard commonplaces of our New England town life a genuine pearl. We will let Mr. Garrison tell the story in his own way:

"Going up-stairs to my office, one day, I observed a letter lying near the door, to my address; which, on opening, I found to contain an original piece of poetry for my paper, the *Free Press*. The ink was very pale, the handwriting very small; and, having at that time a horror of newspaper original poetry—which has rather increased than diminished with the lapse of time—my first impulse was to tear it in pieces, without reading it; the chances of rejection, after its perusal, being as ninety-nine to one; . . . but summoning resolution to read it, I was equally surprised and gratified to find it above mediocrity, and so gave it a place in my journal. . . . As I was anxious to find out the writer, my post-rider, one day, divulged the secret, stating that he had dropped the letter in the manner described, and that it was written by a

Quaker lad, named Whittier, who was daily at work on the shoemaker's bench, with hammer and lapstone, at East Haverhill. Jumping into a vehicle, I lost no time in driving to see the youthful rustic bard, who came into the room with shrinking diffidence, almost unable to speak, and blushing like a maiden. Giving him some words of encouragement, I addressed myself more particularly to his parents, and urged them with great earnestness to grant him every possible facility for the development of his remarkable genius."

Garrison had not only found a true poet, but a true friend as well, in the Quaker lad, John Greenleaf Whittier. The friendship which sprang up between the two was to last during the lifetime of the former. Neither of them in those days of small things could have possibly by any flight of the imagination foreseen how their two lives, moving in parallel lines, would run deep their shining furrows through one of the greatest chapters of human history. But I am anticipating, and that is a vice of which no good storyteller ought to be guilty. So, then, let me incontinently return from this excursion and pursue the even tenor of my tale.

Garrison had stepped down from his elevated position as the publisher and editor of the *Free Press.* He was without work, and, being penniless, it behooved him to find some means of support. With the instinct of the bright New England boy, he determined to seek his fortunes in Boston. If his honesty and independence put him at a disadvantage, as publisher and editor, in the struggle for existence, he had still his trade as a compositor to fall back upon

As a journeyman printer he would earn his bread, and preserve the integrity of an upright spirit. And so without a murmur, and with cheerfulness and persistency, he hunted for weeks on the streets of Boston for a chance to set types. This hunting for a job in a strange city was discouraging enough. Twice before had he visited the place, which was to be his future home. Once when on his way to Baltimore to see his mother, and once afterward when on a sort of pleasure tramp with three companions. But the slight knowledge which he was able to obtain of the town and its inhabitants under these circumstances did not now help him, when from office to office he went in quest of something to do. After many failures and renewed searchings, he found what he was after, an opportunity to practice his trade. Business was dull, which kept our journeyman printer on the wing; first at one and then at another printing office we find him setting types for a living during the year 1827. The winning of bread was no easy matter; but he was not ashamed to work, neither was he afraid of hard work. During this year, he found time to take a hand in a little practical politics. There was in July, 1827, a caucus of the Federal party to nominate a successor to Daniel Webster in the House of Representatives. Young Garrison attended this caucus, and made havoc of its cut and dried programme, by moving the nomination of Harrison Gray Otis, instead of the candidate, a Mr. Benjamin Gorham, agreed upon by the leaders. Harrison Gray Otis was one of Garrison's early and particular idols. He was, perhaps, the one Massachusetts politician whom the young Federalist had placed on a pedestal. And so on this occasion he went into the caucus with a written speech in his hat, eulogistic of his favorite. He had meant to have the speech at his tongue's end, and to get it off as if on the spur of the moment. But the speech stayed where it was put, in the speaker's hat, and failed to materialize where and when it was wanted on the speaker's tongue. As the mountain would not go to Mahomet, Mahomet like a sensible prophet went to the mountain. Our orator in imitation of this illustrious example, bowed to the inevitable and went to his mountain. Pulling his extempore remarks out of his hat, he delivered himself of them to such effect as to create quite an Otis sentiment in the meeting. This performance was, of course, a shocking offence in the eyes of those, whose plans it had disturbed. With one particular old fogy he got into something of a newspaper controversy in consequence. The "consummate assurance" of one so young fairly knocked the breath out of this Mr. Eminent Respectability; it was absolutely revolting to all his "ideas of propriety, to see a stranger, a man who never paid a tax in our city, and perhaps no where else, to possess the impudence to take the lead and nominate a candidate for the electors of Boston!" The "young gentleman of six months standing," was not a whit abashed or awed by the commotion which he had produced. That was simply a case of cause and effect. But he seemed in turn astonished at his opponent's evident ignorance of William Lloyd Garrison. "It is true," he replied, with the proud dignity of conscious power, "it is true that my acquaintance in this city is limited. I have sought none. Let me assure him, however, that if my life be spared, my name shall one day be known to the world—at least to such extent that common inquiry shall be unnecessary. This, I know will be deemed excessive vanity—but time shall prove it prophetic." To the charge of youth he makes this stinging rejoinder, which evinces the progress he was making in the tournament of language: "The little, paltry sneers at my youth by your correspondent have long since become pointless. It is the privileged abuse of old age—the hackneyed allegation of a thousand centuries—the damning *crime* to which all men have been subjected. I leave it to metaphysicians to determine the precise moment when wisdom and experience leap into existence, when, for the first time, the mind distinguishes truth from error, selfishness from patriotism, and passion from reason. It is sufficient for me that I am understood." This was Garrison's first experience with "gentlemen of property and standing" in Boston. It was not his last, as future chapters will abundantly show.

CHAPTER II.

THE MAN HEARS A VOICE: SAMUEL, SAMUEL!

THERE is a moment in the life of every serious soul, when things, which were before unseen and unheard in the world around him become visible and audible. This startling moment comes to some sooner, to others later, but to all, who are not totally given up to the service of self, at sometime surely. From that moment a change passes over such an one, for more and more he hears mysterious voices, and clearer and more clear he sees apparitional forms floating up from the depths above which he kneels. Whence come they, what mean they? He leans over the abyss, and lo! the sounds to which he hearkens are the voices of human weeping and the forms at which he gazes are the apparitions of human woe; they beckon to him, and the voices beseech him in multitudinous accent and heart-break: "Come over, come down, oh! friend and brother, and help us." Then he straightway puts away the things and the thoughts of the past and girding himself with the things, and the thoughts of the divine OUGHT and the almighty MUST, he goes over and down to the rescue.

Such an epochal first moment came to William Lloyd Garrison in the streets of Boston. Amid the hard struggle for bread he heard the abysmal voices, saw the gaunt forms of misery. He was a constant witness of the ravages of the demon of drink—saw how strong men succumbed, and weak ones turned to brutes in its clutch. And were they not his brothers, the strong men and the weak ones alike? And how could he, their keeper, see them desperately beset and not fly to their help? Ah! he could not and did not walk by on the other side, but, stripling though he was, rushed to do battle with the giant vice, which was slaying the souls and the bodies of his fellow citizens. Rum during the three first decades of the present century was, like death, no respecter of persons, entering with equal freedom the homes of the rich, and the hovels of the poor. It was in universal demand by all classes and conditions of men. No occasion was esteemed too sacred for its presence and use. It was an honored guest at a wedding, a christening, or a funeral. The minister whose hands were laid in baptismal blessing on babes, or raised in the holy sacrament of love over brides, lifted also the glass; and the selfsame lips which had spoken the last words over the dead, drank and made merry presently afterward among the decanters on the sideboard. It mattered not for what the building was intended—whether for church, school, or parsonage, rum was the grand master of ceremonies, the indispensable celebrant at the various stages of its completion. The party who dug the parson out after a snow-storm, verily got their reward, a sort of prelibation of the visionary sweets of that land, flowing not, according to the Jewish notion, with milk and *honey*, but according to the revised version of Yankeedom, with milk and *rum*. Rum was, forsooth, a very decent devil, if judged by the exalted character of the company it kept. It stood high on the rungs of the social ladder and pulled and pushed men from it by thousands to wretchedness and ruin. So flagrant and universal was the drinking customs of Boston then that dealers offered on the commons during holidays, without let or hindrance, the drunkard's glass to the crowds thronging by extemporized booths and bars. Shocking as was the excesses of this period "nothing comparatively was heard on the subject of intemperance—it was seldom a theme for the essayist—the newspapers scarcely acknowledged its existence, excepting occasionally in connection with some catastrophes or crimes—the Christian and patriot, while they perceived its ravages, formed no plans for its overthrow—and it did not occur to any that a paper devoted mainly to its suppression, might be made a direct and successful engine in the great work of reform. Private expostulations and individual confessions were indeed sometimes made; but no systematic efforts were adopted to give precision to the views or a bias to the sentiments of the people." Such was the state of public morals and the state of public sentiment up to the year 1826, when there occurred a change. This change was brought about chiefly through the instrumentality of a Baptist city missionary, the Rev. William Collier. His labors among the poor of Boston had doubtless revealed to him the bestial character of intemperance, and the necessity of doing something to check and put an end to the havoc it was working. With this design he established the *National Philanthropist* in Boston, March 4, 1826. The editor was one of Garrison's earliest acquaintances in the city. Garrison went after awhile to board with him, and still later entered the office of the *Philanthropist* as a type-setter. The printer of the paper, Nathaniel H. White and young Garrison, occupied the same room at Mr. Collier's. And so almost before our hero was aware, he had launched his bark upon the sea of the temperance reform. Presently, when the founder of the paper retired, it seemed the most natural thing in the world, that the young journeyman printer, with his editorial experience and ability, should succeed him as editor. His room-mate, White, bought the *Philanthropist*, and in April 1828, formally installed Garrison into its editorship. Into this new work he carried all his moral earnestness and enthusiasm of purpose. The paper grew under his hand in size, typographical appearance, and in editorial force and capacity. It was a wide-awake sentinel on the wall of society; and week after week its columns bristled and flashed with apposite facts, telling arguments, shrewd suggestions, cogent appeals to the community to destroy the accursed thing. No better education could he have had as the preparation for his life work. He began to understand then the strength of deep-seated public evils, to acquaint himself with the methods and instruments with which to attack them. The *Philanthropist* was a sort of forerunner, so far as the training in intelligent and effective agitation was concerned, of the *Genius of Universal Emancipation* and of the *Liberator*. One cannot read his sketch of the progress made by the temperance reform, from which I have already quoted, and published by him in the *Philanthropist* in April, 1828, without being struck by the strong similitude of the temperance to the anti-slavery movement in their beginnings. "When this paper was first proposed," the young temperance editor records, "it met with a repulsion which would have utterly discouraged a less zealous and persevering man than our predecessor. The moralist looked on doubtfully—the whole community esteemed the enterprise desperate. Mountains of prejudice, overtopping the Alps, were to be beaten down to a level—strong interest, connected by a thousand links, severed—new habits formed; Every house, and almost every individual, in a greater or less degree, reclaimed. Derision and contumely were busy in crushing this sublime project in its birth—coldness and apathy encompassed it on every side—but our predecessor, nevertheless, went boldly forward with a giant's strength and more than a giant's heart—conscious of difficulties and perils, though not disheartened, armed with the weapons of truth—full of meekness, yet certain of a splendid victory—and relying on the promises of God for the issue." What an inestimable object-lesson to Garrison was the example of this good man going forth singlehanded to do battle with one of the greatest evils of the age! It was not numerical strength, but the faith of one earnest soul that is able in the world of ideas and human passions to remove mountains out of the way of the onward march of mankind. This truth, we may be sure, sunk many fathoms deep into the mind of the young moralist. And no wonder. For the results of two years agitation and seed sowing were of the most astonishing character. "The change which has taken place in public sentiment," he continues, "is indeed remarkable . . . incorporated as intemperance *was*, and still *is*, into our very existence as a people. . . . A regenerating spirit is everywhere seen; a strong impulse to action has been given, which, beginning in the breasts of a few individuals, and then affecting villages, and cities, and finally whole States, has rolled onward triumphantly through the remotest sections of the republic. As union and example are the levers adopted to remove this gigantic vice, temperance societies have been rapidly multiplied, many on the principle of entire abstinence, and others making it a duty to abstain from encouraging the distillation and consumption of spirituous liquors. Expressions of the deep abhorrence and sympathy which are felt in regard to the awful prevalence of drunkenness are constantly emanating from legislative bodies down to various religious conventions, medical associations, grand juries, etc., etc. But nothing has more clearly evinced the strength of this excitement than the general interest taken in this subject by the conductors of the press. From Maine to the Mississippi, and as far as printing has penetrated—even among the Cherokee Indians—but one sentiment seems to pervade the public papers, viz., the necessity of strenuous exertion for the suppression of intemperance." Such a demonstration of the tremendous power of a single righteous soul for good, we may be sure, exerted upon Garrison lasting influences. What a revelation it was also of the transcendent part which the press was capable of playing in the revolution of popular sentiment upon moral questions; and of the supreme service of organization as a factor in reformatory movements. The seeds sowed were faith in the convictions of one man against the opinions, the prejudices, and the practices of the multitude; and knowledge of and skill in the use of the instruments by which the individual conscience may be made to correct and renovate the moral sense of a nation. But there was another seed corn dropped at this time in his mind, and that is the immense utility of woman in the work of regenerating society. She it is who feels even more than man the effects of social vices and sins, and to her the moral reformer should strenuously appeal for aid. And this, with the instinct of genius, Garrison did in the temperance reform, nearly seventy years ago. His editorials in the *Philanthropist* in the year 1828 on "Female Influence" may be said to be the *courier avant* of the Woman's Christian Temperance Union of to-day, as they were certainly the precursors of the female anti-slavery societies of a few years later.

But now, without his knowing it, a stranger from a distant city entered Boston with a message, which was to change the whole purpose of the young editor's life. It was Benjamin Lundy, the indefatigable friend of the Southern slave, the man who carried within his breast the whole menagerie of Southern slavery. He was fresh from the city which held the dust of Fanny Garrison, who had once written to her boy in Newburyport, how the good God had cared for her in the person of a colored woman. Yes, she had written: "The ladies are all kind to me, and I have a colored woman that waits on me, that is so kind no one can tell how kind she is; and although a slave to man, yet a free-born soul, by the grace of God. Her name is Henny, and should I never see you again, and you should come where she is, remember her, for your poor mother's sake." And now, without his dreaming of it, this devoted Samaritan in black, who, perhaps, had long ago joined her dear friend in the grave, was coming to that very boy, now grown to manhood, to claim for her race what the mother had asked for her, the kind slave-woman. Not one of all those little ones of the nation but who had a home in the many-mansioned heart of Lundy. He had been an eye and ear witness of the barbarism of slavery. "My heart," he sobbed, "was deeply grieved at the gross abomination; I heard the wail of the captive; I felt his pang of distress, and the iron entered my soul." With apostolic faith and zeal he had for a decade been striving to free the captive, and to tie up his bruised spirit. Sadly, but with a great love, he had gone about the country on his self-imposed task. To do this work he had given up the business of a saddler, in which he had prospered, had sacrificed his possessions, and renounced the ease that comes with wealth; had courted unheard-of hardships, and wedded himself for better and worse to poverty and unremitting endeavor. Nothing did he esteem too dear to relinquish for the slave. Neither wife nor children did he withhold. Neither the summer's heat nor the winter's cold was able to daunt him or turn him from his object. Though diminutive and delicate of body, no distance or difficulty of travel was ever able to deter him from doing what his humanity had bidden him do. From place to place, through nineteen States, he had traveled, sowing as he went the seeds of his holy purpose, and watering them with his life's blood. Not Livingstone nor Stanley on the dark continent exceeded in sheer physical exertion and endurance the labors of this wonderful man. He belongs in the category of great explorers, only the irresistible passion and purpose, which pushed him forward, had humanity, not geography, as their goal. Where, in the lives of either Stanley or Livingstone do we find a record of more astonishing activity and achievement than what is contained in these sentences, written by Garrison of Lundy, in the winter of 1828? "Within a few months he has traveled about twenty-four hundred miles, of which upwards of nineteen hundred were performed *on foot!* during which time he has held nearly fifty public meetings. Rivers and mountains vanish in his path; midnight finds him wending his solitary way over an unfrequented road; the sun is anticipated in his rising. Never was moral sublimity of character better illustrated." Such was the marvelous man, whose visit to Boston, in the month of March, of the year 1828, dates the beginning of a new epoch in the history of America. The event of that year was not the "Bill of Abominations," great as was the national excitement which it produced; nor was it yet the then impending political struggle between Jackson and Adams, but the unnoticed meeting of Lundy and Garrison. Great historic movements are born not in the whirlwinds, the earthquakes, and the pomps of human splendor and power, but in the agonies and enthusiasms of grand, heroic spirits. Up to this time Garrison had had, as the religious revivalist would say, no "realizing sense" of the enormity of slave-holding. Occasionally an utterance had dropped from his pen which indicated that his heart was right on the subject, but which evinced no more than the ordinary opposition to its existence, nor any profound convictions as to his own or the nation's duty in regard to its extinction. His first reference to the question appeared in connection with a notice made by him in the *Free Press* of a spirited poem, entitled "Africa," in which the authoress sings of:

> "The wild and mingling groans of writhing millions,
> Calling for vengeance on my guilty land."

He commended the verses "to all those who wish to cherish female genius, and whose best feelings are enlisted in the cause of the poor oppressed sons of Africa." He was evidently impressed, but the impression belonged to the ordinary, transitory sort. His next recorded utterance on the subject was also in the *Free Press.* It was made in relation with some just and admirable strictures on the regulation Fourth of July oration, with its "ceaseless apostrophes to liberty, and fierce denunciations of tyranny." Such a tone was false and mischievous—the occasion was for other and graver matter. "There is one theme," he declares, "which should be dwelt upon, till our whole country is free from the curse—it is slavery." The emphasis and energy of the rebuke and exhortation lifts this second allusion to slavery, quite outside of merely ordinary occurrences. It was not an ordinary personal occurrence for it served to reveal in its lightning-like flash the glow and glare of a conscience taking fire. The fire slumbered until a few weeks before Lundy entered Boston, when there were again the glow and glare of a moral sense in the first stages of ignition on the enormity of slave institutions. The act of South Carolina in making it illegal to teach a colored person to read and write struck this spark from his pen: "There is something unspeakably pitiable and alarming," he writes in the *Philanthropist*, "in the state of that society where it is deemed necessary, for self-preservation, to seal up the mind and debase the intellect of man to brutal incapacity. . . . Truly the alternatives of oppression are terrible. But this state of things cannot always last, nor ignorance alone shield us from destruction." His interest in the question was clearly growing. But it was still in the gristle of sentiment waiting to be transmuted into the bone and muscle of a definite and determined purpose, when first he met Lundy. This meeting of the two men, was to Garrison what the fourth call of God was to Samuel, the Hebrew lad, who afterward became a prophet. As the three previous calls of God and the conversations with Eli had prepared the Jewish boy to receive and understand the next summons of Jehovah, so had Garrison's former experience and education made him ready for the divine message when uttered in his ears by Lundy. All the sense of truth and the passion for righteousness of the young man replied to the voice, "Here am I." The hardening process of growth became immediately manifest in him. Whereas before there was sentimental opposition to slavery, there began then an opposition, active and practical. When Lundy convened many of the ministers of the city to expose to them the barbarism of slavery, Garrison sat in the room, and as

Lundy himself records, "expressed his approbation of my doctrines." The young reformer must needs stand up and make public profession of his new faith and of his agreement with the anti-slavery principles of the older. But it was altogether different with the assembled ministers. Lundy, as was his wont on such occasions, desired and urged the formation of an anti-slavery society, but these sons of Eli of that generation were not willing to offend their slave-holding brethren in the South. Eyes they had, but they refused to see; ears, which they stopped to the cry of the slave breaking in anguish and appeal from the lips of this modern man of God. Garrison, eleven years later, after the lips, which were eloquent then with their great sorrow, were speechless in the grave, told the story of that ministers' meeting. And here is the story:

"He (Lundy) might as well have urged the stones in the streets to cry out in behalf of the perishing captives. Oh, the moral cowardice, the chilling apathy, the criminal unbelief, the cruel skepticism, that were revealed on that memorable occasion! My soul was on fire then, as it is now, in view of such a development. Every soul in the room was heartily opposed to slavery, but, it would terribly alarm and enrage the South to know that an anti-slavery society existed in Boston. But it would do harm rather than good openly to agitate the subject. But *perhaps a select* committee might be formed, to be called by some name that would neither give offence, nor excite suspicion as to its real design! One or two only were for bold and decisive action; but as they had neither station nor influence, and did not rank among the wise and prudent, their opinion did not weigh very heavily, and the project was finally abandoned. Poor Lundy! that meeting was a damper to his feelings." There is no doubt that Garrison was one of the very few present, who "were for bold and decisive action" against the iniquity. The grief and disappointment of his brave friend touched his heart with a brother's affection and pity. The worldly wisdom and lukewarmness of the clergy kindled a righteous indignation within his freedom-loving soul. This was his first bitter lesson from the clergy. There were, alas, many and bitterer experiences to follow, but of them he little recked at the time. As this nineteenth-century prophet mused upon the horrible thing the fires of a life purpose burned within him. And oftener thenceforth we catch glimpses of the glow and glare of a soul bursting into flame. The editorials in the *Philanthropist*, which swiftly followed Lundy's visit, began to throw off more heat as the revolving wheels of an electrical machine throw off sparks. The evil that there was in the world, under which, wherever he turned, he saw his brother man staggering and bleeding, was no longer what it had been, a vague and shadowy apparition, but rather a terrible and tremendous reality against which he must go forth to fight the fight of a lifetime. And so he girded him with his life purpose and flung his moral earnestness against the triple-headed curse of intemperance, slavery, and war. A mighty human love had begun to flow inward and over him. And as the tide steadily rose it swallowed and drowned all the egoism of self and race in the altruism of an all-embracing humanity. When an apprentice in the office of the Newburyport

Herald, and writing on the subject of South American affairs he grew hot over the wrongs suffered by American vessels at Valparaiso and Lima. He was for finishing "with cannon what cannot be done in a conciliatory and equitable manner, where justice demands such proceedings." This was at seventeen when he was a boy with the thoughts of a boy. Six years later he is a man who has looked upon the sorrows of men. His old boy-world is far behind him, and the ever-present sufferings of his kind are in front of him. War now is no longer glorious, for it adds immeasurably to the sum of human misery. War ought to be abolished with intemperance and slavery. And this duty he began to utter in the ears of his country. "The brightest traits in the American character will derive their luster, not from the laurels picked from the field of blood, not from the magnitude of our navy and the success of our arms," he proclaimed, "but from our exertions to banish war from the earth, to stay the ravages of intemperance among all that is beautiful and fair, to unfetter those who have been enthralled by chains, which we have forged, and to spread the light of knowledge and religious liberty, wherever darkness and superstition reign. . . . The struggle is full of sublimity, the conquest embraces the world." Lundy himself did not fully appreciate the immense gain, which his cause had made in the conversion of Garrison into an active friend of the slave. Not at once certainly. Later he knew. The discovery of a kindred spirit in Boston exerted probably no little influence in turning for the second time his indefatigable feet toward that city. He made it a second visit in July, 1828, where again he met Garrison. His experience with the ministers did not deter him from repeating the horrible tale wherever he could get together an audience. This time he secured his first public hearing in Boston. It was in the Federal Street Baptist Church. He spoke not only on the subject of slavery itself, the growth of anti-slavery societies, but on a new phase of the general subject, viz., the futility of the Colonization Society as an abolition instrument. Garrison was present, and treasured up in his heart the words of his friend. He did not forget how Lundy had pressed upon his hearers the importance of petitioning Congress for the abolition of slavery in the District of Columbia, as we shall see further on. But poor Lundy was unfortunate with the ministers. He got this time not the cold shoulder alone but a clerical slap in the face as well. He had just sat down when the pastor of the church, Rev. Howard Malcolm, uprose in wrath and inveighed against any intermeddling of the North with slavery, and brought the meeting with a high hand to a close. This incident was the first collision with the church of the forlorn hope of the Abolition movement. Trained as Garrison was in the orthodox creed and sound in that creed almost to bigotry, this behavior of a standard-bearer of the church, together with the apathy displayed by the clergy on a former occasion, caused probably the first "little rift within the lute" of his creed, "that by and by will make the music mute, and, ever widening, slowly silence all." For in religion as in love, "Unfaith in aught is want of faith in all." The Rev. Howard Malcolm's arbitrary proceeding had prevented the organization of an anti-slavery committee.

But this was affected at a second meeting of the friends of the slave. Garrison was one of the twenty gentlemen who were appointed such a committee. His zeal and energy far exceeded the zeal and energy of the remaining nineteen. He did not need the earnest exhortation of Lundy to impress upon his memory the importance of "activity and steady perseverance." He perceived almost at once that everything depended on them. And so he had formed plans for a vigorous campaign against the existence of slavery in the District of Columbia. But before he was ready to set out along the line of work, which he had laid down for Massachusetts, the scene of his labors shifted to Bennington, Vermont. Before he left Boston, Lundy had recognized him as "a valuable coadjutor." The relationship between the two men was becoming beautifully close. The more Lundy saw of Garrison, the more he must have seemed to him a man after his own heart. And so no wonder that he was solicitous of fastening him to his cause with hooks of steel. The older had written the younger reformer a letter almost paternal in tone—he must do thus and thus, he must not be disappointed if he finds the heavy end of the burthen borne by himself, while those associated with him do little to keep the wheels moving, he must remember that "a few will have the labor to perform and the honor to share." Then there creeps into his words a grain of doubt, a vague fear lest his young ally should take his hands from the plough and go the way of all men, and here are the words which Paul might have written to Timothy: "I hope you will persevere in your work, steadily, but not make too large calculations on what may be accomplished in a particularly stated time. You have now girded on a holy warfare. Lay not down your weapons until honorable terms are obtained. *The God of hosts is on your side.* Steadiness and faithfulness will most assuredly overcome every obstacle." The older apostle had yet to learn that the younger always did what he undertook in the field of morals and philanthropy.

But the scene had shifted from Boston to Bennington, and with the young reformer goes also his plan of campaign for anti-slavery work. The committee of twenty, now nineteen since his departure, slumbered and slept in the land of benevolent intentions, a practical illustration of Lundy's pungent saying, that "philanthropists are the slowest creatures breathing. They think forty times before they act." The committee never acted, but its one member in Vermont did act, and that promptly and powerfully as shall shortly appear. Garrison had gone to Bennington to edit the *Journal of the Times* in the interest of the reëlection of John Quincy Adams to the Presidency. For this object he was engaged as editor of the paper. What he was engaged to do he performed faithfully and ably, but along with his fulfillment of his contract with the friends of Mr. Adams, he carried the one which he had made with humanity likewise. In his salutatory he outlined his intentions in this regard thus: "We have three objects in view, which we shall pursue through life, whether in this place or elsewhere—namely, the suppression of intemperance and its associate vices, the gradual emancipation of every slave in the republic, and the perpetuity of national peace. In discussing these topics what is wanting in vigor shall be made up in zeal." From the issue of that first number if the friends of Adams had no cause to complain of the character of his zeal and vigor in their service, neither had the friends of humanity. What he had proposed doing in Massachusetts as a member of the anti-slavery committee of twenty, he performed with remarkable energy and success in Vermont. It was to obtain signatures not by the hundred to a petition for the abolition of slavery in the District of Columbia, but by the thousands, and that from all parts of the State. He sent copies of the petition to every postmaster in Vermont with the request that he obtain signatures in his neighborhood. Through his exertions a public meeting of citizens of Bennington was held and indorsed the petition. The plan for polling the anti-slavery sentiment of the State worked admirably. The result was a monster petition with 2,352 names appended. This he forwarded to the seat of Government. It was a powerful prayer, but as to its effect, Garrison had no delusions. He possessed even then singularly clear ideas as to how the South would receive such petitions, and of the course which it would pursue to discourage their presentation. He was no less clear as to how the friends of freedom ought to carry themselves under the circumstances. In the *Journal of the Times* of November, 1828, he thus expressed himself: "It requires no spirit of prophecy to predict that it (the petition) will create great opposition. An attempt will be made to frighten Northern 'dough-faces' as in case of the Missouri question. There will be an abundance of furious declamation, menace, and taunt. Are we, therefore, to approach the subject timidly—with half a heart—as if we were treading on forbidden ground? No, indeed, but earnestly, fearlessly, as becomes men, who are determined to clear their country and themselves from the guilt of oppressing God's free and lawful creatures." About the same time he began to make his assaults on the personal representatives of the slave-power in Congress, cauterizing in the first instance three Northern "dough-faces," who had voted against some resolutions, looking to the abolition of the slave-trade and slavery itself in the District of Columbia. So while the South thus early was seeking to frighten the North from the agitation of the slavery question in Congress, Garrison was unconsciously preparing a countercheck by making it dangerous for a Northern man to practice Southern principles in the National Legislature. He did not mince his words, but called a spade a spade, and sin, sin. He perceived at once that if he would kill the sin of slaveholding, he could not spare the sinner. And so he spoke the names of the deliquents from the housetop of the *Journal of the Times*, stamping upon their brows the scarlet letter of their crime against liberty. He had said in the October before: "It is time that a voice of remonstrance went forth from the North, that should peal in the ears of every slaveholder like a roar of thunder. . . . For ourselves, we are resolved to agitate this subject to the utmost; nothing but death shall prevent us from denouncing a crime which has no parallel in human depravity; we shall take high ground. *The alarm must be perpetual.*" A voice of remonstrance, with thunder growl accompaniment, was rising higher and clearer from the pen of the young editor. His tone of earnestness was deepening to the stern bass of the moral reformer, and the storm breath of enthusiasm was blowing to a blaze the glowing coals of his humanity. The wail of the fleeing fugitive from the house of bondage sounded no longer far away and unreal in his ears, but thrilled now right under the windows of his soul. The masonic excitement and the commotion created by the abduction of Morgan he caught up and shook before the eyes of his countrymen as an object lesson of the million-times greater wrong daily done the slaves. "All this fearful commotion," he pealed, "has arisen from the abduction of *one man.* More than two millions of unhappy beings are groaning out their lives in bondage, and scarcely a pulse quickens, or a heart leaps, or a tongue pleads in their behalf. 'Tis a trifling affair, which concerns nobody. Oh! for the spirit that rages, to break every fetter of oppression!" Such a spirit was fast taking possession of the writer.

Of this Lundy was well informed. He had not lost sight of his young coadjutor, but had watched his course with great hope and growing confidence. In him he found what he had discovered in no one else, anti-slavery activity and perseverence. He had often found men who protested loudly their benevolence for the negro, but who made not the slightest exertion afterward to carry out their good wishes. "They will pen a paragraph, perhaps an article, or so—and then—*the subject is exhausted!*" It was not so with his young friend, the Bennington editor. He saw that "argument and useful exertion on the subject of African emancipation can never be exhausted until the system of slavery itself be totally annihilated." He was faithful among the faithless found by Lundy. To reassure his doubting leader, Garrison took upon himself publicly a vow of perpetual consecration to the slave. "Before God and our country," he declares, "we give our pledge that the liberation of the enslaved Africans shall always be uppermost in our pursuits. The people of New England are interested in this matter, and they must be aroused from their lethargy as by a trumpet-call. They shall not quietly slumber while we have the management of a press, or strength to hold a pen." The question of slavery had at length obtained the ascendency over all other questions in his regard. And when Lundy perceived this he set out from Baltimore to Bennington to invite Garrison to join hands with him in his emancipation movement at Baltimore. He performed the long journey on foot, with staff in hand in true apostolic fashion. The two men of God met among the mountains of Vermont, and when the elder returned from the heights the younger had resolved to follow him to the vales where men needed his help, the utmost which he could give them. He agreed to join his friend in Baltimore and there edit with him his little paper with the grand name (*The Genius of Universal Emancipation*), devoted to preaching the gospel of the gradual abolishment of American slavery. Garrison was to take the position of managing editor, and Lundy to look after the subscription list. The younger to be resident, the elder itinerant partner in the publication of the paper. Garrison closed his relations with the *Journal of the Times*, March 27, 1829, and delivered his valedictory to its readers. This valedictory strikes with stern hammer-stroke the subject of his thoughts. "Hereafter," it reads, "the editorial charge of this paper will devolve on another person. I am invited to occupy a broader field, and to engage in a higher enterprise; that field embraces the whole country—that enterprise is in behalf of the slave population."

"To my apprehension, the subject of slavery involves interests of greater moment to our welfare as a republic, and demands a more prudent and minute investigation than any other which has come before the American people since the Revolutionary struggle—than all others which now occupy their attention. No body of men on the face of the earth deserve their charities, and prayers, and united assistance so much as the slaves of this country; and yet they are almost entirely neglected. It is true many a cheek burns with shame in view of our national inconsistency, and many a heart bleeds for the miserable African. It is true examples of disinterested benevolence and individual sacrifices are numerous, particularly in the Southern States; but no systematic, vigorous, and successful measures have been made to overthrow this fabric of oppression. I trust in God that I may be the humble instrument of breaking at least one chain, and restoring one captive to liberty; it will amply repay a life of severe toil." The causes of temperance and peace came in also for an earnest parting word, but they had clearly declined to a place of secondary importance in the writer's regard. To be more exact, they had not really declined, but the slavery question had risen in his mind above both.

They were great questions, but it was *the* question—had become *his* cause.

Lundy, after his visit to Garrison at Bennington, started on a trip to Hayti with twelve emancipated slaves, whom he had undertaken to colonize there. Garrison awaited in Boston the return of his partner to Baltimore. The former, meanwhile, was out of employment, and sorely in need of money Never had he been favored with a surplusage of the root of all evil. He was deficient in the money-getting and money-saving instinct. Such was plainly not his vocation, and so it happened that wherever he turned, he and poverty walked arm in arm, and the interrogatory, "wherewithal shall I be fed and clothed on the morrow?" was never satisfactorily answered until the morrow arrived. This led him at times into no little embarrassment and difficulty. But since he was always willing to work at the case, and to send his "pride on a pilgrimage to Mecca," the embarrassment was not protracted, nor did the difficulty prove insuperable.

The Congregational societies of Boston invited him in June to deliver before them a Fourth of July address in the interest of the Colonization Society. The exercises took place in Park Street Church. Ten days before this event he was called upon to pay a bill of four dollars for failure to appear at the May muster. Refusing to do so, he was thereupon summoned to come into the Police Court on the glorious Fourth to show cause why he ought not to pay the amercement. He was in a quandary. He did not owe the money, but as he could not be in two places at the same time, and, inasmuch as he wanted very much to deliver his address before the Congregational Societies, and did not at all long to make the acquaintance of his honor, the Police Court Judge, he determined to pay the fine. But, alack and alas! he had "not a farthing" with which to discharge him from his embarrassment. Fortunately, if he wanted money he did not want friends. And one of these, Jacob Horton, of Newburyport, who had married his "old friend and playmate, Harriet Farnham," came to his rescue with the requisite amount.

On the day and place appointed Garrison appeared before the Congregational Societies with an address, to the like of which, it is safe to say, they had never before listened. It was the Fourth of July, but the orator was in no holiday humor. There was not, in a single sentence of the oration the slightest endeavor to be playful with his audience. It was rather an eruption of human suffering, and of the humanity of one man to man. What the Boston clergy saw that afternoon, in the pulpit of Park Street Church, was the vision of a soul on fire. Garrison burned and blazed as the sun that July afternoon burned and blazed in the city's streets. None without escaped the scorching rays of the latter, none within was able to shun the fervid heat of the former. Those of my readers who have watched the effects of the summer's sun on a track of sandy land and have noted how, about midday, the heat seems to rise in sparkling particles and exhalations out of the hot, surcharged surface, can form some notion of the moral fervor and passion of this Fourth of July address, delivered more than sixty years ago, in Boston. Through all the pores of it, over all the length and breadth of it, there went up bright, burning particles from the sunlit sympathy and humanity of the young reformer.

In beginning, he animadverted, among other things, on the spread of intemperance, of political corruption, on the profligacy of the press, and, amid them all, the self-complacency and boastfulness of the national spirit, as if it bore a charmed life.

"But," he continued, "there is another evil which, if we had to contend against nothing else, should make us quake for the issue. It is a gangrene preying upon our vitals—an earthquake rumbling under our feet—a mine accumulating material for a national catastrophe. It should make this a day of fasting and prayer, not of boisterous merriment and idle pageantry—a day of great lamentation, not of congratulatory joy. It should spike every cannon, and haul down every banner. Our garb should be sackcloth—our heads bowed in the dust—our supplications for the pardon and assistance of Heaven.

"Sirs, I am not come to tell you that slavery is a curse, debasing in its effects, cruel in its operations, fatal in its continuance. The day and the occasion require no such revelation. I do not claim the discovery as my own, that 'all men are born equal,' and that among their inalienable rights are 'life, liberty, and the pursuit of happiness.' Were I addressing any other than a free and Christian assembly, the enforcement of this truth might be pertinent. Neither do I intend to analyze the horrors of slavery for your inspection, nor to freeze your blood with authentic recitals of savage cruelty. Nor will time allow me to explore even a furlong of that immense wilderness of suffering which remains unsubdued in our land. I take it for granted that the existence of these evils is acknowledged, if not rightly understood. My object is to define and enforce our duty, as Christians and philanthropists."

This was, by way of exordium, the powerful skirmish line of the address. Assuming the existence of the evil, he advanced boldly to his theme, viz., the duty of abolishing it. To this end he laid down four propositions, as a skillful general plants his cannon on the heights overlooking and commanding his enemies' works. The first, broadly stated, asserted the kinship of the slave to the free population of the republic. They were men; they were natives of the country; they were in dire need. They were ignorant, degraded, morally and socially. They were the heathen at home, whose claims far outranked those in foreign lands; they were higher than those of the "Turks or Chinese, for they have the privileges of instruction; higher than the Pagans, for they are not dwellers in a Gospel land; higher than our red men of the forest, for we do not bind them with gyves, nor treat them as chattels."

Then he turned hotly upon the Church, exclaiming:

"What has Christianity done by direct effort for our slave population? Comparatively nothing. She has explored the isles of the ocean for objects of commiseration; but, amazing stupidity! she can gaze without emotion on a multitude of miserable beings at home, large enough to constitute a nation of freemen, whom tyranny has heathenized by law. In her public services they are seldom remembered, and in her private donations they are forgotten. From one end of the country to the other her charitable societies form golden links of benevolence, and scatter their contributions like rain drops over a parched heath; but they bring no sustenance to the perishing slave. The blood of souls is upon her garments, yet she heeds not the stain. The clanking of the prisoner's chains strike upon her ear, but they cannot penetrate her heart."

Then, with holy wrath upon the nation, thus:

"Every Fourth of July our Declaration of Independence is produced, with a sublime indignation, to set forth the tyranny of the mother country, and to challenge the admiration of the world. But what a pitiful detail of grievances does this document present, in comparison with the wrongs which our slaves endure? In the one case it is hardly the plucking of a hair from the head; in the other, it is the crushing of a live body on the wheel—the stings of the wasp contrasted with the tortures of the Inquisition. Before God I must say that such a glaring contradiction as exists between our creed and practice the annals of six thousand years cannot parallel. In view of it I am ashamed of my country. I am sick of our unmeaning declamation in praise of liberty and equality; of our hypocritical cant about the inalienable rights of man. I would not for my right hand stand up before a European assembly, and exult that I am an American citizen, and denounce the usurpations of a kingly government as wicked and unjust; or, should I make the attempt, the recollection of my country's barbarity and despotism would blister my lips, and cover my cheeks with burning blushes of shame."

Passing to his second proposition, which affirmed the right of the free States to be in at the death of slavery, he pointed out that slavery was not sectional but national in its influence. If the consequences of slave-holding did not flow beyond the limits of the slave section, the right would still exist, on the principle that what affected injuriously one part must ultimately hurt the whole body politic. But it was not true that slavery concerned only the States where it existed—the parts where it did not exist were involved by their constitutional liability to be called on for aid in case of a slave insurrection, as they were in the slave representation clause of the national compact, through which the North was deprived of its "just influence in the councils of the nation." And, furthermore, the right of the free States to agitate the question inhered in the principle of majority rule —the white population of the free States being almost double that of the slave States, "and the voice of this overwhelming majority should be potential." He repelled in strong language the wrongfulness of allowing the South to multiply the votes of those freemen by the master's right to count three for every five slaves, "because it is absurd and anti-republican to suffer property to be represented as men, and *vice versa*, because it gives the South an unjust ascendancy over other portions of territory, and a power which may be perverted on every occasion."

He looked without shrinking upon the possibility of disunion even then.

"Now I say that, on the broad system of equal rights," he declared, "this inequality should no longer be tolerated. If it cannot be speedily put down—not by force but by fair persuasion—if we are always to remain shackled by unjust constitutional provisions, when the emergency that imposed them has long since passed away; if we must share in the guilt and danger of destroying the bodies and souls of men *as the price of our Union;* if the slave States will haughtily spurn our assistance, and refuse to consult the general welfare, then the fault is not ours if a separation eventually takes place."

Considering that he was in his twenty-fourth year, and that the Abolition movement had then no actual existence, the orator evinced surprising prescience in his forecast of the future, and of the strife and hostility which the agitation was destined to engender.

"But the plea is prevalent," he said, "that any interference by the free States, however benevolent or cautious it might be, would only irritate and inflame the jealousies of the South, and retard the cause of emancipation. If any man believes that slavery can be abolished without a struggle with the worst passions of human nature, quietly, harmoniously, he cherishes a delusion. It can never be done, unless the age of miracles returns. No; we must expect a collision, full of sharp asperities and bitterness. We shall have to contend with the insolence, and pride, and selfishness of many a heartless being.

"Sirs, the prejudices of the North are stronger than those of the South; they bristle like so many bayonets around the slaves; they forge and rivet the chains of the nation. Conquer them and the victory is won. The enemies of emancipation take courage from our criminal timidity. . . . We are . . . afraid of our own shadows, who have been driven back to the wall again and again; who stand trembling under their whips; who turn pale, retreat, and surrender at a talismanic threat to dissolve the Union. . . ." But the difficulties did not daunt him, nor the dangers cow him. He did not doubt, but was assured, that truth was mighty and would prevail. "Moral influence when in vigorous exercise," he said, "is irresistible. It has an immortal essence. It can no more be trod out of existence by the iron foot of time, or by the ponderous march of iniquity, than matter can be annihilated. It may disappear for a time; but it lives in some shape or other, in some place or other, and will rise with renovated strength. Let us then be up and doing. In the simple and stirring language of the stout-hearted Lundy, all the friends of the cause must go to work, keep to work, hold on, and never give up.". The closing paragraph is this powerful peroration: "I will say, finally, that I despair of the republic while slavery exists therein. If I look up to God for success, no smile of mercy or forgiveness dispels the gloom of futurity; if to our own resources, they are daily diminishing; if to all history our destruction is not only possible but almost certain. Why should we slumber at this momentous crisis? If our hearts were dead to every thought of humanity; if it were lawful to oppress, where power is ample; still, if we had any regard for our safety and happiness, we should strive to crush the vampire which is feeding upon our life-blood. All the selfishness of our nature cries aloud for a better security. Our own vices are too strong for us, and keep us in perpetual alarm; how, in addition to these, shall we be able to contend successfully with millions of armed and desperate men, as we must, eventually, if slavery do not cease?" Exit the apprentice, enter the master. The period of preparation is ended, the time of action begun. The address was the fiery cry of the young prophet ere he plunged into the unsubdued wilderness of American slavery.

CHAPTER III.

THE MAN BEGINS HIS MINISTRY.

Some time in August, 1829, Garrison landed in Baltimore, and began with Lundy the editorship of *The Genius of Universal Emancipation.* Radical as the Park Street Church address was, it had, nevertheless, ceased to represent in one essential matter his anti slavery convictions and principles. The moral impetus and ground-swell of the address had carried him beyond the position where its first flood of feeling had for the moment left him. During the composition of the address he was transported with grief and indignation at the monstrous wrong which slavery did the slaves and the nation. He had not thought out for himself any means to rid both of the curse. The white heat of the address destroyed for the instant all capacity for such thinking. "Who can be amazed, temperate, and furious—in a moment? No man. The expedition of his violent love outran the pauser reason" He had accepted the colonization scheme as an instrument for removing the evil, and called on all good citizens "to assist in establishing auxiliary colonization societies in every State, county, and town"; and implored "their direct and liberal patronage to the parent society." He had not apparently, so much as dreamed of any other than gradual emancipation. "The emancipation of all the slaves of this generation is most assuredly out of the question," he said; "the fabric which now towers above the Alps, must be taken away brick by brick, and foot by foot, till it is reduced so low that it may be overturned without burying the nation in its ruins. Years may elapse before the completion of of the achievement; generations of blacks may go down to the grave, manacled and lacerated, without a hope for their children." He was on the Fourth of July a firm and earnest believer in the equity and efficacy of gradualism. But after that day, and some time before nis departure for Baltimore, he began to think on this subject. The more he thought the less did gradualism seem defensible on moral grounds. John Wesley had said that slavery was the "sum of all villainies"; it was indeed the sin of sins, and as such ought to be abandoned not gradually but immediately. Slave-holding was sin and slaveholders were sinners. The sin and sinner should both be denounced as such and the latter called to instant repentance, and the duty of making immediate restitution of the stolen liberties of their slaves. This was the tone ministers of religion held everywhere toward sin and sinners, and this should be the tone held by the preachers of Abolition toward slavery, and slaveholders. To admit the principle of gradualism was for Abolition to emasculate itself of its most virile quality. Garrison, consequently rejected gradualism as a weapon, and took up instead the great and quickening doctrine of immediatism. Lundy did not know of this change in the convictions of his coadjutor until his arrival in Baltimore. Then Garrison frankly unburdened himself and declared his decision to conduct his campaign against the national iniquity along the lines of immediate and unconditional emancipation. The two on this new radicalism did not see eye to eye. But Lundy with sententious shrewdness and liberality suggested to the young radical: "Thee may put thy initials to thy articles and I will put my initials to mine, and each will bear his own burden." And the arrangement pleased the young radical, for it enabled him to free his soul of the necessity which was then sitting heavily upon it. The precise state of his mind in respect of the question at this juncture in its history and in his own is made plain enough in his salutatory address in *The Genius of Universal Emancipation.* The vow made in Bennington ten months before to devote his life to philanthrophy, and the dedication of himself made six months afterward to the extirpation of American slavery, he solemnly renews and reseals in Baltimore. He does not hate intemperance and war less, but slavery more, and those, therefore, he formally relegates thenceforth to a place of secondary importance in the endeavors of the future. It is obvious that the colonization scheme has no strong hold upon his intelligence. He does not conceal his respect for it as an instrument of freedom, but he puts no high value on its utility. "It may pluck a few leaves," he remarks, "from the Bohon Upas, but can neither extract its roots nor destroy its withering properties. Viewed as an auxiliary, it deserves encouragement; but as a remedy it is altogether inadequate." But this was not all. As a remedy, colonization was not only altogether inadequate, its influence was indirectly pernicious, in that it lulled the popular mind into "a belief that the monster has received his mortal wound." He perceived that this resultant indifference and apathy operated to the advantage of slavery, and to the injury of freedom. Small, therefore, as was the good which the Colonization Society was able to achieve, it was mixed with no little ill. Although Garrison has not yet begun to think on the subject, to examine into the motives and purposes of the society, it does not take a prophet to foresee that some day he will. He had already arrived at conclusions in respect of the rights of the colored people "to choose their own dwelling place," and against the iniquity of their expatriation, which cut directly at the roots of the colonization scheme. Later the pro-slavery character of the society will be wholly revealed to him. But truth in the breast of a reformer as of others must needs follow the great law of moral growth, first the blade, then the ear, and then the full corn in the ear. It is enough that he has made the tremendous step from gradual to immediate and unconditional emancipation on the soil.

At this period he tested the disposition of slaveholders to manumit their slaves. The Colonization Society had given it out that there was no little desire on the part of many masters to set their slaves free. All that was wanted for a practical domonstation in this direction was the assurance of free transportation out of the country for the emancipated slaves. Lundy had made arrangement for the transportation of fifty slaves to Hayti and their settlement in that country. So he and Garrison advertised this fact in the *Genius*, but they waited in vain for a favorable response from the South—notwithstanding the following humane inducement which this advertisement offered: "THE PRICE OF PASSAGE WILL BE ADVANCED, and everything furnished of which they may stand in need, until they shall have time to prepare their houses and set in to work." No master was moved to take advantage of the opportunity. This was discouraging to the believers in the efficacy of colonization as a potent anti-slavery instrument. But Garrison was no such believer. With unerring moral instinct he had from the start placed his reliance "on nothing but the eternal principles of justice for the speedy overthrow of slavery."

He obtained at this period an intimate personal knowledge of the free colored people. He saw that they were not essentially unlike other races—that there was nothing morally or intellectually peculiar about them, and that the evil or the good which they manifested was the common property of mankind in similar circumstances. He forthwith became their brave defender against the common slanders of the times. "There is a prevalent disposition among all classes to traduce the habits and morals of our free blacks," he remarked in the *Genius*. "The most scandalous exaggerations in regard to their condition are circulated by a thousand mischievous tongues, and no reproach seems to them too deep or unmerited. Vile and malignant indeed is this practice, and culpable are they who follow it. We do not pretend to say that crime, intemperance, and suffering, to a considerable extent, cannot be found among the free blacks; but we do assert that they are as moral, peaceable, and industrious as that class of the whites who are, like them, in indigent circumstances—and far less intemperate than the great body of foreign immigrants who infest and corrupt our shores." This idea of the natural equality of the races he presented in the *Genius* a few weeks before with Darwinian breadth in the following admirable sentences: "I deny the postulate that God has made, by an irreversible decree, or any inherent qualities, one portion of the human race superior to another. No matter how many breeds are amalgamated—no matter how many shades of color intervene between tribes or nations give them the same chances to improve, and a fair start at the same time, and the result will be equally brilliant, equally productive, equally grand."

At the same time that he was making active, personal acquaintance with the free colored people, he was making actual personal acquaintance with the barbarism of slavery also. "The distinct application of a whip, and the shrieks of anguish" of the slave, his residence in Baltimore had taught him was "nothing uncommon" in that city. Such an instance had come to him while in the street where the office of the *Genius* was located. It was what was occuring at almost all hours of the day and in almost all parts of the town. He had not been in Baltimore a month when he saw a specimen of the brutality of slavery on the person of a negro, who had been mercilessly flogged. On his back were thirty-seven gashes made with a cowskin, while on his head were many bruises besides. It was a Sunday morning, fresh from his terrible punishment, that the poor fellow had found the editors of the *Genius*, who, with the compassion of brothers, took him in, dressed his wounds, and cared for him for two days. Such an experience was no new horror to Lundy, but it was doubtless Garrison's first lesson in that line, and it sank many fathoms deep into his heart.

Maryland was one of the slave-breeding States and Baltimore a slave emporium. There was enacted the whole business of slavery as a commercial enterprise. Here the human chattels were brought and here warehoused in jails and other places of storage and detention. Here they were put up at public auction, and knocked down to the highest bidder, and from here they were shipped to New Orleans, the great distributing center for such merchandise. He heard what Lundy had years before heard, the wail of captive mothers and fathers, wives, husbands and children, torn from each other; like Lundy, "he felt their pang of distress; and the iron entered his soul." He could not hold his peace in the midst of such abominations, but boldly exposed and denounced them. His indignation grew hot when he saw that Northern vessels were largely engaged in the coastwise slave-trade; and when, to his amazement, he learned that the ship *Francis*, owned by Francis Todd, a Newburyport merchant, had sailed for New Orleans with a gang of seventy-five slaves, his indignation burst into blaze. He blazoned the act and the name of Francis Todd in the *Genius*, and did verily what he had resolved to do, viz., "to cover with thick infamy all who were concerned in this nefarious business," the captain as well as the owner of the ill-freighted ship. He did literally point at these men the finger of scorn. Every device known to the printer's art for concentrating the reader's attention upon particular words and sentences, Garrison made skillful use of in his articles—from the deep damnation of the heavy black capitals in which he printed the name Francis Todd, to the small caps in which appeared the words, "sentenced to solitary confinement for life," and which he flanked with two terrible indices. But the articles did not need such embellishment. They were red hot branding irons without them. One can almost smell the odor of burning flesh as he reads the words: "It is no worse to fit out piratical cruisers or to engage in the foreign slave-trade, than to pursue a similar trade along our coast; and the men who have the wickedness to participate therein, for the purpose of keeping up wealth should be ☞ SENTENCED TO SOLITARY CONFINEMENT FOR LIFE; ☜ *they are the enemies of their own species —highway robbers, and murderers;* and their final doom will be, unless they speedily repent, *to occupy the lowest depths of perdition.* I know that our laws make a distinction in this matter. I know that the man who is allowed to freight his vessel with slaves at home, for a distant market, would be thought worthy of death if he should take a similar freight on the coast of Africa; but I know, too, that this distinction is absurd, and at war with the common sense of mankind, and that God and good men regard it with abhorrence.

"I recollect that it was always a mystery in Newburyport how Mr. Todd contrived to make profitable voyages to New Orleans and other places, when other merchants, with as fair an opportunity to make money, and sending to the same ports at the same time invariably made fewer successful speculations.

The mystery seems to be unravelled. Any man can gather up riches if he does not care by what means they are obtained."

A copy of the *Genius*, containing this article Garrison sent to the owner of the ship *Francis*. What followed made it immediately manifest that the branding irons of the reformer had burned home with scarifying effect. Mr. Todd's answer to the strictures was a suit at law against the editors of the *Genius* for five thousand dollars in damages. But this was not all. The Grand Jury for Baltimore indicted them for publishing "a gross and malicious libel against Francis Todd and Nicholas Brown." This was at the February Term, 1830. On the first day of March following, Garrison was tried. He was ably and eloquently defended by Charles Mitchell, a young lawyer of the Baltimore Bar. But the prejudice of judge and jury rendered the verdict of guilty a foregone conclusion. April 17, 1830, the Court imposed a penalty of fifty dollars and costs, which, with the fine amounted in all to nearly one hundred dollars. The fine and costs Garrison could not pay, and he was therefore committed to jail as a common malefactor. His confinement lasted seven weeks. He did not languish during this period. His head and hands were in fact hardly ever more active than during the term of his imprisonment. Shut out by Maryland justice from work without the jail, he found and did that which needed to be done within "high walls and huge." He was an extraordinary prisoner and was treated with extraordinary consideration by the Warden. He proved himself a genuine evangel to the prisoners, visiting them in their cells, cheering them by his bouyant and benevolent words, giving them what he had, a brother's sympathy, which to these ill-fated ones, was more than gold or silver. He indited for such of them as he deemed deserving, letters and petitions to the Governor praying their pardon; and he had the great satisfaction of seeing many of his efforts in this regard crowned with success.

But more than this his imprisonment afforded him an opportunity for a closer acquaintance with the barbarism of slavery than he could possibly have made had he lived otherwise in Baltimore. A Southern jail was not only the place of detention of offenders against social justice, but of slaves waiting for the next market-day, of recaptured fugitives waiting for their owners to reclaim them. Here they were huddled and caged, pitiful and despairing in their misery. Such scenes sickened the young reformer every day. God had opened to him the darkest chapter in the book of the negroes' wrongs. Here is a page from that black volume of oppression and cruelty, the record of which he has preserved in the following graphic narrative: "During my late incarceration in Baltimore prison, four men came to obtain a runaway slave. He was brought out of his cell to confront his master, but pretended not to know him—did not know that he had ever seen him before—could not recollect his name. Of course the master was exceedingly irritated. 'Don't you remember,' said he, 'when I gave you not long since thirty-nine lashes under the apple-tree? Another time when I gave you a sound flogging in the barn? Another time when you was scourged for giving me the lie, by saying that the horse was in a good condition?' 'Yes,' replied the slave, whose memory was thus quickened, 'I do recollect. You have beaten me cruelly without cause; you have not given me enough to eat and drink; and I don't want to go back again. I wish you to sell me to another master. I had rather even go to Georgia than to return home!'

"'I'll let you know, you villain,' said the master, 'that my wishes and not *yours*, are to be consulted. I'll learn you how to run away again.'"

The other men advised him to take the black home, and cut him up in inch pieces for his impudence, obstinacy, and desertion—swearing tremendously all the while. The slave was ordered back to his cell. Then ensued the following colloquy between Garrison and the master:

G.—"Sir, what right have you to that poor creature?"

M.—"My father left him to me."

G.—"Suppose your father had broken into a bank and stolen ten thousand dollars, and safely bequeathed that as a legacy; could you conscientiously keep the money? For myself, I had rather rob any bank to an indefinite amount than kidnap a fellow-being, or hold him in bondage; the sin would be less injurious to society, and less sinful in the sight of God."

M.—"Perhaps you would like to buy the slave and give him his liberty?"

G.—"Sir, I am a poor man; and were I ever so opulent, it would be necessary, on your part, to make out a clear title to the services of the slave before I could conscientiously make a bargain."

M —" Well, sir, I can prove from the Bible that slavery is right."

G.—" Ah! that is a precious book—the rule of conduct. I have always supposed that its spirit was directly opposed to everything in the shape of fraud and oppression. However, sir, I should be glad to hear your text."

M. (hesitatingly) — " Ham — Noah's curse, you know."

G. (hastily)—" Oh, sir, you build on a very slender foundation. Granting even—what remains to be proved—that the Africans are the descendants of Ham, Noah's curse was a *prediction* of future servitude, and not an injunction to oppress. Pray, sir, is it a careful desire to fulfill the Scriptures, or to make money, that induces you to hold your fellow-men in bondage ? "

M. (excitedly)—" Why, sir, do you really think that the slaves are beings like ourselves ?—that is, I mean do you believe that they possess the same faculties and capacities as the whites ? "

G. (energetically)—" Certainly, sir, I do not know that there is any moral or intellectual quality in the curl of the hair, or the color of the skin. I cannot conceive why a black man may not as reasonably object to my color, as I to his. Sir, it is not a black face that I detest, but a black heart—and I find it very often under a white skin."

M. (derisively)—" Well, sir, how should you like to see a black man President of the United States ? "

G. (severely)—" As to that, sir, I am a true Republican, and bow to the will of the majority. If the people prefer a black President, I should cheerfully submit; and if he be qualified for the station, may peradventure give him my vote."

M. (triumphantly)—"How should you like to have a black man marry your daughter?"

G. (making a home thrust and an end of the dialogue)—"I am not married—I have no daughter. Sir, I am not familiar with *your* practices; but allow me to say, that slaveholders generally should be the last persons to affect fastidiousness on that point; for they seem to be enamored with *amalgamation.*"

Garrison's pen was particularly busy during the term of his imprisonment. He paid his respects to the State's Attorney who prosecuted him, to the judge who condemned him, and to Francis Todd, the owner of the ship *Francis.* He prepared and scattered broadcast a true account of his trial, showing how the liberty of the press had been violated in the case. He did not doubt that it would astonish Europe if it were known there "that *an American citizen lies incarcerated in prison, for having denounced slavery and its abettors in his own country.*" The fact created no little astonishment in America. Slavery became distinctly connected for the first time with abridgments of the freedom of the press, and the right of free speech. And the cause of the slave became involved with the Constitutional liberties of the republic. In punishing Garrison, the Abolitionist, the rights of Garrison the white freeman were trampled on. And white freemen in the North, who cared nothing for Abolitionism, but a great deal for their right to speak and write freely, resented the outrage. This fact was the most important consequence, which flowed from the trial and imprisonment of the young editor of

The Genius of Universal Emancipation. "As the news of my imprisonment became extensively known," he wrote, "and the merits of the case understood, not a mail rolled into the city but it brought me consolatary letters from individuals hitherto unknown to me, and periodicals of all kinds from every section of the Union (not even excepting the South), all uniting to give me a triumphant acquittal—all severely reprehending the conduct of Mr. Todd—and all regarding my trial as a mockery of justice." This unexpected result was one of those accidents of history, which "have laws as fixed as planets have."

The prosecution and imprisonment of Garrison was without doubt designed to terrorize him into silence on the subject of slavery. But his persecutors had reckoned without a knowledge of their victim. Garrison had the martyr's temperament and invincibility of purpose. His earnestness burned the more intensely with the growth of opposition and peril. Within "gloomy walls close pent," he warbled gay as a bird of a freedom which tyrants could not touch, nor bolts confine:

"No chains can bind it, and no cell enclose,
Swifter than light, it flies from pole to pole,
And in a flash from earth to heaven it goes!"

or with deep, stern gladness sang he to "The Guiltless Prisoner" how:

"A martyr's crown is richer than a king's!
Think it an honor with thy Lord to bleed,
And glory 'midst intensest sufferings;
Though beat—imprisoned—put to open shame
Time shall embalm and magnify thy name."

"Is it supposed by Judge Brice," the guiltless prisoner wrote from his cell, "that his frowns can intimidate me, or his sentence stifle my voice on the subject of African oppression? He does not know me. So long as a good Providence gives me strength and intellect, I will not cease to declare that the existence of slavery in this country is a foul reproach to the American name; nor will I hesitate to proclaim the guilt of kidnappers, slave abettors, or slaveowners, wheresoever they may reside, or however high they may be exalted. I am only in the *alphabet* of my task; time shall perfect a useful work. It is my shame that I have done so little for the people of color; yea, before God, I feel humbled that my feelings are so cold, and my language so weak. A few white victims must be sacrificed to open the eyes of this nation, and to show the tyranny of our laws. I expect and am willing to be persecuted, imprisoned, and bound for advocating African rights; and I should deserve to be a slave myself if I shrunk from that duty or danger." The story of the trial of William Lloyd Garrison, from which the above brave words are taken, fell into the hands of that noble man and munificent merchant, Arthur Tappan, of New York. From the reading of it he rose "with that deep feeling of abhorrence of slavery and its abettors which every one must feel who is capable of appreciating the blessings of liberty," and thereupon notified Lundy to draw upon him for one hundred dollars if that amount would give the young editor his liberty The fine and costs of court were accordingly paid and just forty-nine days after entering Baltimore jail a prisoner, Garrison recovered his freedom. The civil action of Todd against him was still pending. Nothing daunted Garrison went North two days after his discharge to obtain certain evidence deemed important by his counsel to his defence. He took with him an open letter from Lundy looking to the renewal of the the weekly *Genius* under their joint control. Prior to Garrison's trial the paper had fallen into great stress for want of money. Lundy and he had made a division of their labors, the latter doing the editorial and office work, while the former traveled from place to place soliciting subscriptions and collecting generally the sinews of war. But the experiment was not successful from a business standpoint. For as Garrison playfully observed subsequently: "Where friend Lundy could get one new subscriber, I could knock a *dozen* off, and I did so. It was the old experiment of the frog in the well, that went two feet up and fell three feet back, at every jump." Where the income of the paper did not exceed fifty dollars in four months and the weekly expenditure amounted to at least that sum, the financial failure of the enterprise was inevitable. This unhappy event did actually occur six weeks before the junior editor went to jail; and the partnership was formally dissolved in the issue of the *Genius* of March 5, 1830. But when Arthur Tappan made his generous offer of a hundred dollars to effect Garrison's release, he made at the same time an offer of an equal amount to aid the editors in reëstablishing the *Genius*. This proposition led to hopes on the part of the two friends to a renewal of their partnership in the cause of emancipation. And so Garrison's visit to the North was taken advantage of to test the disposition of Northern philanthropy to support such a paper. But what he found was a sad lack of interest in the slave. Everywhere he went he encountered what appeared to him to be the most monstrous indifference and apathy on the subject. The prejudices of the free States seemed to him stronger than were those of the South. Instead of receiving aid and encouragement to continue the good work of himself and coadjutor, and for the doing of which he had served a term of seven weeks in prison, men, even his best friends sought to influence him to give it up, and to persuade him to forsake the slave, and to turn his time and talents to safer and more profitable enterprises nearer home. He was informed by these worldly wise men and Job's counselors that his "scheme was visionary, fanatical, unattainable." "Why should he make himself," they argued, "an exile from home and all that be held dear on earth, and sojourn in a strange land, among enemies whose hearts were dead to every noble sentiment?" Ah! he himself confessed that all were against his return to Baltimore. But his love of the slave was stronger than the strength of the temptation. He put all these selfish objections behind him. As he has recorded the result of this experience: "Opposition served only to increase my ardor, and confirm my purpose." Strange and incomprehensible to his fellows is the man who prefers "persecution, reproach, and poverty" with duty, to worldly ease and honor and riches without it. When a man appears in society who is not controlled by motives which usually govern the conduct of other men he becomes at first an object of pity, then of contempt, and, lastly, of hate. Garrison we may be sure at the end of this visit had made rapid transit from the first to the second of these stages in the esteem of his generation.

His experience was not all of this deplorable kind. He left Baltimore without the money required to pay his way North, depending literally upon the good God to provide for him the necessary means to complete his journey. And such help was more than once providentially afforded the young apostle of liberty. At New York, when he did not know how he was to go farther for want of means, he met a Mr. Samuel Leggett who gave him a pass on the "splendid steamboat *President*." It seems that this friend in his need had read with indignation the story of his trial. The bread which he had scattered from his prison on the waters of public sentiment had thus returned to him after many days in the timely assistance of a sympathetic soul. And then, again, when he was in Boston in sore distress for a little money, suddenly, beautifully, the desire of his heart was satisfied. But let him tell the incident in his own touching way. His face was turned toward Baltimore: "But how was I to return?" he asks. "I had not a dollar in my pocket, and my time was expired. No one understood my circumstances. I was too proud to beg, and ashamed to borrow. My friends were prodigal of pity, but of nothing else. In the extremity of my uneasiness, I went to the Boston post-office, and found a letter from my friend Lundy, inclosing a draft for $100 from a stranger and as a remuneration for my poor inefficient services in behalf of the slaves!" The munificent stranger was Ebenezer Dole, of Hallowell, Maine. Money thus acquired was a sacred trust to this child of Providence. "After deducting the expenses of traveling," he goes on to say, "the remainder of the above-named sum was applied in discharging a few of the debts incurred by the unproductiveness of the *Genius.*"

Garrison returned to Baltimore, but he did not tarry long in that slave-ruled city. Todd's suit against him was tried after his departure, and the jury soothed the Newburyport merchant's wounded pride with a verdict for a thousand dollars. He never attempted, however, to enforce the payment of the same being content probably with the "vindication," which his legal victory gave him.

Before the reformer left Baltimore he had definitely abandoned the plans looking to a revival of his interest in the *Genius.* He determined instead to publish a sheet devoted to the abolition of slavery under his sole management and control. This paper he proposed to call the *Public Liberator*, and to issue from Washington. The prospectus of this journalistic project bearing date, August, 1830, declares in its opening sentence its "primary object" to be "the abolition of slavery, and the moral and intellectual elevation of our colored population." "I shall spare no efforts," he pledged himself, "to delineate the withering influence of slavery upon our national prosperity and happiness, its awful impiety, its rapid extension, and its inevitable consequences if it be suffered to exist without hindrance. It will also be my purpose to point out the path of safety, and a remedy for the disease." This comprehensive and aggressive plan of campaign signalized the rise of an Abolitionism wholly unlike the Abolitionism of any previous time in the history of the country. It did in fact date the opening of a new era in the slavery struggle in America.

With Northern indifference and apathy on the subject of emancipation, Garrison's previous visit to the North had acquainted him. Their existence he saw interposed the main obstacle to the success of his new venture in journalism. "The cause of this callous state of feeling," he believed, "was owing to their exceeding ignorance of the horrors of slavery." He accordingly made up his mind to throw the light which he possessed into the midst of this darkness. He had written in prison three lectures on "Slavery and Colonization." What better could he now do than to deliver those lectures at the North? If the good people and their religious leaders knew what he knew, they would presently feel as he did on the question. He was loath to leave Baltimore without giving this testimony against slavery. But unable to procure a room for this purpose was finally compelled to content himself with the witness he had already borne in the *Genius* and in prison in behalf of the slave. In Philadelphia he well-nigh failed to obtain a hall for his lectures, but did finally succeed in getting the Franklin Institute, where, to small audiences, he lifted up his voice against the iniquity of the times. He repeated his lectures in New York, New Haven, and Hartford. But not many came out to hear him. The nation, its churches, and politicians had thrust their fingers in their ears to every cry coming up from the slave. Why should they go to sup with a madman on horrors, with which as patriotic people they were forbidden to concern themselves. And so for the most part Garrison could do nothing with communities, which had eyes. but obstinately refused to see with them upon any subject relating to the abominations of slavery. In his own town of Newburyport, officers of Christian churches not only refused to hear his message themselves, but debarred others from listening to the woes and wrongs of fellow-creatures in bondage. As Mr. Garrison truly said at the time: "If I had visited Newburyport to plead the cause of twenty white men in chains, every hall and every meeting-house would have been thrown open, and the fervor of my discourses anticipated and exceeded by my fellow-townsmen. The fact that two millions of colored beings are groaning in bondage, in this land of liberty, excites no interest nor pity." If these damning facts are remembered sixty years after their occurrence to the shame of the trustees of the two churches, viz., the Presbyterian Church on Harris street and the Second Congregational Church, it is also remembered to the honor of the two pastors, Rev. Dr. Daniel Dana, and the Rev. Dr. Luther F. Dimmick, that they had thrown open to the prophet the doors of their meeting-houses, which the trustees afterward slammed in his face.

In Boston the same hard luck followed him. In all that city of Christian churches he could not obtain the use of a single meeting-house, "in which to vindicate the rights of TWO MILLIONS of American citizens, who are now groaning in servile chains in this boasted land of liberty; and also to propose just, benevolent, and constitutional measures for their relief." So ran an advertisement in the Boston *Courier* of the sorely tried soul. For two weeks he had gone up and down the town in search of a room free of cost, in which to deliver his message. The door of every sanctuary was locked against his cause. It was then, as a final recourse, that he turned to the *Courier*, and made his last appeal to the Christian charity of the city. The prayer of the prophet was answered from an unexpected quarter. It was that ecclesiastical dragon of the times, Abner Kneeland, and his society of "blasphemers," who proved afresh the truth of that scripture which says: "Not every one that saith unto me, Lord, Lord, shall enter into the kingdom of heaven; but he that doeth the will of my Father which is in heaven." It was they that gave to liberty a hearing, to the prophet of righteousness a chance to deliver his message. It was in their meeting-house, in Julian Hall, that Garrison gave his lectures, giving the first one on the evening of October 15, 1830.

Samuel J. May, who was present, has preserved his impressions of the lecture and lecturer. "Never before," he records many years afterward, "was I so affected by the speech of man. When he had ceased speaking I said to those around me: 'That is a providential man; he is a prophet; he will shake our nation to its center, but he will shake slavery out of it. We ought to know him, we ought to help him. Come, let us go and give him our hands.' Mr. Sewall and Mr. Alcott went up with me and we introduced each other. I said to him, 'Mr. Garrison, I am not sure that I can indorse all you have said this evening. Much of it requires careful consideration. But I am prepared to embrace you. I am sure you are called to a great work, and I mean to help you.' Mr. Sewall cordially assured him of his readiness also to coöperate with him. Mr. Alcott invited him to his home. He went and we sat with him until twelve that night, listening to his discourse, in which he showed plainly that *immediate, unconditional emancipation, without expatriation, was the right of every slave, and could not be withheld by his master an hour without sin.* That night my soul was baptised in his spirit, and ever since I have been a disciple and fellow-laborer of William Lloyd Garrison." A new force had arisen in our history, and a new epoch had broken bolts for humanity.

CHAPTER IV.

THE HOUR AND THE MAN.

THE providential man was not yet twenty-five. In personal appearance he was quite the reverse of his friend Lundy. Garrison was gifted with a body that matched his mind, strong, straight, sound in every part, and proportioned in every member. As he stood he was much above the medium height. His dark hair had already partially left the crown of the high dome-shaped head. His forehead combined height with breadth, which, taken in connection with the brown eyes covered with the now habitual glasses, lent to his countenance a striking air of moral serenity and elevation. Force, firmness, no ordinary self-reliance and courage found masterly expression in the rest of the face. There was through the whole physical man a nice blending of strength and delicacy of structure. The impression of fineness and finish was perhaps mainly owing to the woman-like purity and freshness of skin and color, which overspread the virile lines and features of the face from brow to chin. What one saw in that face was the quality of justice made flesh, good-will to men personified.

This characterization of the reformer's countenance may be considered absurd by some readers. But absurd it is not. People who had read his stern denunciations of slave-holding and slaveholders, and who had formed their image of the man from his "hard language" and their own prejudices could not recognize the original when they met him. His manner was peculiarly winning and attractive, and in personal intercourse almost instantly disarmed hostility. The even gentleness of his rich voice, his unfailing courtesy and good temper, his quick eye for harmless pleasantries, his hearty laugh, the Quaker-like calmness, deliberateness, and meekness, with which he would meet objections and argue the righteousness of his cause, his sweet reasonableness and companionableness were in strange contrast to popular misconceptions and caricatures of him. No one needed to be persuaded, who had once conversed with him, that there was no hatred or vindictiveness in his severities of language toward slaveholders. That he was no Jacobin, no enemy of society, was perceived the moment one looked into his grave, kind face, or caught the warm accents of his pacific tones, or listened to the sedate intensity, and humanity of his discourses on the enormity of American slavery as they fell from him in conversations between man and man. Here is a case in point, a typical incident in the life of the reformer; it occurred, it is true, when he was twenty-seven, but it might have occurred at twenty-five quite as well; it is narrated by Samuel J. May in his recollections of the anti-slavery conflict: On his way from New York to Philadelphia with Garrison, Mr. May fell into a discussion with a pro-slavery passenger on the vexed question of the day. There was the common pro-slavery reasoning, which May answered as well as he was able. Presently Mr. Garrison drew near the disputants, whereupon May took the opportunity to shift the anti-slavery burden of the contention to his leader's shoulders. All of his most radical and unpopular Abolition doctrines Garrison immediately proceeded to expound to his opponent. "After a long conversation," says Mr. May, "which attracted as many as could get within hearing, the gentleman said, courteously : 'I have been much interested, sir, in what you have said, and in the exceedingly frank and temperate manner in which you have treated the subject. If all Abolitionists were like you, there would be much less opposition to your enterprise. But, sir, depend upon it, that hair-brained, reckless, violent fanatic, Garrison, will damage, if he does not shipwreck, any cause.' Stepping forward, I replied, 'Allow me, sir, to introduce you to Mr. Garrison, of whom you entertain so bad an opinion. The gentleman you have been talking with is he.'"

Or take Harriet Martineau's first impressions on seeing him. "His aspect put to flight in an instant what prejudices his slanderers had raised in me. I was wholly taken by surprise. It was a countenance glowing with health, and wholly expressive of purity, animation and gentleness. I did not wonder at the citizen who, seeing a print of Garrison at a shop window without a name to it, went in and bought it, and framed it as the most saintlike of countenances."

The appearance of such a man on the stage of our history as a nation, at this hour, was providential. His coming was in the fulness of time. A rapid review of events anterior to the advent of Garrison will serve to place this matter more clearly before the general reader. To begin, then, at the beginning we have two ships off the American coast, the one casting anchor in Plymouth harbor, the other discharging its cargo at Jamestown. They were both freighted with human souls. But how different ! Despotism landed at Jamestown, democracy at Plymouth. Here in the germ was the Southern idea, slave labor, slave institutions ; and here also was the Northern idea, free labor, free institutions. Once planted they grew, each seed idea multiplying after its kind. In course of time there arose on one side an industrial system in which the plantation principle, race-rule and race-slavery, were organic centers ; and, on the other, a social system in which the principle of popular power and government, the town meeting, and the common school were the ganglia of social expansion. Contrary ideas beget naturally enough contrary interests and institutions. So it is no matter for surprise that the local interests and institutions of the thirteen revolted colonies lacked homogeneity and identity. What was calculated to promote the general welfare of the Northern one, it was quite possible might work a totally opposite result in the Southern. For, indeed, while there were slaves in them all, the slave system had taken root in Southern soil only ; and while on the other hand the spirit of freedom was existent in each, free labor had rooted itself in Northern ground solely.

As the war of the Revolution was an uprising against arbitrary power, and for the establishment of political liberty, it pushed easily into the foreground the larger subject of human rights. Most of the leading actors felt the inconsistency of keeping some men in bondage, when they were fighting to rid themselves of a tyranny which, in comparison to the other, was a state of honorable freedom. Their humanity condemned African slavery, and they earnestly desired its extinction. The Declaration of Independence proves to how high a level the tide of freedom rose in the colonies. The grand truths by it proclaimed the signers of that instrument did not restrict in their application to some men to the exclusion of other men. They wrote "All men," and they meant exactly what they wrote. Too simply honest and great they were to mean less than their solemn and deliberate words.

On political as well as on moral grounds they desired emancipation. But there was a difficulty which at the time proved insuperable. The nation-making principle, the idea of country, was just emerging out of the nebulous civil conditions and relations of the ante-Revolutionary epoch. There was no existent central authority to reach the evil within the States except the local governments of the States respectively. And States in revolt against the central authority of the mother country would hardly be disposed to divest themselves of any part of their newly asserted right to govern themselves for the purpose of conferring the same upon any other political body. To each State, then, the question was necessarily left for settlement.

The war, during its continuance, absorbed the united resources and energies of the people and their leaders. The anti-slavery movement made accordingly but small progress. Reforms thrive only when they get a hearing. Public attention is the food on which they thrive. But precious little of this food was the Abolition cause able to snatch in those bitter years. It could not grow. It remained in the gristle —hardly more than a sentiment. But the sentiment was a seed, the promise and potency of kindlier times. With the close of the long struggle other questions arose; got the people's ears; fixed the attention of the leaders. Scant notice could emancipation extort from men who had to repair the ravages of an exhausting war, reconstruct shattered fortunes, restore civil socicietv in parts tumbling into ruinous disorder. The instinct of self-preservation was altogether too masterful for the moral starveling. It succumbed to circumstances, content to obtain an occasional sermon, an annual address, a few scattered societies to keep a human glow in the bosom of the infant Confederacy.

The Confederation failed. The formation of a more perfect union was demanded and undertaken. This transcendent task straightway thrust into the background every other enterprise and interest. The feeble activity of the freedom-making principle was checked, for the time being, by the energy of the nation-making power. They were not antagonistic forces—only in the natural order of things, the earliest stages in the evolution of the former had to come after the first steps were taken in the development of the latter. Before there could start a general movement against American slavery there must needs be an American nation. An American nation was, in the year 1787, in process of successful development. With the adoption of the Constitution, the national principle entered on a period of marvelous expansion and activity.

Let it not, however. be hastily concluded that freedom meanwhile was in total eclipse, that the anti-slavery sentiment was absolutely without influence. For it unquestionably inspired the Ordinance of 1787. The Northwest Territory, out of which were subsequently organized the States of Ohio, Indiana, Illinois, Michigan, and Wisconsin, was thereby, forever secured to the Northern idea, and free labor. Supplementary to this grand act was the Constitutional prohibition of the African slave-trade after the year 1808. Together they were intended to discourage the growth of slavery—the first by restricting its territorial extension, the second, by arresting its numerical increase. And without doubt they would have placed the evil in the way of ultimate extinction had other and far reaching causes not intervened to produce adverse social and political conditions.

The first of these causes, in point of time, were certain labor-saving inventions in England, which vastly enhanced the demand for raw cotton. Arkwright's invention of the spinning machine about twenty years prior to the adoption of the Constitution, perfected by the spinning-jenny of Hargreaves, and the mule of Crompton, "turned Lancashire," the historian Green says, "into a hive of industry." The then rapid demand for cotton operated in time as a stimulus to its production in America. Increased productivity raised the value of slave property and slave soil. But the slow and tedious hand method of separating the fiber of the cotton bulb from the seed greatly limited the ability of the Cotton States to meet and satisfy the fast growing demand of the English manufacturers, until Eli Whitney, in 1793, by an ingenious invention solved the problem of supply for these States. The cotton gin was not long in proving itself the other half—the other hand of the spinning machine.

From that year the slave interests of the South rose in market value, and its industrial system assumed unexpected importance in the economic world. The increased production of cotton led directly to increased demand for slave labor and slave soil. The increased demand for slave labor the Constitutional provision relating to the African slave trade operated in part to satisfy. The increased demand for slave soil was likewise satisfied by the cession to the United States by Georgia and North Carolina of the Southwest Territory, with provisos practically securing it to slavery. Out of this new national territory were subsequently carved the slave States of Tennessee, Mississippi, and Alabama.

Slave soil unlike free soil, is incapable of sustaining a dense population. Slave labor calls for large spaces within which to multiply and prosper. The purchase of Louisiana and the acquisition of Florida met this agrarian necessity on the part of the South. Immense, unsettled areas thus fell to the lot of the slave system at the crisis of its material expansion and prosperity. The domestic slave-trade under the impetus of settling these vast regions according to the plantation principle, became an enormous and spreading industry. The crop of slaves was not less profitable than the crop of cotton. A Southern white man had but to buy a score of slaves and a few hundred acres to get "rich beyond the dreams of avarice." So at least calculated the average Southern man.

This revival of slavery disappointed the humane expectation of its decline and ultimate extinction entertained by the founders of the republic. It built up instead a growing and formidable slave class, and interest in the Union. With the rise of giant slave interests, there followed the rise of a power devoted to their encouragement and protection.

Three far-reaching concessions the slave States obtained in the convention of 1787, viz., the right to import slaves from Africa until 1808; the rendition of fugitive slaves escaping into the free States, and the three-fifths slave representation clause of the Constitution—all of which added vastly to the security and value of this species of property, and as a consequence contributed to the slave revival.

The equality of the States in the upper branch of the National Legislature, taken in connection with the right of the slave States to count five slaves as three freemen in the apportionment of representatives to the lower House of Congress, gave the Southern section an almost immediate ascendency in the Federal Government. To the South was thus opened by an unexpected combination of circumstances a wide avenue for the acquisition of fabulous wealth, and to Southern public men an incomparable arena for the exercise of political abilities and leadership. An institution, which thus ministered to two of the strongest passions of mankind—avarice and ambition—was certain to excite the most intense attachment. Its safety naturally, therefore, became among the slave class an object of prime importance. Southern jealousy in this regard ultimated inevitably in Southern narrowness, Southern sectionalism, which early manifested themselves in the exclusion from lead in national affairs of Northern public men, reputed to be unfriendly to slavery. Webster as late as 1830, protested warmly against this intolerance. Like begets like. And the proscribing of anti-slavery politicians by the South, created in turn not a little sectional feeling at the North, and helped to stimulate there a consciousness of sectional differences, of antagonism of interests between the two halves of the Union.

Discontent with the original basis of the Union, which had given the South its political coign of vantage, broke out first in New England. The occasion, though not the cause, of this discontent was, perhaps, the downfall of the Federal party, whose stronghold was in the East. The commercial and industrial crisis brought on by the embargo, and which beggared, on the authority of Webster, "thousands of families and hundreds of thousands of individuals" fanned this Eastern dissatisfaction into almost open disaffection towards a government dominated by Southern influence, and directed by Southern statesmanship. To the preponderance of this Southern element in national legislation New England traced her misfortunes. She was opposed to the War of 1812, but was overruled to her hurt by the South. In these circumstances New England went for correcting the inequalities of the original basis of the Union, which gave to the South its undue preponderance in shaping national laws and policies. This was the purpose of the Hartford Convention, which proposed the abrogation of the slave representation clause of the Constitution, and the imposition of a check upon the admission of new States into the Union. The second proposition did not say "new slave States," but new slave States was, nevertheless, intended by the Convention. Here in point of time and magnitude, was the first distinct collision of the two sets of ideas and interests of the Republic.

Following the Treaty of Ghent other and imperious questions engaged the public attention—questions of the tariff, of finance, internal improvements, national defence, a new navy, forts and fortifications. Hard times, too, engrossed an enormous share of this attention. The immediate needs and problems of the hour pushed into the background all less pressing ones. The slavery question amidst the clamor and babel of emergent and material interests, lost something of its sectional heat and character. But its fires were not extinguished, only banked as events were speedily to reveal.

The application of Missouri for admission into the Union as a slave State four years after the Hartford Convention blew to a blaze the covered embers of strife between the sections. The North was violently agitated. For the admission of a new slave State meant two more slave votes in the Senate, and an increase on the old inequitable basis of slave representation in the lower House of Congress. It meant to the Northern section indefinite Southern ascendency, prolonged Southern lead in national legislation. All the smouldering passions of the earlier period, of embargo, and non-intercourse, and the war of 1812, flamed suddenly and fiercely in the heart of the free States.

The length and bitterness of that controversy excited the gravest apprehensions for the stability of the Union. The dread of disunion led to mutual concessions, to the Missouri Compromise. The slave-holding section got its immediate claim allowed, and the free States secured the erection of a line to the north of which slavery was forever prohibited. And besides this, the admission of Maine was supposed to neutralize whatever political advantages, which would accrue to the South from the admission of Missouri as a slave State. Both sections were content, and the slavery question was thought to be permanently settled. With this final disposition of an ugly problem, the peace and permanence of the Union were viewed universally as fixed facts. Still, considering the gravity of the case, a little precaution would not go amiss. The slavery question had shaken men's faith in the durability of the republic. It was therefore adjudged a highly dangerous subject. The political physicians with one accord prescribed on the ounce-of-prevention principle, *quiet*, SILENCE, and OBLIVION, to be administered in large and increasing doses to both sections. Mum was the word, and mum the country solemnly and suddenly became from Maine to Georgia. But, alas! beneath the ashes of this Missouri business, deep below the unnatural silence and quiet, inextinguishable fires were burning and working again to the surface of politics. In such circumstances a fresh outbreak of old animosities must occur as soon as the subterranean heat should reach the point of highest combustibility in the federal system. The tariff proved to be that point of highest combustibility.

Alexander Hamilton inaugurated the policy of giving governmental aid to infant manufactures. The wisdom of diversifying the industries of the young nation was acquiesced in by the leading statesmen of both sections. Beset as the republic then was by international forces hostile to democratic institutions, it was natural enough that the great men who presided over its early years should seek by Federal legislation to render it, as speedily and completely as possible, industrially self-dependent and self-supporting. The war of 1812 enforced anew upon the attention of statesmen the importance of industrial independence. The war debt, together with certain governmental enterprises and expenditures growing out of the war, was largely, if not wholly, responsible for the tariff of 1816. This act dates the rise of our American system of protection. It is curious to note that Southern men were the leaders of this new departure in the national fiscal policy. Calhoun, Clay, and Lowndes were the guiding spirits of that period of industrial ferment and activity. They little dreamt what economic evils were to fall in consequence upon the South. That section was not slow to feel the unequal action of the protective principle. The character of its labor incapacitated the South from dividing the benefits of the new revenue policy with its free rival. The South of necessity was restricted to a single industry, the tillage of the earth. Slave labor did not possess the intelligence, the skill, the patience, the mechanical versatility to embark successfully in manufacturing enterprises. Free labor monopolised the protected industries, and Northern capital caught all the golden showers of fiscal legislation. What the South needed, from an economic point of view, was unrestricted access to the markets of the world for her products, and the freest competition of the world in her own markets. The limitations imposed upon the slave States by their industrial system was in itself a tremendous handicap in their struggle for an advantageous place in the New World of the nineteenth century; in their struggle with their free sisters for political leadership in the Union. But with the development of the protective principle those States fell into sore financial distress, were ground between the upper millstone of the protective system and the nether millstone of their own industrial system. Prosperity and plenty did presently disappear from that section and settled in the North. In 1828 Benton drew this dark picture of the state of the South :

" In place of wealth, a universal pressure for money was felt ; not enough for common expenses ; the price of all property down ; the country drooping and languishing ; towns and cities decaying, and the frugal habits of the people pushed to the verge of universal self-denial for the preservation of their family estates."

He did not hesitate to charge to Federal legislation the responsibility for all this poverty and distress, for he proceeds to remark that :

" Under this legislation the exports of the South have been made the basis of the Federal revenue. The twenty odd millions annually levied upon imported goods are deducted out of the price of their cotton, rice, and tobacco, either in the diminished prices which they receive for those staples in foreign ports, or in the increased price which they pay for the articles they have to consume at home."

A suffering people are not apt to reason clearly or justly on the causes which have brought them to indigence. They feel their wretchedness and reach out for a victim. And the law-making power usually happens to be that victim. As the distress of the South increased, the belief that Federal legislation was responsible for it increased likewise. The spread and deepening of this conviction in the Southern States precipitated among them an ominous crisis in their attachment to the Union. Nullification and an embittered sectionalism was the hateful legacy bequeathed to the republic by the tariff controversy. It left the South in a hyper-sensitive state in all matters relating to her domestic interests. It left the North in a hyper-sensitive condition on all matters touching the peace and stability of the Union. The silence and oblivion policy on the subject of slavery was renewed with tenfold intensity. Ulysses-like the free States bound themselves, their right of free speech, and their freedom of the press on this subject, for fear of the Siren voices which came thrilling on every breeze from the South. Quiet was the word, and quiet the leaders in Church and State sought to enforce upon the people, to the end that the vision of "States dissevered, discordant, belligerent, of a land rent with civil feuds, or drenched it may be, in fraternal blood," might not come to pass for their "glorious Union."

The increasing friction and heat between the sections during twenty-five years, had effected every portion of the Federal system, and created conditions favorable to a violent explosion. Sectional differences of a political and industrial complexion, forty years had sufficed to develop. Sectional differences of a moral and social character forty years had also sufficed to generate. To kindle all those differences, all that mass of combustible feelings and forces into a general conflagration a spark only was wanted. And out of the glowing humanity of one man the spark was suddenly struck.

It is curious to note that in the year 1829, the very year in which William Lloyd Garrison landed in Baltimore, and began the editorship of *The Genius of Universal Emancipation*, the American Convention, or national assembly of the old State societies for the abolition of slavery, fell into desuetude. It was as if Providence was clearing the débris of an old dispensation out of the way of the new one which his prophet was beginning to herald, as if guarding against all possibility of having the new wine, then soon to be pressed from the moral vintage of the nation, put into old bottles. The Hour for a new movement against slavery had come, and with its arrival the Man to hail it had also come.

Other men had spoken and written against slavery, and labored for the freedom of the slave before Garrison had thought upon the subject at all. Washington and Jefferson, Franklin, Jay, and Hamilton had been Abolitionists before he was born, but theirs was a divided interest. The establishment of a more perfect union was the paramount object of their lives. John Wesley had denounced slavery in language quite as harsh as Garrison's, but his, too, was a divided interest, the religious revival of the eighteenth century being his distinctive mission. Benezet, Woolman, and Lundy were saints, who had yearned with unspeakable sympathy for the black bondmen, and were indefatigable in good works in his behalf, but they had not that stern and iron quality without which reforms cannot be launched upon the attention of mankind. What his predecessors lacked, Garrison possessed to a marvelous degree—the undivided interest, the supremacy of a single purpose, the stern stuff out of which the moral reformer is made, and in which he is panoplied. They were all his, but there was another besides—immediatism. This element distinguished the movement against slavery, started by him, from all other movements begun before he arrived on the stage, for the emancipation of the slaves in the Union.

This doctrine of immediate as opposed to gradual emancipation, was not original with Garrison, nor was he the first to enunciate it. More than a dozen years before he was converted to it, Rev. George Bourne, in "The Book and Slavery Irreconcilable," had shown that "the system (of slavery) is so entirely corrupt that it admits of no cure but by a *total and immediate abolition*. For a gradual emancipation is a virtual recognition of the right, and establishes the rectitude of the practice. If it be just for one moment, it is hallowed forever; and if it be inequitable, not a day should it be tolerated." In 1824, eight years after the publication of Bourne's book, and five years before Garrison announced the doctrine in the *Genius*, the Rev. James Duncan maintained it, in his "Treatise on Slavery," with no uncertainty of sense or conviction. But neither Bourne nor Duncan had been able to effect an incarnation of the doctrine, without which the good which it aimed at could not be achieved. What they failed to effect, it is the glory of Garrison that he achieved in his own person. He was "*total and immediate Abolition*" personified. "Truth is mighty and will prevail," is a wise saying and worthy of acceptation. But this ultimate prevailing of TRUTH depends mainly upon individual effort, applied not intermittently, but steadily to a particular segment of the circle of conduct. It is the long, strong, never-ending pull and tug upon the wheels of conduct, which marks the great reformer. He finds his age or country stuck in some Serbonian bog of iniquity. He prays, but he prays with his shoulders braced strenuously against the body of society, and he does not cease his endeavors until a revolution in conduct places his age or country on firm ground beyond its Serbonian bog. The coming of such a man is no accident. When the Hour is ready and the Man comes, a new epoch in the life of a people arises from the conjunction. Of such vast consequence verily was the coming into American history of William Lloyd Garrison.

CHAPTER V.

THE DAY OF SMALL THINGS.

AFTER leaving Baltimore, Garrison clung pathetically to the belief that, if he told what he had seen of the barbarism of slavery to the North, he would be certain to enlist the sympathy and aid of its leaders, political and ecclesiastical, in the cause of emancipation. The sequel to his efforts in this regard proved that he was never more mistaken in his life. He addressed letters to men like Webster, Jeremiah Mason, Lyman Beecher, and Dr. Channing, "holding up to their view the tremendous iniquity of the land, and begging them, ere it should be too late, to interpose their great power in the Church and State, to save our country from the terrible calamities which the sin of slavery was bringing upon us." But there is no evidence that this appeal produced the feeblest ripple in the lives of the two first; and upon the two last it was equally barren of result. Dr. Channing, indeed, did not take the trouble to hear any one of the three lectures of the young philanthropist. Dr. Beecher, however, was at the pains to be present at the first lecture given at Julien Hall. But he betrayed no real interest in the subject. He had no time to devote to anti-slvavery, had, in fine, too many irons in the fire already. To this impotent apology of the great preacher of immediatism in his dealing with all kinds of sin, except the sin of slave-holding, for not espousing the cause of the slave, Mr. Garrison made his famous retort:

"Then you had better let all your irons burn than neglect your duty to the slave."

What more did this poor and friendless man, with his one idea and his harsh language, know of duties and dangers than Daniel Webster, who was busy saving the Union; than Lyman Beecher, who was not less busy saving souls; or than Dr. Channing, who was quite as busy saving liberalism in matters of religion? What folly and presumption it must have seemed to these mighty men this attempt of Garrison to impress upon them a proper sense of their obligations to their country.

"Your zeal," said Dr. Beecher to him, with unlimited condescension of tone—"your zeal is commendable, but you are misguided. If you will give up your fanatical notions and be guided by us (the clergy) we will make you the Wilberforce of America."

And so what was the young man, burning up with his one idea, to do in presence of such a failure to win these men to the leadership of the anti-slavery movement? He could not hold his peace; his message he was compelled to deliver in the ears of the nation whether its leaders would hear or forbear. Perhaps the common people would hearken to what the wise and powerful had rejected. At any rate they should hear what was resting upon his soul with the weight of a great woe, the force of a supreme command. But how was he, penniless and friendless, to roll from his bosom the burden which was crushing it; to pause long enough in the battle for bread to fight the battle of the slave? Ah, if he had money! but no money did he have, not a dollar in his pocket! Oh, if he had rich friends who would dedicate their riches to the preaching of the gospel of freedom! but alas! rich friends there were none. Oh, if he could cry to the Church for help in this hour of his need! but it was slowly dawning on him that not from the Church would help come to his cause; for a grievous thing had happened to the Church. The slave gorgon sat staring from the pews, and turning the pulpits to stone, turning also to stone the hearts of the people.

Undismayed by the difficulties which were closing in around him, Garrison resolutely set himself to accomplish his purpose touching the establishment of a weekly paper devoted to the abolition of slavery. He had promised in his *Prospectus* to issue the first number of the *Public Liberator* "as soon as subscriptions thereto may authorize the attempt." But had he waited for the fulfillment of this condition, the experiment could never have been tried. When subscribers did not come in, the paper, he determined should go forth all the same. But there are some things in the publication of a paper which no man can dispense with, which indispensable somethings are: types, a press, an office, and an assistant. All these requisites were wanting to the man whose sole possession seemed an indomitable will, a faith in himself, and in the righteousness of his cause, which nothing could shake, nor disappointment nor difficulty, however great, was able to daunt or deter. To such an unconquerable will, to such an invincible faith obstacles vanish; the impossible becomes the attainable. As Garrison burned to be about his work, help came to him from a man quite as penniless and friendless as himself. The man was Isaac Knapp, an old companion of his in Newburyport, who had also worked with him in the office of the *Genius*, in Baltimore. He was a practical printer, and was precisely the sort of assistant that the young reformer needed at this juncture in the execution of his purpose; a man like himself acquainted with poverty, and of unlimited capacity for the endurance of unlimited hardships. Together they worked out the financial problems which blocked the way to the publication of the paper. The partners took an office in Merchants' Hall building, then standing on the corner of Congress and Water streets, Boston, which gave their joint enterprise a local habitation. It had already a name. They obtained the use of types in the printing office of the *Christian Examiner*, situated in the same building. The foreman, Stephen Foster, through his ardent interest in Abolition, made the three first numbers of the paper possible. The publishers paid for the use of the types by working during the day at the case in the *Examiner's* office. They got the use of a press from another foreman with Abolition sympathies, viz., James B. Yerrington, then the printer of the Boston *Daily Advocate*. Thus were obtained the four indispensables to the publication of the *Liberator*—types, a press, an office, and an assistant.

When at length the offspring of such labor and sacrifices made its appearance in the world, which was on January 1, 1831, it was, in point of size, insignificant enough. It did not look as if its voice would ever reach beyond the small dark chamber where it saw the light. Picture, oh ! reader, a wee sheet with four columns to the page, measuring fourteen inches one way and nine and a quarter the other, and you will get an idea of the diminutiveness of the *Liberator* on the day of its birth. The very paper on which it was printed was procured on credit. To the ordinary observer it must have seemed such a weakling as was certain to perish from inanition in the first few months of its struggle for existence in the world of journalism. It was domiciled during successive periods in four different rooms of the Merchant's Hall building, until it reached No. 11, "under the eaves," whence it issued weekly for many years to call the nation to repentance. A photographic impression of this cradle-room of the anti-slavery movement has been left by Oliver Johnson, an eye-witness. Says Mr. Johnson : "The dingy walls ; the small windows, bespattered with printer's ink ; the press standing in one corner ; the composing-stands opposite ; the long editorial and mailing table, covered with newspapers ; the bed of the editor and publisher on the floor—all these make a picture never to be forgotten." For the first eighteen months the partners toiled fourteen hours a day, and subsisted "chiefly upon bread and milk, a few cakes, and a little fruit, obtained from a baker's shop opposite, and a petty cake and fruit shop in the basement," and, alas, "were on short commons even at that." Amid such hard and grinding poverty was the *Liberator* born. But the great end of the reformer glorified the mean surroundings :

"O truth! O Freedom! how are ye still born
In the rude stable, in the manger nursed;
What humble hands unbar those gates of morn
Through which the splendors of the New Day burst."

About the brow of this "infant crying in the night," shone aureole-like the sunlit legend: *Our country is the world—our countrymen are mankind.* The difference between this motto of the *Liberator* and that of the *Free Press: Our country, our whole country, and nothing but our country*—measures the greatness of the revolution which had taken place in the young editor. The grand lesson he had learned, than which there is none greater, that beneath diversities of race, color, creed, language, there is the one human principle, which makes all men kin. He had learned at the age of twenty-five to know the mark of brotherhood made by the Deity Himself: "Behold! my brother is man, not because he is American or Anglo-Saxon, or white or black, but because he is a fellow-man," is the simple, sublime acknowledgment, which thenceforth he was to make in his word and life.

It was Mr. Garrison's original design, as we have seen, to publish the *Liberator* from Washington. Lundy had, since the issue of the *Prospectus* for the new paper, removed the *Genius* to the capital of the nation. This move of Lundy rendered the establishment of a second paper devoted to the abolition of slavery in the same place, of doubtful utility, but, weighty as was this consideration from a mere business point of view, in determining Garrison to locate the *Liberator* in another quarter, it was not decisive. Just what was the decisive consideration, he reveals in his salutatory address in the *Liberator*. Here it is:

"During my recent tour for the purpose of exciting the minds of the people by a series of discourses on the subject of slavery," he confides to the reader, "every place that I visited gave fresh evidence of the fact, that a greater revolution in public sentiment was to be effected in the free States—*and particularly in New England*—than at the South. I found contempt more bitter, opposition more active, detraction more relentless, prejudice more stubborn, and apathy more frozen than among slaveowners themselves. Of course there were individual exceptions to the contrary. This state of things afflicted, but did not dishearten me. I determined, at every hazard, to lift up the standard of emancipation in the eyes of the nation, *within sight of Bunker Hill, and in the birthplace of liberty*." This final choice of Boston as a base from which to operate against slavery was sagacious, and of the greatest moment to the success of the experiment and to its effective service to the cause.

If the reformer changed his original intention respecting the place of publication for his paper, he made no alteration of his position on the subject of slavery. "I shall strenuously contend," he declares in the salutatory, "for the immediate enfranchisement of our slave population." "In Park Street Church," he goes on to add, "on the Fourth of July, 1829, in an address on slavery, I unreflectingly assented to the popular but pernicious doctrine of *gradual* abolition. I seize this opportunity to make a full and unequivocal recantation, and thus publicly to ask pardon of my God, of my country, and of my brethren, the poor slaves, for having uttered a sentiment so full of timidity, injustice, and absurdity."

To those who find fault with his harsh language he makes reply: "I *will* be as harsh as truth, and as uncompromising as justice. On this subject, I do not wish to think, or speak, or write, with moderation. No! no! Tell a man whose house is on fire to give a moderate alarm; tell him to moderately rescue his wife from the hands of the ravisher; tell the mother to gradually extricate her babe from the fire into which it has fallen—but urge me not to use moderation in a cause like the present. I am in earnest—I will not equivocate—I will not excuse—I will not retreat a single inch—AND I WILL BE HEARD." Martin Luther's "Here I take my stand," was not braver or grander than the "I will be heard," of the American reformer. It did not seem possible that a young man, without influence, without money, standing almost alone, could ever make good those courageous words. The country, in Church and State, had decreed silence on the subject of slavery; the patriotism of the North, its commerce, its piety, its labor and capital had all joined hands to smother agitation, and stifle the discussion of a question that imperilled the peace and durability of Webster's glorious Union. But one man, tearing the gag from his lips, defying all these, cried, "Silence, there shall not be!" and forthwith the whole land began to talk on the forbidden theme:

"O small beginnings ye are great and strong,
Based on a faithful heart and weariless brain!
Ye build the future fair, ye conquer wrong.
Ye earn the crown, and wear it not in vain!"

CHAPTER VI.

THE HEAVY WORLD IS MOVED.

ARCHIMEDES with his lever desired a place to stand that he might move the world of matter. Garrison with his paper, having found a place for his feet, demonstrated speedily his ability to push from its solid base the world of mind. His plan was very simple, viz., to reveal slavery as it then existed in its naked enormity, to the conscience of the North, to be "as harsh as truth and as uncompromising as justice." And so, week after week, he packed in the columns of the *Liberator* facts, the most damning facts, against slaveholders, their cruelty and tyranny. He painted the woes of the slaves as if he, too, had been a slave. For the first time the masters found a man who rebuked them as not before had they been rebuked. Others may have equivocated, but this man called things by their proper names, a spade, a spade, and sin, sin. Others may have contented themselves with denunciations of the sins and with excuses for the sinner, as a creature of circumstances, the victim of ancestral transgressions, but this man offered no excuses for the slave-holding sinner. Him and his sin he denounced in language, which the Eternal puts only into the mouths of His prophets. It was, as he had said, "On this subject I do not wish to think, or speak, or write, with moderation." The strength and resources of his mother-tongue seemed to him wholly inadequate for his needs, to express the transcendent wickedness of slave-holding. All the harsh, the stern, the terrible and tremendous energies of the English speech he drew upon, and launched at slaveholders. Amid all of this excess of the enthusiast there was the method of a calculating mind. He aimed to kindle a conflagration because he had icebergs to melt. "The public shall not be imposed upon," he replied to one of his critics, "and men and things shall be called by their right names. I retract nothing, I blot out nothing. My language is exactly such as suits me; it will displease many, I know; to displease them is my intention." He was philosopher enough to see that he could reach the national conscience only by exciting the national anger. It was not popular rage, which he feared but popular apathy. If he could goad the people to anger on the subject of slavery he would soon be rid of their apathy. And so week after week he piled every sort of combustible material, which he was able to collect on board the *Liberator* and lighting it all, sent the fiery messenger blazing among the icebergs of the Union. Slaveholders were robbers, murderers, oppressors; they were guilty of all the sins of the decalogue, were in a word the chief of sinners. At the same moment that the reformer denied their right of property in the slave, he attacked their character also, held them up in their relation of masters to the reprobation of the nation and of mankind as monsters of injustice and inhumanity. The tone which he held toward them, steadily, without shadow of change, was the tone of a righteous man toward the workers of iniquity. The indifference, the apathy, the pro-slavery sympathy and prejudice of the free States rendered the people of the North hardly less culpable. They were working iniquity with the people of the South. This was the long, sharp goad, which the young editor thrust in between the bars of the Union and stirred the guilty sections to quick and savage outbursts of temper against him and the bitter truths which he preached. Almost directly the proofs came to him that he was HEARD at the South and at the North alike. Angry growls reached his ears in the first month of the publication of the *Liberator* from some heartless New England editors in denunciation of his "violent and intemperate attacks on slaveholders." The *Journal*, published at Louisville, Kentucky, and edited by George D. Prentice, declared that, "some of his opinions with regard to slavery in the United States are no better than lunacy." The *American Spectator* published at the seat of the National Government, had hoped that the good sense of the "late talented and persecuted junior editor" of the *Genius*, "would erelong withdraw him even from the side of the Abolitionists." And from farther South the growl which the reformer heard was unmistakably ferocious. It was from the State of South Carolina and the Camden *Journal*, which pronounced the *Liberator* "a scandalous and incendiary budget of sedition." These were the beginning of the chorus of curses, which soon were to sing their serpent songs about his head. Profane and abusive letters from irate slaveholders and their Northern sympathisers began to pour into the sanctum of the editor. Within a few months after the first issue of the *Liberator* the whole aspect of the world without had changed toward him. "Foes are on my right hand, and on my left," he reported to some friends. "The tongue of detraction is busy against me. I have no communion with the world—the world none with me. The timid, the lukewarm, the base, affect to believe that my brains are disordered, and my words the ravings of a maniac. Even many of my friends—they who have grown up with me from my childhood—are transformed into scoffers and enemies." The apathy of the press, and the apathy of the people were putting forth signs that the long winter of the land was passing away.

To a colored man belongs the high honor of having been the *courier avant* of the slavery agitation. This man was David Walker, who lived in Boston, and who published in 1829 a religio-political discussion of the status of the negroes of the United States in four articles. The wretchedness of the blacks in consequence of slavery he depicted in dark and bitter language. Theodore Parker, many years afterward, said that the negro was deficient in vengeance, the lowest form of justice. "Walker's Appeal" evinced no deficiency in this respect in its author. The pamphlet found its way South, and was the cause of no little commotion among the master-class. It was looked upon as an instigation to servile insurrection. The "Appeal" was proscribed, and a price put upon the head of the author. Garrison deprecated the sanguinary character of the book. For he himself was the very reverse of Walker. Garrison was a full believer in the literal doctrine of non-resistance as enunciated by Jesus. He abhorred all war, and physical collisions of every description, as wicked and inhuman. He sang to the slave :

"Not by the sword shall your deliverance be;
Not by the shedding of your master's blood,
Not by rebellion—or foul treachery,
Upspringing suddenly, like swelling flood;
Revenge and rapine ne'er did bring forth good.
God's *time is best!*—nor will it long delay;
Even now your barren cause begins to bud,
And glorious shall the fruit be!—watch and pray,
For lo! the kindling dawn that ushers in the day."

He considered "Walker's Appeal" "a most injudicious publication, yet warranted by the creed of an independent people." He saw in our Fourth-of-July demonstrations, in our glorification of force as an instrument for achieving liberty, a constant incentive to the slaves to go and do likewise. If it was right for the men of 1776 to rise in rebellion against their mother-country, it surely could not be wrong were the slaves to revolt against their oppressors, and strike for their freedom. It certainly did not lie in the mouth of a people, who apotheosized force, to condemn them. What was sauce for the white man's goose was sauce for the black man's gander.

The South could not distinguish between this sort of reasoning, and an express and positive appeal to the slaves to cut the throats of their masters. The contents of the *Liberator* were quite as likely to produce a slave insurrection as was "Walker's Appeal," if the paper was allowed to circulate freely among the slave population. It was, in fact, more dangerous to the lives and interests of slaveholders by virtue of the pictorial representation of the barbarism and abomination of the peculiar institution, introduced as a feature of the *Liberator* in its seventeenth number, in the shape of a slave auction, where the slaves are chattels, and classed with "horses and other cattle," and where the tortures of the whipping-post are in vigorous operation. Here was a message, which every slave, however ignorant and illiterate could read. His instinct would tell him, wherever he saw the pictured horror, that a friend, not an enemy, had drawn it, but for what purpose? What was the secret meaning, which he was to extract from a portrayal of his woes at once so real and terrible. Was it to be a man, to seize the knife, the torch, to slay and burn his way to the rights and estate of a man? Garrison had put no such bloody import into the cut. It was designed not to appeal to the passions of the slaves, but to the conscience of the North. But the South did not so read it, was incapable, in fact, of so reading it. What it saw was a shockingly realistic representation of the wrongs of the slaves, the immediate and inevitable effect of which upon the slaves would be to incite them to sedition, to acts of revenge. Living as the slave-holders were over mines of powder and dynamite, it is not to be marveled at that the first flash of danger filled them with apprehension and terror. The awful memories of San Domingo flamed red and dreadful against the dark background of every Southern plantation and slave community. In the "belly" of the *Liberator's* picture were many San Domingos. Extreme fear is the beginning of madness; it is, indeed, a kind of madness. The South was suddenly plunged into a state of extreme fear toward which the *Liberator* and "Walker's Appeal" were hurrying it, by one of those strange accidents or coincidences of history.

This extraordinary circumstance was the slave insurrection in Southampton, Virginia, in the month of August, 1831. The leader of the uprising was the now famous Nat Turner. Brooding over the wrongs of his race for several years, he conceived that he was the divinely appointed agent to redress them. He was cast in the mould of those rude heroes, who spring out of the sides of oppression as isolated trees will sometimes grow out of clefts in a mountain. With his yearning to deliver his people, there mingled not a little religious frenzy and superstition. Getting his command from Heaven to arise against the masters, he awaited the sign from this same source of the moment for beginning the work of destruction. It came at last and on the night of August 21st; he and his confederates made a beginning by massacring first his own master, Mr. Joseph Travis, and his entire family. Turner's policy was remorseless enough. It was to spare no member of the white race, whether man, woman, or child, the very infant at the mother's breast was doomed to the knife, until he was able to collect such an assured force as would secure the success of the enterprise. This purpose was executed with terrible severity and exactness. All that night the work of extermination went on as the slave leader and his followers passed like fate from house to house, and plantation to plantation, leaving a wide swathe of death in their track. Terror filled the night, terror filled the State, the most abject terror clutched the bravest hearts. The panic was pitiable, horrible. James McDowell, one of the leaders of the Old Dominion, gave voice to the awful memories and sensations of that night, in the great anti-slavery debate, which broke out in the Virginia Legislature, during the winter afterward. One of the legislators, joined to his idol, and who now, that the peril had passed, laughed at the uprising as a "petty affair." McDowell retorted—"Was that a 'petty affair,' which erected a peaceful and confiding portion of the State into a military camp, which outlawed from pity the unfortunate beings whose brothers had offended; which barred every door, penetrated every bosom with fear or suspicion, which so banished every sense of security from every man's dwelling, that let but a hoof or horn break upon the silence of the night, and an aching throb would be driven to the heart? The husband would look to his weapon, and the mother would shudder and weep upon her cradle. Was it the fear of Nat Turner and his deluded, drunken handful of followers which produced such effects? Was it this that induced distant counties, where the very name of Southampton was strange, to arm and equip for a struggle? No, sir, it was the *suspicion eternally attached to the slave himself*,—a suspicion that a Nat Turner might be in every family, that the same bloody deed might be acted over at any time and in any place, that the materials for it were spread through the land, and were always ready for a like explosion."

Sixty-one whites and more than a hundred blacks perished in this catastrophe. The news produced a profound sensation in the Union. Garrison himself, as he records, was horror-struck at the tidings. Eight months before he had in a strain of prophecy penetrated the future and caught a glimpse of just such an appalling tragedy:

"Wo, if it come with storm, and blood, and fire,
When midnight darkness veils the earth and sky!
Wo to the innocent babe—the guilty sire—
Mother and daughter—friends of kindred tie!
Stranger and citizen alike shall die!
Red-handed slaughter his revenge shall feed,
And havoc yell his ominous death-cry,
And wild despair in vain for mercy plead—
While hell itself shall shrink and sicken at the deed!"

After the Southampton insurrection the slavery agitation increased apace, and the *Liberator* and its editor became instantly objects of dangerous notoriety in it. The eyes of the country were irresistibly drawn to them. They were at the bottom of the uprising, they were instigating the slaves to similar outbreaks. The savage growlings of a storm came thrilling on every breeze from the South, and wrathful mutterings against the agitator and his paper grew thenceforth more distinct and threatening throughout the free States. October 15, 1831, Garrison records in the *Liberator* that he "is constantly receiving from the slave States letters filled with the most diabolical threats and indecent language." In the same month Georgetown, S. C., in a panic made it unlawful for a free colored person to take the *Liberator* from the post-office. In the same month the Charleston *Mercury* announced that "gentlemen of the first respectability" at Columbia had offered a reward of fifteen hundred dollars for the arrest and conviction of any white person circulating the *Liberator*, Walker's pamphlet, "or any other publication of seditious tendency." In Georgia the same symptoms of fright were exhibited. In the same month the grand jury at Raleigh, N. C., indicted William Lloyd Garrison and Isaac Knapp for circulating the *Liberator* in that county. It was even confidently expected that a requisition would be made by the Executive of the State upon the Governor of Massachusetts for their arrest, when they would be tried under a law, which made their action felony. "Whipping and imprisonment for the first offence, and death, without benefit of clergy, for the second." Governor Floyd said in his message to the Virginia Legislature in December that there was good cause to suspect that the plans of the Southampton massacre were "designed and matured by unrestrained fanatics in some of the neighboring States." Governor Hamilton sent to the South Carolina Legislature in the same month an excited message on the situation. He was in entire accord with the Virginia Executive as to the primary and potent agencies which led to the slave uprising in Virginia. They were "incendiary newspapers and other publications put forth in the non-slave-holding States, and freely circulated within the limits of Virginia." As specimens of "incendiary newspapers and other publications, put forth in the non-slave-holding States," the South Carolina official sent along with his message, copies of the *Liberator* and of Mr. Garrison's address to the "Free People of Color," for the enlightenment of the members of the Legislature. But it remained for Georgia to cap the climax of madness when her Legislature resolved: 'That the sum of five thousand dollars be, and the same is hereby appropriated, to be paid to any person or persons who shall arrest, bring to trial and prosecute to conviction, under the laws of this State, the editor or publisher of a certain paper called the *Liberator*, published in the town of Boston and State of Massachusetts ; or who shall arrest and bring to trial and prosecute to conviction, under the laws of this State, any other person or persons who shall utter, publish, or circulate within the limits of this State said paper called the *Liberator*, or any other paper, circular, pamphlet, letter, or address of a seditious character." This extraordinary resolve was signed Dec. 26, 1831, by "Wilson Lumpkin, Governor." The whole South was in a state of terror. In its insane fright it would have made short shrift of the editor of the *Liberator*, had he by accident, force, or fraud have fallen into the clutches of its laws. The Georgia reward of five thousand dollars was as Mr. Garrison put it, "a bribe to kidnappers." The Southern method of dealing with the agitation within the slave States was violent and effective. There could be no agitation after the agitators were abolished. And the Southern method was to abolish the agitators.

The suppression of Abolitionism within the slave States was no difficult matter, but its suppression at the North was a problem of a wholly different nature, as the South was not long in finding out. It would not understand why its violent treatment of the disease within its jurisdiction could not be prescribed as a remedy by the non-slave-holding half of the Union within its borders. And so the South began to call loudly and fiercely for the suppression of a movement calculated to incite the slaves to insubordination and rebellion. This demand of the South had its influence at the North. Such newspapers as the *National Intelligencer*, and the Boston *Courier* suggested amendments to the laws whereby the publication of incendiary writings in the free States might be prohibited. The latter journal allowed that under the criminal code of Massachusetts "every man has a right to advocate Abolition, or conspiracy, or murder; for he may do all these without breaking our laws, although in any Southern State public justice and public safety would require his punishment. "But," the editor goes on to remark, "if we have no laws upon the subject, it is because the exigency was not anticipated . . . Penal statutes against treasonable and seditious publications are necessary in all communities. We have them for our own protection; if they should include provisions for the protection of our neighbors it would be no additional encroachment upon the liberty of the press." The Governors of Virginia and Georgia remonstrated with Harrison Gray Otis, who was Mayor of Boston in the memorable year of 1831, "against an incendiary newspaper published in Boston, and, as they alleged, thrown broadcast among their plantations, inciting to insurrection and its horrid results." As a lawyer Mayor Otis, however, "perceived the intrinsic, if not insuperable obstacles to legislative enactments made to prevent crimes from being consummated beyond the local jurisdiction." But the South was not seeking a legal opinion as to what it could or could not do. It demanded, legal or illegal, that Garrison and the *Liberator* be suppressed. To the Boston mayor the excitement over the editor and his paper seemed like much ado about nothing The cause appeared to his supercilious mind altogether inadequate to the effect. And so he set to work to reduce the panic by exposing the vulgarity and insignificance of the object, which produced it. That he might give the Southern bugaboo its *quietus*, he directed one of his deputies to inquire into a publication, of which "no member of the city government, nor any person," of his honor's acquaintance, "had ever heard." The result of this inquiry Mayor Otis reported to the Southern functionaries.

"Some time afterward," he wrote, "it was reported to me by the city officers that they had ferreted out the paper and its editor; that his office was an obscure hole, his only visible auxiliary a negro boy, and his supporters a very few insignificant persons of all colors."

With this bare bodkin Harrison Gray Otis thought to puncture the Southern panic. But the slaveholders had correcter notions of the nature and tendency of the Abolition enterprise than had the Boston mayor. They had a strange, an obstinate presentiment of disaster from the first instant that the *Liberator* loomed upon their horizon. It was a battery whose guns, unless silenced, would play havoc with Southern interests and the slave system; *ergo*, the paper must be suppressed; *ergo*, its editor must be silenced or destroyed. And so when Otis, from his serene height, assured them of his "belief that the new fanaticism had not made, nor was likely to make, proselytes among the respectable classes of our people," they continued to listen to their fears, and to cry the louder for the suppression of the "incendiary newspaper published in Boston."

The editor of that paper never flinched before the storm of malignity which was gathering about his head. He pursued the even tenor of his way, laboring at the case more than fourteen hours every day, except Sundays, upon the paper, renewing, week after week, his assaults upon the citadel of the great iniquity, giving no quarter to slave-holding sinners, but carrying aloft the banner of IMMEDIATE AND UNCONDITIONAL EMANCIPATION. Otis had looked to numbers and respectability as his political barometer and cue; but when, after diligent search with official microscopes, he failed to observe the presence of either in connection with this "new fanaticism," wise man that he was, he turned over and renewed his slumbers on the edge of a volcano whose ominous rumbling the Southern heart had heard and interpreted aright. He was too near to catch the true import of the detonations of those subterranean forces which were sounding, week after week, in the columns of the *Liberator*. They seemed trivial, harmless, contemptible, like the toy artillery of children bombarding Fort Independence. Garrison's moral earnestness and enthusiasm seemed to the Boston mayor like the impotent rage of a man nursing memories of personal injuries suffered at the South.

If there was panic in the South, there was none in the office of the *Liberator*. Unterrified by the commotion which his composing-stick was producing near and far, he laughed to scorn the abuse and threats of his enemies. When the news of the reward of the State of Georgia "for the abduction of his person" reached him, he did not quail, great as was his peril, but boldly replied:

"Of one thing we are sure: all Southern threats and rewards will be insufficient to deter us from pur suing the work of emancipation. As citizens of the United States we know our rights and dare maintain them. We have committed no crime, but are expending our health, comfort, and means for the salvation of our country, and for the interests and security of infatuated slaveholders, as well as for the relief of the poor slaves."

Archimedes with his lever had moved the world. Archimedes "in a small chamber, unfurnitured and mean," had set a world of pro-slavery passions and prejudices spinning away into space:

"Such earnest natures are the fiery pith,
The compact nucleus, 'round which systems grow;
Mass after mass becomes inspired therewith,
And whirls impregnate with the central glow."

CHAPTER VII.

MASTER STROKES.

"HELP came but slowly" to the reformer. With a single instrument he had stirred the nation, as no other man had done, on the slavery question. He had thrown the South into widespread excitement, and thawed the apathy of the North into widespread attention. He had won an almost instant hearing for his cause. But he knew that this was not enough. Effective as he had shown the weapon of the press to be, it alone was unequal to the conduct of prolonged agitation. And prolonged agitation Garrison clearly apprehended was to be the price of abolition. Back of him and the *Liberator* he needed an organized force, coadjutors like Aaron and Hur to hold up his arms during the mighty conflict on which he had now entered with the slave interests of the country. Those interests were organized, and because they were organized they were powerful. The sentiment of freedom he determined to organize and to render it thereby invincible. To organized wrong he designed to oppose organized right, confident that organized right would prevail in the end. He had knowledge of the utility of temperance societies in advancing the cause of sobriety among the people. He had learned from Lundy how much he had relied upon the union of men as anti-slavery helps. Garrison determined to summon to his side the powerful agency of an anti-slavery society devoted to immediate and unconditional emancipation. He had already made converts ; he had already a small following. At Julien Hall, on the occasion of his first lecture on the subject of slavery, he had secured three remarkable men to the movement, viz., Rev. Samuel J. May, then a young Unitarian minister, Samuel E. Sewall, a young member of the Bar, and A. Bronson Alcott, a sage even in his early manhood. They had all promised him aid and comfort in the great task which he had undertaken. A little later two others, quite as remarkable as those first three were drawn to the reformer's side, and abetted him in the treason to iniquity, which he was prosecuting through the columns of the *Liberator* with unrivaled zeal and devotion. These disciples were Ellis Grey Loring and David Lee Child. They were a goodly company, were these five conspirators, men of intellect and conscience, of high family and social connections, of brilliant attainments and splendid promises for the future. To this number must be added a sixth, Oliver Johnson, who was at the time editing *The Christian Soldier*, disciple of Garrison then, and ever after his devoted friend. The early promises of this noble half dozen friends of the slave were more than fulfilled in after years. Often to the dingy room "under the eaves" in Merchants' Hall they climbed to carry aid and comfort to "one poor, unlearned young man," and to sit at his feet in this cradle-room of the new movement. It was there in communion with the young master that suggestions looking to the formation of an anti-slavery society, were doubtless first thrown out.

"The place was dark, unfurnitured and mean;
Yet there the freedom of a race began."

It was not all clear sailing for the editor of the *Liberator* even with such choice spirits. They did not always carry aid and comfort to him, but differences of opinions sometimes as well. He did not sugar-coat enough the bitter truth which he was telling to the nation. Some of them would have preferred *The Safety Lamp* to the *Liberator* as a title less likely to offend the prejudices of many good people. Some again objected to the pictorial heading of the paper as an altogether unwise proceeding, and positively mischievous. He had the same experience when the formation of an Abolition society was under consideration. He was confronted with this benevolent aversion to giving offence by calling things by their right names. But much as he desired to have his friends and followers organized for associated action, where a principle was at stake he was with them as with slavery itself absolutely inflexible and uncompromising. He was for organizing on the principle of immediate emancipation. A few deemed that ground too radical and revolutionary, and were for ranging themselves under the banner of Gradualism, thinking to draw to their ranks a class of people, who would be repelled by Immediatism. But Garrison was unyielding, refused to budge an inch to conciliate friend or foe—not even such stanch supporters as were Sewall and Loring, who supplied him again and again with money needed to continue the publication of the *Liberator*. No, he was right and they were wrong, and they, not he, ought accordingly to yield. The contention between the leader and his disciples was not what was expedient, but what was right. It was on the part of the leader the assertion of a vital principle, and on this ground he was pledged against retreat. The mountain could not go to Mahomet, therefore Mahomet must needs go to the mountain. Garrison could not abandon his position, wherefore in due time Loring, Child, and Sewall surrendered theirs. Finely has Lowell expressed this righteous stubborness, and steadfastness to principle in three stanzas of his poem entitled, "The Day of Small Things," and which have such an obvious lesson for our own times that I shall venture to quote them in this place :

"Who is it will not dare himself to trust?
Who is it hath not strength to stand alone?
Who is it thwarts and bilks the inward MUST?
He and his works, like sand from earth are blown.

"Men of a thousand shifts and wiles look here!
See one straightforward conscience put in pawn
To win a world! See the obedient sphere
By bravery's simple gravitation drawn!

"Shall we not heed the lesson taught of old,
And by the Present's lips repeated still,
In our own single manhood to be bold,
Fortressed in conscience and impregnable will?"

The history of the making of this first society is an interesting story. There were four meetings in all before it was found possible to complete the work of its organization. These meetings extended over a space of nearly three months, so obstinate were a minority against committing the proposed society to the principle of immediate emancipation. The very name which was to be given to the association provoked debate and disagreement. Some were for christening it "Philo-African," while Garrison would no such milk-and-water title, but one which expressed distinctly and graphically the real character of the organization, viz., "New England Anti-Slavery Society." He would sail under no false or neutral colors, but beneath the red flag of open and determined hostility to slavery. It should be a sign which no one could possibly mistake. The first meeting was held at the office of Samuel E. Sewall, November 13, 1831. At the third meeting, convened New Year's evening of 1832, which was the first anniversary of the publication of the *Liberator*, the work of organization was finished, with a single important exception, viz., the adoption of the preamble to the constitution. The character of the preamble would fix the character of the society. Therefore that which was properly first was made to come last. The fourth meeting took place on the night of January 6th in the African Baptist Church on what was then Belknap but now known as Joy street. The young leader and fourteen of his followers met that evening in the school-room for colored children, situated under the auditorium of the church. They could hardly have fallen upon a more obscure or despised place for the consummation of their enterprise in the city of Boston than was this selfsame negro church and school-room. The weather added an ever memorable night to the opprobrium of the spot. A fierce northeaster accompanied with "snow, rain, and hail in equal proportions" was roaring and careering through the city's streets. To an eye-witness, Oliver Johnson, "it almost seemed as if Nature was frowning upon the new effort to abolish slavery; but," he added, "the spirits of the little company rose superior to all external circumstances."

If there was strife of the elements without, neither was there sweet accord within among brethren. "The spirits of the little company" may have risen superior to the weather, but they did not rise superior to the preamble, with the principle of immediatism incorporated in it. Eleven stood by the leader and made it the chief of the corner of the new society, while three, Messrs. Loring, Sewall, and Child, refused to sign the Constitution and parted sorrowfully from the small band of the New England Anti-Slavery Society. But the separation was only temporary, for each returned to the side of the reformer, and proved his loyalty and valor in the trying years which followed.

The preamble which was the bone of so much contention declared that: "We, the undersigned, hold that every person, of full age and sane mind, has a right to immediate freedom from personal bondage of whatsoever kind, unless imposed by the sentence of the law for the commission of some crime. We hold that man cannot, consistently with reason, religion, and the eternal and immutable principles of justice, be the property of man. We hold that whoever retains his fellow-man in bondage is guilty of a grievous wrong. We hold that a mere difference of complexion is no reason why any man should be deprived of any of his natural rights, or subjected to any political disability. While we advance these opinions as the principles on which we intend to act, we declare that we will not operate on the existing relations of society by other than peaceful and lawful means, and that we will give no countenance to violence or insurrection."

Twelve, the apostolic number, affixed to the preamble and constitution their names, and thus formed the first Garrisonian Society for the abolition of slavery in the United States. The names of these apostolic men it is well to keep in mind. They are William Lloyd Garrison, Oliver Johnson, Robert B. Hall, Arnold Buffum, William J. Snelling, John E. Fuller, Moses Thatcher, Joshua Coffin, Stillman B. Newcomb, Benjamin C. Bacon, Isaac Knapp, and Henry K. Stockton. The band of reformers, their work done, had risen to pass out of the low, rude room into the dark night. The storm was still raging. They themselves had perchance been sobered by the experiences of the evening. They had gone in fifteen, they were returning twelve. And, after all, what had they accomplished? What could they a mere handful do to abolish slavery entrenched as it was in Church and State? It is possible that some such dim discouragement, some such vague misgiving of the futility of the evening's labor, was in the hearts of those wearied men, and that their leader divined as much, for the spirit of prophecy fell upon Garrison just as they "were stepping out into the storm and darkness." "We have met to-night," he said, "in this obscure school-house; our numbers are few and our influence limited; but, mark my prediction, Faneuil Hall shall erelong echo with the principles we have set forth. We shall shake the nation by their mighty power." Then the little band dispersed "into the storm and darkness," carrying with them these words charged with hope and courage.

The fruitful seed of organized agitation Garrison had securely planted in soil fertile and ready for its reception. Its growth constitutes one of the marvels of reforms. Within a few brief years it multiplied into hundreds and thousands of societies throughout the free States. But its beginnings were small and humble enough. "The objects of the society" were according to the second article of the constitution, "to endeavor by all means sanctioned by law, humanity, and religion, to effect the abolition of slavery in the United States, to improve the character and condition of the free people of color, to inform and correct public opinion in relation to their situation and rights, and to obtain for them equal civil and political rights and privileges with the whites." The means which were immediately adopted by the society for the accomplishment of these objects were mainly three, than which none others could have been more effective. These were petitioning Congress on the subject of slavery. The publication and circulation of anti-slavery addresses and tracts, and the employment of anti-slavery agents, "in obtaining or communicating intelligence, in the publication and distribution of tracts, books, or papers, or in the execution of any measure which may be adopted to promote the objects of the society." Such was the simple but unequaled machinery which the New England Anti-Slavery Society relied upon for success in the war, which it had declared against American slavery. The executive power of the body, and the operation of its machinery were lodged in a board of managers of which Garrison's was the leading, originating mind. The society started out bravely in the use of its means by memorializing Congress for the abolition of slavery, "in the District of Columbia and in the Territories of the United States under their jurisdiction," and by preparing and distributing an address in maintenance of the doctrine of immediate emancipation. The board of managers set the machinery in motion as far and as fast as the extremely limited pecuniary ability of the society would permit. The membership was not from the rich classes. It was Oliver Johnson who wittily remarked that not more than one or two of the original twelve, "could have put a hundred dollars into the treasury without bankrupting themselves." The remark was true, and was quite as applicable to any dozen of the new-comers as to the original twelve. The society was never deficient in zeal, bnt it was certainly sadly wanting in money. And money was even to such men and to such a movement an important factor in revolutionizing public opinion.

The *Liberator* was made the official organ of the society, and in this way was added to its other weapons that of the press. This was a capital arrangement, for by it both the paper and the society were placed under the direction of the same masterly guidance. There was still one arrow left in the moral quiver of the organization to reach the conscience of the people, and that was the appointment of an agent to spread the doctrines of the new propaganda of freedom. In August the board of managers, metaphorically speakin g, shot this arrow by making Garrison the agent of the society to lecture on the subiect of slavery "for a period not exeeeding three months." This was the first drop from a cloud then no bigger than a hand, but which was to grow and spread until, covering the North, was, at the end of a few short years, to flood the land with anti-slavery agents and lecturers.

Our anti-slavery agent visited portions of Massachusetts, Maine, and Rhode Island, preaching the Abolition gospel in divers places, and to many people—notably at such centers of population as Worcester, Providence, Bangor, and Portland, making at the latter city a signal conversion to his cause in the person of General Samuel Fessenden, distinguished then as a lawyer, and later as the father of William Pitt Fessenden. The anti-slavery schoolmaster was abroad, and was beginning to turn New England and the North into one resounding schoolhouse, where he sat behind the desk and the nation occupied the forms.

So effective was the agitation prosecuted by the society during the first year of its existence that it was no empty declaration or boast of the *Abolitionist*, the new monthly periodical of the society, that "probably, through its instrumentality, more public addresses on the subject of slavery, and appeals in behalf of the contemned free people of color, have been made in New England, during the past year (1832) than were elicited for forty years prior to its organization."

The introduction of the principle of association into the slavery agitation, and the conversion of it into an organized movement was an achievement of the first importance. To Garrison, more than to any man, or to all others put together, belongs the authorship of this immense initiative. He it was, who, having "announced the principle, arranged the method" of the Abolition movement. The marshaling of the anti-slavery sentiment of New England under a common standard, in a common cause, was a master stroke of moral generalship. This master stroke the leader followed up promptly with a second stroke not less masterly. That second stroke was his "Thoughts on African Colonization," published in the summer succeeding the formation of the New England Anti-Slavery Society.

Garrison's championship of the cause of the slave had started with strong faith in the efficacy and disinterestedness of the colonization scheme as an instrument of emancipation. It commanded, therefore, his early support. In his Park Street Church address he evinced himself in earnest sympathy with the friends of colonization. But after his arrival in Baltimore a change began to exhibit itself in this regard. He began to qualify his confidence in its utility; began to discern in it influences calculated to retard general emancipation. As these doubts and misgivings arose within him he expressed them frankly in the *Genius.* Lundy had been suspicious of the pro-slavery purposes or interests of the enterprise for many years. He could not reconcile himself to the significant or, at least, singular fact of so many slaveholders being in the membership and the offices of the association. Then, in addition to this lack of confidence on the part of Lundy in the scheme, Garrison became acquainted, for the first time, with the objects of the society's philanthropy—the class of free people of color. He found that these people were not at all well affected to the society; that they had no appreciation of its benevolent intentions in respect to themselves. He found, on the contrary, that they were positively embittered toward it and toward its designs for their removal from the country as toward their worst enemy. This circumstance was undoubtedly a poser to their young friend. How could he reconcile this deep-seated and widespread disbelief in the purity of the motives of the Colonization Society, with the simple integrity and humanity of the enterprise itself? Later, his acquaintance with such representatives of the free people of color in Philadelphia as James Forten and his son-in-law, Robert Purvis, served but to confirm those first impressions which he received in Baltimore from the Watkinses and the Greeners. It was the same experience in New York and New Haven, in Boston and Providence. He learned that from the very beginning, in the year 1817, that the free people of color in Richmond and Philadelphia had, by an instinctive knowledge of threatened wrong and danger, met and resolved against the society and its sinister designs upon themselves. These people did not wish to leave the country; they did not wish to be sent to Liberia; but the society, bent on doing them good against their will, did want them to leave the country, did want to send them to Liberia.

And why did the society desire to remove the free people of color out of the country? Was it from moives of real philanthropy? The colored people were the first to detect its spurious humanity, the first to see through the artful disguises employed to impose upon the conscience of the republic. Their removal, they intuitively divined, was proposed not to do their race a benefit, but rather to do a service to the owners of slaves. These objects of the society's pseudo-philanthropy had the sagacity to perceive that, practically, their expatriation tended to strengthen the chains of their brethren then in slavery; for if the South could get rid of its free colored population, its slave property would thereby acquire additional security, and, of consequence, increased market value. Like cause, like effect. If the operation of the colonization scheme was decidedly in the interest of the masters, it was the part of wisdom to conclude as the free colored people did actually conclude that the underlying motive, the hidden purpose of the society was also in the interest of the masters.

Garrison did not reach his conclusions as to the pro-slavery character and tendency of the society abruptly. The scales fell away gradually from his eyes. He was not completely undeceived until he had examined the reports of the society and found in them the most redundant evidence of its insincerity and guilt. It was out of its own mouth that he condemned it. When he saw the society in its true character, he saw what he must do. It was a wolf in sheep's skin running at large among the good shepherd's flock, and inflicting infinite hurt upon his poor sheep. He no longer wondered at the horror which the colonization scheme inspired among the free people of color. They were right. The society was their dangerous and determined enemy; it was the bulwark of the slave-holding classes. With the instinct of a great purpose he resolved to carry this powerful bulwark of slavery by assault. To the attack he returned week after week in the *Liberator*, during a year and a half. Then he hurled himself upon it with all his guns, facts, arguments, denunciations, blowing away and burning up every shred of false covering from the doctrines, principles, and purposes of the society, revealing it to mankind in its base and monstrous character.

The society's one motive "to get rid of the free people of color," was outrageous enough, but this was not its only sin. There was another phase to the mischief it was working, which lifted it to the rank of a great sinner. It was not only harmful in its principles and purposes. "It imperatively and effectually seals up the lips," so Garrison accused it, "of a vast number of influential and pious men, who, for fear of giving offence to those slaveholders with whom they associate, and thereby leading to a dissolution of the compact, dare not expose the flagrant enormities of the system of slavery, nor denounce the crime of holding human beings in bondage. They dare not lead to the onset against the forces of tyranny; and if they shrink from the conflict, how shall the victory be won? I do not mean to aver that in their sermons, or addresses, or private conversations, they never allude to the subject of slavery; for they do so frequently, or at least every Fourth of July. But my complaint is that they content themselves with representing slavery as an evil—a misfortune—a calamity which has been entailed upon us by former generations,—*and not as an individual* CRIME, embracing in its folds, robbery, cruelty, oppression, and piracy. *They do not identify the criminal;* they make no direct, pungent, earnest appeal to the consciences of men-stealers." This was a damning bill, but it was true in every particular; and the evidence which Garrison adduced to establish his charges was overwhelming and irrefragable.

Nearly fifty years afterward, Elizur Wright described the baleful influence of the society upon the humanity and philanthropy of the nation. "The humanity and philanthropy," he said, "which could not otherwise be disposed of, was ingeniously seduced into an African Colonization Society, whereby all slaves who had grown seditious and troublesome to their masters could be transplanted on the pestiferous African coast. That this wretched and seemingly transparent humbug could have deluded anybody, must now seem past belief; but I must with shame confess the fact that I for one was deluded by it. And that fact would put me in doubt of my own sanity at the time if I did not know that high statesmen, presidents of colleges, able editors, and that most undoubted of firm philanthropists, Gerrit Smith, shared the same delusion. Bible and missionary societies fellowshipped that mean and scurvy device of the kidnapper, in their holy work. It was spoken of as the most glorious of Christian enterprises, had a monthly magazine devoted to itself, and taxed about every pulpit in the land for an annual sermon in its favor."

Such was the Colonization Society, and its entrenched strength in the piety and philanthropy of the country at the moment when Garrison published his "Thoughts." It did not seem possible that a single arm however powerful, was able to start its roots;

but, directly upon the launching of this bolt, the roots of the Bohun Upas, as Garrison graphically designated the society, were seen to have started, and the enterprise appeared blasted as by fire. The deluded intellect and conscience of the free States saw in the fierce light, which the pamphlet of the reformer threw upon the colonization scheme how shamefully imposed upon they had been. They had believed the society "the most glorious of Christian enterprises," and, lo! it stood revealed to them a "scurvy device of the kidnapper." The effect was extraordinary. The book was seized and its contents devoured by some of the finest minds of the North. Here is an example of the interest which it excited and the converts which it made: "Last Monday evening was our Law Club meeting, and I had the great satisfaction of hearing Judge Mellen, our Chief-Justice, say he had read your 'Thoughts,' was a thorough convert to your views, and was ready to do all in his power to promote them. Mr. Longfellow [father of Henry W. Longfellow] was present also, and with equal warmth and clearness expressed himself also in favor of your views. This is getting the two first men in the State for talents and influence in benevolent effort. I have no doubt they will head the list of those who will subscribe to form here an anti-slavery society. Mr. Greenleaf [Simon] also, will cordially come in, and I need not say he is one of the first [men] in the State, for his character is known." This quotation is made from a letter of General Samuel Fessenden, of Portland, Me., to Mr. Garrison, dated December 14. 1832. Among the remarkable minds which the "Thoughts" disillusioned in respect of the character and tendency of the Colonization Society were Theodore D. Weld, Elizur Wright, and Beriah Green, N. P. Rogers, William Goodell, Joshua Leavitt, Amos A. Phelps, Lewis Tappan, and James Miller McKim.

Garrison's assertion that "the overthrow of the Colonization Society was the overthrow of slavery itself," was, from the standpoint of a student of history, an exaggerated one. We know now that the claim was not founded on fact, that while they did stand together they did not fall together. But the position was, nevertheless, the strongest possible one for the anti-slavery movement to occupy at the time. In the disposition of the pro-slavery forces on the field of the opening conflict in 1832, the colonization scheme commanded the important approaches to the citadel of the peculiar institution. It cut off the passes to public opinion, and to the religious and benevolent influences of the land. To reach these it was necessary in the first place to dislodge the society from its coign of vantage, its strategical point in the agitation. And this is precisely what "The Thoughts on African Colonization" did. It dislodged the society from its powerful place in the moral sentiment of the North. The capture of this position was like the capture of a drawbridge, and the precipitation of the assaulting column directly upon the the walls of a beseiged castle. Within the pamphlet was contained the whole tremendous enginery of demolition. The anti-slavery agent and lecturer thenceforth set it up wherever he spoke.

To him it was not only the catapult, it furnished the missile-like facts and arguments for breaching the walls of this pro-slavery stronghold as well.

The effect of the publication of "The Thoughts" in this country was extraordinary, but the result of their circulation in England was hardly less so. It produced there as here a revolution in public sentiment upon the subject. The philanthropy and piety of Great Britain had generally prior to the unmasking of the society, looked upon it as an instrument of Emancipation, and had accordingly given it their powerful countenance, and not a little material support. But from the moment that the pamphlet reached England a decided change in this regard became manifest. The society made fruitless attempts to break the force of the blow dealt it by Garrison in the United States. But wherever its emissaries traveled "The Thoughts" confronted and confounded them. So that Mr. Garrison was warranted in saying that "all that sophistry or misrepresentation could effect to overthrow its integrity has been attempted in vain. The work, as a whole, stands irrefutable." The attempts made to maintain its hold upon the British public were characterized by duplicity and misrepresentation beyond anything practiced in America. The work of deceiving the philanthropy of Great Britain was conducted by the emissary of the society, Elliott Cresson, a man perfectly fitted to perform his part with remarkable thoroughness and industry. Three thousand miles away from America, and practically secure from contradiction, he went about making outrageous statements as to the anti-slavery character and purpose of the colonization enterprise. As there was no one in England sufficiently acquainted with the operations and designs of the society, he was enabled to falsify facts, to conceal the real principles of the scheme with astonishing audacity and activity. He approached Wilberforce, and duped Clarkson into a belief in the antislavery aim of the society.

Unmasked in America, the time had come when the interests of the Abolition movement on this side of the Atlantic required that it should be stripped of its disguises on the other side also. No better instrument could be selected for this purpose than the man who had torn the mask from its features in the United States. And so in March, 1833, the Board of Managers of the New England Anti-Slavery Society notified the public of the appointment of "William Lloyd Garrison as their agent, and that he would proceed to England as soon as the necessary arrangements can be made, for the purpose of procuring funds to aid in the establishment of the proposed MANUAL LABOR SCHOOL FOR COLORED YOUTH, and of disseminating in that country the truth in relation to American slavery, and to its ally, the American Colonization Society." The managers offered in justification of their step the fact that "Elliott Cresson is now in England as an agent for the Colonization Society, and that he has procured funds to a considerable amount by representing that the object of the society is 'to assist in the emancipation of all the slaves now in the United States.' It is important that the philanthropists of that country should be undeceived, and that the real principles and designs of the Colonization Society should be there made known."

In pursuance of this mission Garrison sailed from New York, May 2, 1833. Twenty days later he landed in Liverpool. His arrival was opportune, for all England was watching the closing scene in the drama of West India Emancipation. He was an eye-witness of the crowning triumph of the English Abolitionists, viz., the breaking by Act of Parliament of the fetters of eight hundred thousand slaves. He was in time to greet his great spiritual kinsman, William Wilberforce, and to undeceive him in respect of the Colonization Society, before death claimed his body, and to follow him to his last resting-place by the side of Pitt and Fox, in Westminster Abbey.

A highly interesting incident of this visit is best told in Mr. Garrison's own words. He said:

"On arriving in London I received a polite invitation by letter from Mr. Buxton to take breakfast with him. Presenting myself at the appointed time, when my name was announced, instead of coming forward promptly to take me by the hand, he scrutinized me from head to foot, and then inquired, 'Have I the pleasure of addressing Mr. Garrison, of Boston, in the United States?' 'Yes, sir,' I replied, 'I am he; and I am here in accordance with your invitation.' Lifting up his hands he exclaimed, 'Why, my dear sir, I thought you were a black man! And I have consequently invited this company of ladies and gentlemen to be present to welcome Mr. Garrison, the black advocate of emancipation, from the United States of America.' I have often said that that is the only compliment I have ever had paid to me that I care to remember or to tell of! For Mr. Buxton had somehow or other supposed that no white American could plead for those in bondage as I had done, and therefore I must be black!"

Garrison promptly threw down his challenge to Elliott Cresson, offering to prove him an impostor and the Colonization Society "corrupt in its principles, proscriptive in its measures, and the worst enemy of the free colored and slave population of the United States." From the first it was apparent that Cresson did not mean to encounter the author of the "Thoughts" in public debate. Even a mouse when cornered will show fight, but there was no manly fight in Cresson. Garrison sent him a letter containing seven grave charges against his society, and dared him to a refutation of them in a joint discussion. This challenge was presented four times before the agent of colonization could be pursuaded to accept it. Garrison was bent on a joint public discussion between himself and Mr. Cresson. But Mr. Cresson was bent on avoiding his opponent. He skulked under one pretext or another from vindicating the colonization scheme from the seven-headed indictment preferred against it by the agent of the New England Anti-Slavery Society. As Cresson could not be driven into a joint discussion with him there was nothing left to Garrison but to go on without him. His arraignment and exposure of the society in public and private was thorough and overwhelming. He was indefatigable in the prosecution of this part of his mission. And his labor was not in vain. For in less than three months after his reaching England he had rendered the Colonization Society as odious there as his "Thoughts" had made it in America. The great body of the anti-slavery sentiment in Great Britain promptly condemned the spirit and object of the American Colonization Society. Such leaders as Buxton and Cropper "termed its objects *diabolical;*" while Zachary Macaulay, father of the historian, did not doubt that "the unchristian prejudice of color (which alone has given brith to the Colonizatian Society, though varnished over with other more plausible pretences, and veiled under a profession of a Christian regard for the temporal and spiritual interests of the negro which is belied by the whole course of its reasonings and the spirit of its measures) is so detestable in itself that I think it ought not to be tolerated, but, on the contrary, ought to be denounced and opposed by all humane, and especially by all pious persons in this country."

The protest against the Colonization Society "signed by Wilberforce and eleven of the most distinguished Abolitionists in Great Britain," including Buxton, Macaulay, Cropper, and Daniel O'Connell, showed how thoroughly Garrison had accomplished his mission. The protest declares, thanks to the teachings of the agent of the New England Anti-Slavery Society, that the colonization scheme "takes its roots from a cruel prejudice and alienation in the whites of America against the colored people, slave or free. This being its source the effects are what might be expected; that it fosters and increases the spirit of caste, already so unhappily predominant; that it widens the breach between the two races—exposes the colored people to great practical persecution, in order to *force* them to emigrate; and, finally, is calculated to swallow up and divert that feeling which America, as a Christian and free country, cannot but entertain, that slavery is alike incompatible with the law of God and with the well-being of man, whether the enslaver or the enslaved." The solemn conclusion of the illustrious signers of this mighty protest was that: "That society is, in our estimation, not deserving of the countenance of the British public." This powerful instrument fell, as Garrison wrote at the time, "like a thunderbolt upon the society." The damage inflicted upon it was immense, irreparable. The name of Thomas Clarkson was conspicuous by its absence from the protest. He could not be induced to take positive ground against the society. Garrison had visited him for this purpose. But the venerable philanthropist, who was then blind, had taken position on *neutral ground*, and conld not, after an interview of four hours, be induced to abandon it. But, fortunately, potent as the name of Clarkson would have been in opposition to the society, it was not indispensable to its overthrow in Great Britain. Garrison had won to his side "all the staunch anti-slavery spirits," while Cresson was able to retain only "a few titled, wealthy, high-pretending individuals."

The success of the mission was signal, its service to the movement against slavery in America manifold. Garrison writing from London to the board of managers, summarized the results produced by it as follows: "1st, awakening a general interest among the friends of emancipation in this country, and securing their efficient coöperation with us in the abolition of slavery in the United States; 2d, dispelling the mists with which the agent of the American

Colonization Society has blinded the eyes of benevolent men in relation to the design and tendency of the society; 3d, enlisting able and eloquent advocates to plead our cause; 4th, inducing editors of periodicals and able writers to give us the weight of their influence; 5th, exciting a spirit of emulation in the redemption of our slave population among the numerous female anti-slavery societies; 6th, procuring a large collection of anti-slavery documents, tracts, pamphlets, and volumes, which will furnish us with an inexhaustible supply of ammunition." These were indeed some of the grand results of laborious weeks. His mission was ended. He was profoundly grateful to the good God for its success. The great movement which he had started against oppression in his own country was awaiting his aggressive leadership. He did not tarry abroad, therefore, but set sail from London August 18, 1833, for New York, where he landed six weeks later.

CHAPTER VIII.

COLORPHOBIA.

GARRISON'S Abolitionism was of the most radical character. It went the whole length of the humanity of the colored race, and all that that implied. They were, the meanest members, whether bond or free, his brothers and his sisters. From the first he regarded them as bone of his bone and blood of his blood, as children with him of a common father. Poor and enslaved and despised to be sure, wronged by all men, and contemned by all men, but for that very reason they were deserving of his most devoted love and labor. He never looked down upon them as wanting in any essential respect the manhood which was his. They were men and as such entitled to immediate emancipation. They were besides entitled to equality of civil and political rights in the republic, entitled to equality and fraternity in the church, equality and fraternity at the North, equality and fraternity always and everywhere. This is what he preached, this is what he practiced. In not a single particular was he ever found separating himself from his brother in black, saying to him "thus far but no farther." He never drew the line in public or private between him and the people whose cause was his cause—not even socially. He went into their homes and was in all things one with them. He forgot that he was white, forgot that they were black, forgot the pride of race, forgot the stigma of race too in the tie of human kinship which bound him to them. If he had what they did not possess, the rights of a man, the civil and political position of a man in the State, the equality of a brother in the church, it could not make him feel better than they, it filled him instead with a righteous sense of wrong, a passionate sympathy, a supreme desire and determination to make his own rights the measure of theirs.

"I lose sight of your present situation," he said in his address before Free People of Color, "and look at it only in futurity. I imagine myself surrounded by educated men of color, the Websters, and Clays, and Hamiltons, and Dwights, and Edwardses of the day. I listen to their voice as judges and representatives, and rulers of the people—the whole people." This glowing vision was not the handiwork of a rhetorician writing with an eye to its effect upon his hearers. The ardent hope of the reformer was rather the father of the golden dream.

This practical recognition of the negro as a man and a brother was the exact opposite of the treatment which was his terrible lot in the country. Never in all history was there a race more shamefully oppressed by a dominant race than were the blacks by the whites of America. Held as slaves in the South, they were stamped as social outcasts at the North. There was no one, however mean or vicious, who if he possessed a white skin, was not treated more humanely than were they. In the most enlightened of the free States they were discriminated against by public laws and proscribed by public opinion. They were in a word pariahs of the republic. They were shut out from all the common rights, and privileges and opportunities enjoyed by the lowest of the favored race. They were denied equality in the public school. The principle of popular education had no application to a class which was not of the people, a class which the common sentiment of a Christian nation had placed at the zero point of political values, and meant to keep forever at that point. Entrance to the trades were barred to the blacks. What did they want with such things where there was no white trash so forgetful of his superiority as to consent to work by their side. Nowhere were they allowed the same traveling accommodations as white men, and they were everywhere excluded from public inns. Neither wealth nor refinement was able to procure them admission into other than "Jim Crow cars." If heart-sick at the outrages by every one heaped upon them they turned for consolation to the house of God, even there the spirit of proscription and caste prejudice met them, and pointed to the "negro pew" where they sat corraled from the congregation as if they had no equal share in the salvation which the pulpit preached. Everywhere the white man had the right of way, even on the highway to heaven! And in no place was the negro made to feel the prejudice against his color more gallingly than in churches arrogating the name of Christian. He had no rights on earth, he had none in trying to get into the bosom of the founder of Christianity, which the white sinners or saints were bound to respect. Even the liberty-loving Quakers of Philadelphia were not above the use of the "negro seat" in their meetings. Somehow they discerned that there was a great gulf separating in this life at least the white from the black believer. That God had made of one blood all nations of men, St. Paul had taught, but the American church had with one accord in practice drawn the line at the poor despised colored man. He was excluded from ecclesiastical equality, for he was different from other men for whom Christ died. The Bible declared that man was made but a little lower than the angels; the American people in their State and Church supplemented this sentiment by acts which plainly said that the negro was made but a little above the brute creation.

Here are instances of the length to which the prejudice against color carried the churches in those early years of the anti-slavery movement:

In 1830, a colored man, through a business transaction with a lessee of one of the pews in Park Street Church, came into possession of it. Thinking to make the best use of his opportunity to obtain religious instruction for himself and family from this fountain of orthodoxy, the black pew-holder betook him, one Sunday, to "Brimstone Corner." But he was never permitted to repeat the visit. "Brimstone Corner" could not stand him another Lord's day, and thereupon promptly expelled him and his family out of its midst. The good deacons displayed their capacity for shielding their flock from consorting with "niggers," by availing themselves of a technicality to relet the pew to a member who was not cursed with a dark skin. On another Lord's day, in another stronghold of Boston Christianity, Oliver

Johnson ran the battery of "indignant frowns of a large number of the congregation" for daring to take a fellow-Christian with a skin not colored like his own into his pew, to listen to Dr. Beecher. The good people of the old Baptist meeting-house, at Hartford, Conn., had evidently no intention of disturbing the heavenly calm of their religious devotions by so much as a thought of believers with black faces; for by boarding up the "negro pews" in front and leaving only peep-holes for their occupants, they secured themselves from a sight of the obnoxious creatures, while Jehovah, who is no respecter of persons, was in His holy place. Incredible as it may seem, a church in the town of Stoughton, Mass., to rid itself of even a semblance of Christian fellowship and equality with a colored member, did actually cut the floor from under the colored member's pew!

These cruel and anti-Christian distinctions in the churches affected Garrison in the most painful manner. He says:

"I never can look up to these wretched retreats for my colored brethren without feeling my soul overwhelmed with emotions of shame, indignation, and sorrow."

He had such an intimate acquaintance with members of this despised caste in Boston and Philadelphia, and other cities, and appreciated so deeply their intrinsic worth and excellence, as men and brethren, that he felt their insults and injuries as if they were done to himself. He knew that beneath many a dark skin he had found real ladies and gentlemen, and he knew how sharper than a serpent's tooth to them was the American prejudice against their color. In 1832, just after a visit to Philadelphia, where he was the guest of Robert Purvis, and had seen much of the Fortens, he wrote a friend :

"I wish you had been with me in Philadelphia to see what I saw, to hear what I heard, and to experience what I felt in associating with many colored families. There are colored men and women, young men and young ladies, in that city, who have few superiors in refinement, in moral worth, and in all that makes the human character worthy of admiration and praise."

Strange to say, notwithstanding all their merits and advancement, the free people of color received nothing but disparagement and contempt from eminent divines like Dr. Leonard W. Bacon and the emissaries of the Colonization Society. They were "the most abandoned wretches on the face of the earth" ; they were "all that is vile, loathsome, and dangerous" ; they were "more degraded and miserable than the slaves," and *ad infinitum* through the whole gamut of falsehood and traduction. It was human for the American people to hate a class whom they had so deeply wronged, and altogether human for them to justify their atrocious treatment by blackening before the world the reputation of the said class. That this was actually done is the best of all proofs of the moral depravity of the nation which slavery had wrought.

Garrison's vindication of the free people of color in Exeter Hall, London, on July 13, 1833, from this sort of detraction and villification is of historic value:

"Sir," said he, addressing the chair, "it is not possible for the mind to coin, or the tongue to utter baser libels against an injured people. Their condition is as much superior to that of the slaves as the light of heaven is more cheering than the darkness of the pit. Many of their number are in the most affluent circumstances, and distinguished for their refinement, enterprise, and talents. They have flourishing churches, supplied by pastors of their own color, in various parts of the land, embracing a large body of the truly excellent of the earth. They have public and private libraries. They have their temperance societies, their debating societies, their moral societies, their literary societies, their benevolent societies, their saving societies, and a multitude of kindred associations. They have their infant schools, their primary and high schools, their sabbath schools, and their Bible classes. They contribute to the support of foreign and domestic missions to Bible and tract societies, etc. In the city of Philadelphia alone they have more than fifty associations for moral and intellectual improvement. In fact, they are rising up, even with mountains of prejudice piled upon them, with more than Titanic strength, and trampling beneath their feet the slanders of their enemies. A spirit of virtuous emulation is pervading their ranks, from the young child to the gray head. Among them is taken a large number of daily and weekly newspapers, and of literary and scientific periodicals, from the popular monthlies up to the grave and erudite *North American* and *American Quarterly Reviews.* I have at this moment, to my own paper, the *Liberator*, one thousand subscribers among this people; and, from an occupancy of the editorial chair for more than seven years, I can testify that they are more punctual in their payments than any five hundred white subscribers whose names I ever placed indiscriminately in my subscription book."

There was an earnest desire on the part of the free people of color to raise the level of their class in the Union. At a convention held by them in Philadelphia, in 1831, they resolved upon a measure calculated to make up, to some extent, the deprivations which their children were suffering by being excluded from the higher schools of learning in the land. So they determined to establish a college on the manual-labor system for the education of colored youth. They appealed for aid to their benevolent friends, and fixed upon New Haven as the place to build their institution. Arthur Tappan, with customary beneficence, "purchased several acres of land, in the southerly part of the city, and made arrangements for the erection of a suitable building, and furnishing it with needful supplies, in a way to do honor to the city and country."

The school, however, was never established owing to the violent hostility of the citizens, who with the Mayor, Aldermen, and Common Council resolved in public meeting to "*resist* the establishment of the proposed college in this place by every lawful means."

The free people of color were derided because of their ignorance by their persecutors, but when they and their friends proposed a plan to reduce that ignorance, their persecutors bitterly opposed its execution. New Haven piety and philanthropy, as embodied in the Colonization Society, were not bent on the education of this class but on its emigration to the coast of Africa solely. In such sorry contradictions and cruelties did American prejudice against color involve American Christianity and humanity.

This outrage was perpetrated in 1831. Two years afterward Connecticut enacted altogether the most shameful crime in her history. There lived in the year 1833, in the town of Canterbury, in that State, an accomplished young Quaker woman, named Prudence Crandall. Besides a superior education, she possessed the highest character. And this was well; for she was the principal of the Female Boarding School located in that town. The institution was, in 1833, at the beginning of its third year, and in a flourishing condition. While pursuing her vocation of a teacher, Miss Crandall made the acquaintance of the *Liberator* through a "nice colored girl," who was at service in the school. Abhorring slavery from childhood, it is no wonder that the earnestness of the *Liberator* exerted an immediate and lasting influence upon the sympathies of the young principal. The more she read and the more she thought upon the subject the more aroused she became to the wrongs of which her race was guilty to the colored people. She, too, would lend them a helping hand in their need. Presently there came to her a colored girl who was thirsting for an education such as the Canterbury Boarding School for young ladies was dispensing to white girls. This was Miss Crandall's opportunity to do something for the colored people, and she admitted the girl to her classes. But she had no sooner done so than there were angry objections to the girl's remaining.

"The wife of an Episcopal clergyman who lived in

the village," Miss Crandall records, "told me that if I continued that colored girl in my school it would not be sustained."

She heroically refused to turn the colored pupil out of the school, and thereby caused a most extraordinary exhibition of Connecticut chivalry and Christianity.

Seeing how matters stood with her in these circumstances, Prudence Crandall conceived the remarkable purpose of devoting her school to the education of colored girls exclusively. She did not know whether her idea was practicable, and so in her perplexity she turned for counsel to the editor of the *Liberator*. She went to Boston for this purpose, and there, at the old Marlboro' Hotel, on Washington street, on the evening of January 29, 1833, she discussed this business with Mr. Garrison. This visit and interview confirmed the brave soul in her desire to change her school into one for the higher education of colored girls. It was expected that a sufficient number of such pupils could be obtained from well-to-do colored families in cities like Boston, Providence, and New York to assure the financial success of the enterprise. When Miss Crandall had fully matured her plans in the premises she announced them to the Canterbury public. But if she had announced that she contemplated opening a college for the spread of contagious diseases among her townspeople, Canterbury could not possibly have been more agitated and horrified. Every door in the village was slammed in her face. She was denounced in town meetings, and there was not chivalry enough to cause a single neighbor to speak in her defence. Samuel J. May had to come from an adjoining town for this purpose. "But," says Mr. May, "they would not hear me. They shut their ears and rushed upon me with threats of personal violence."

As there was nothing in the statutes of Connecticut which made the holding of such a school as that of Miss Crandall's illegal, the good Canterbury folk procured the passage of a hasty act through the Legislature, which was then in session, "making it a penal offence, punishable by fine and imprisonment, for any one in that State keeping a school to take as his or her pupils the children of colored people of other States." But the heart of the young Quaker woman was the heart of a heroine. She dared to disregard the wicked law, was arrested, bound over for trial, and sent to jail like a common malefactor. It was no use, persecution could not cow the noble prisoner into submission to the infamous statute. In her emergency truth raised up friends who rallied about her in the unparalleled contest which raged around her person and her school. There was no meanness or maliciousness to which her enemies did not stoop to crush and ruin her and her cause. "The newspapers of the county and of the adjoining counties teemed with the grossest misrepresentations, and the vilest insinuations," says Mr. May, "against Miss Crandall, her pupils, and her patrons; but for the most part, peremptorily refused us any room in their columns to explain our principles and purposes, or to refute the slanders they were circulating." Four or five times within two years she was forced into court to defend her acts against the determined malignity of men who stood high in the Connecticut Church and State. The shops in the town boycotted her, the churches closed their doors to her and her pupils. Public conveyances refused to receive them, and physicians to prescribe for them. It is said that the heroic soul was cut off from intercourse with her own family, in the hope doubtless that she would the sooner capitulate to the negro-hating sentiment of her neighbors. But firm in her resolve the fair Castellan never thought of surrendering the citadel of her conscience at the bidding of iniquitous power. Then, like savages, her foes defiled with the excrement of cattle the well whence the school drew its supply of water, attacked the house with rotten eggs and stones, and daubed it with filth. This drama of diabolism was fitly ended by the introduction of the fire fiend, and the burning of the detestable building devoted to the higher education of "niggers." Heathenism was, indeed, outdone by Canterbury Christianity.

The circumstances of this outrage kindled Garrison's indignation to the highest pitch. Words were inadequate to express his emotions and agony of soul. In the temper of bold and clear-eyed leadership he wrote George W. Benson, his future brother-in-law, " we may as well, first as last," meet this proscriptive spirit, *and conquer it.* We—*i. e.*, all the friends of the cause—must make this a common concern. The New Haven excitement has furnished a bad precedent—a second must not be given or I know not what we can do to raise up the colored population in a manner which their intellectual and moral necessities demand. In Boston we are all excited at the Canterbury affair. Colonizationists are rejoicing and Abolitionists looking sternly." Like a true general Garrison took in from his *Liberator* outlook the entire field of the struggle. No friend of the slave, however distant, escaped his quick sympathy or ready reinforcements. To him the free people of color turned for championship, and to the *Liberator* as a mouthpiece. The battle for their rights and for the the freedom of their brethren in the South advanced apace. Everywhere the army of their friends and the army of their foes were in motion, and the rising storm winds of justice and iniquity were beginning "to bellow through the vast and boundless deep" of a nation's soul.

CHAPTER IX.

AGITATION AND REPRESSION.

William Lloyd Garrison's return from his English mission was signalized by two closely related events, viz., the formation of the New York City Anti-Slavery Society, and the appearance of the first of a succession of anti-slavery mobs in the North. The news of his British successes had preceded him, and prepared for him a warm reception on the part of his pro-slavery countrymen. For had he not with malice prepense put down the "most glorious of Christian enterprises," and rebuked his own country in the house of strangers as recreant to freedom? And when O'Connell in Exeter Hall pointed the finger of scorn at America and made her a by-word and a hissing in the ears of Englishmen, was it not at a meeting got up to further the designs of this "misguided young gentlemen who has just returned from England whither he has recently been for the sole purpose as it would seem [to the *Commercial Advertiser*] of traducing the people and institutions of his own country." Had he not caught up and echoed back the hissing thunder of the great Irish orator :—*Shame on the American Slaveholders!* Base wretches should we shout in chorus—base wretches, how dare you profane the temple of national freedom, the sacred fane of Republican rites, with the presence and the sufferings of human beings in chains and slavery!"

The noise of these treasons on a foreign shore, "deafening the sound of the westerly wave, and riding against the blast as thunder goes," to borrow O'Connell's graphic and grandiose phrases, had reached the country in advance of Mr. Garrison. The national sensitiveness was naturally enough stung to the quick. Here is a pestilent fellow who is not content with disturbing the peace of the Union with his new fanaticism, but must needs presume to make the dear Union odious before the world as well. And his return, what is it to be but the signal for increased agitation on the slavery question. The conquering hero comes and his fanatical followers salute him forthwith with a new anti-slavery society, which means a fresh instrument in his hands to stir up strife between the North and the South. "Are we tamely to look on, and see this most dangerous species of fanaticism extending itself through society?" shrieked on the morning of Mr. Garrison's arrival in New York Harbor, the malignant editor of the *Courier and Enquirer*.

The pro-slavery and lawless elements of the city were not slow to take the cue given by metropolitan papers, and to do the duty of patriots upon their country's enemies. Arthur Tappen and his anti-slavery associates outwitted these patriotic gentlemen, who attended in a body at Clinton Hall on the evening of October 2, 1833, to perform the aforesaid duty of patriots, while the objects of their attention were convened at Chatham Street Chapel and organizing their new fanaticism. The mob flew wide of its mark a second time, for when later in the evening it began a serenade more expressive than musical before the entrance to the little chapel on Chatham street the members of the society "folded their tents like the Arabs and as silently stole away." The Abolitionists accomplished their design and eluded their enemies at the same time. But the significance of the riotous demonstration went not unobserved by them and their newly arrived leader. It was plain from that night that if the spirit of Abolitionism had risen, the spirit of persecution had risen also.

A somewhat similar reception saluted the reformer in Boston. An inflammatory handbill announced to his townsmen his arrival. "The true American has returned, *alias* William Lloyd Garrison, the 'Negro Champion,' from his disgraceful mission to the British metropolis," etc., etc., and wound up its artful list of lies with the malignant suggestion that "He is now in your power—do not let him escape you, but go this evening, armed with plenty of *tar and feathers* and administer to him justice at his abode at No. 9 Merchant's Hall, Congress street." In obedience to this summons, a reception committee in the shape of "a dense mob, breathing threatenings which forboded a storm," did pay their respects to the "true American" in front of his abode at the *Liberator* office. Fortunately the storm passed over without breaking that evening on the devoted head of the "Negro Champion." But the meaning of the riotous demonstration it was impossible to miss. Like the mob in New York it clearly indicated that the country was on the outer edge of an area of violent disturbances on the subject of slavery.

The peril which Garrison had twice escaped was indeed grave, but neither it nor the certainty of future persecution could flutter or depress his spirits. "For myself," he wrote subsequently in the *Liberator*, "I am ready to brave any danger even unto death. I feel no uneasiness either in regard to my fate or to the success of the cause of Abolition. Slavery must speedily be abolished ; the blow that shall sever the chains of the slaves may shake the nation to its center—may momentarily disturb the pillars of the Union—but it shall redeem the character, extend the influence, establish the security, and increase the prosperity of our great republic." It was not the rage and malice of his enemies which the brave soul minded, but the ever-present knowledge of human beings in chains and slavery whom he must help. Nothing could separate him from his duty to them. neither dangers present nor persecutions to come. The uncertainty of life made him only the more zealous in their behalf. The necessity of doing, doing, and yet ever doing for the slave was plainly pressing deep like thorns into his thoughts. "I am more and more impressed;" he wrote a friend a few weeks later, "I am more and more impressed with the importance of 'working whilst the day lasts.' If 'we all do fade as a leaf,' if we are 'as the sparks that fly upward,' if the billows of time are swiftly removing the sandy foundation of our life, what we intend to do for the captive, and for our country, and for the subjugation of a hostile world, must be done quickly. Happily 'our light afflictions are but for a moment.'"

This yearning of the leader for increased activity in the cause of immediate emancipation was shared by friends and disciples in different portions of the country. Few and scattered as were the Abolitionists, they so much the more needed to band together for the great conflict with a powerful and organized evil. This evil was organized on a national scale, the forces of righteousness which were rising against it, if they were ever to overcome it and rid the land of it, had needs to be organized on a national scale also. Garrison with the instinct of a great reformer early perceived the immense utility of a national anti-slavery organization for mobilizing the whole available Abolition sentiment of the free States in a moral agitation of national and tremendous proportions.

He had not long to wait after his return from England before this desire of his soul was satisfied. It was in fact just a month afterward that a call for a convention for the formation of the American Anti-Slavery Society went out from New York to the friends of immediate emancipation throughout the North. As an evidence of the dangerously excited state of the popular mind on the subject of slavery there stands in the summons the significant request to delegates to regard the call as confidential. The place fixed upon for holding the convention was Philadelphia, and the time December 4, 1833.

Garrison bestirred himself to obtain for the convention a full representation of the friends of freedom. He sent the call to George W. Benson, at Providence, urging him to spread the news among the Abolitionists of his neighborhood and to secure the election of a goodly number of delegates by the society in Rhode Island. He forthwith bethought him of Whittier on his farm in Haverhill, and enjoined his old friend to fail not to appear in Philadelphia. But while the young poet longed to go to urge upon his Quaker brethren of that city "to make their solemn testimony against slavery visible over the whole land—to urge them, by the holy memories of Woolman and Benezet and Tyson to come up as of old to the standard of Divine Truth, though even the fires of another persecution should blaze around them," he feared that he would not be able to do so. The spirit was surely willing but the purse was empty, "as thee know," he quaintly adds, "our farming business does not put much cash in our pockets." The cash he needed was generously supplied by Samuel E. Sewall, and Whittier went as a delegate to the convention after all. The disposition on the part of some of the poorer delegates was so strong to be present at the convention that not even the lack of money was sufficient to deter them from setting out on the expedition. Two of them, David T. Kimball and Daniel E. Jewett, from Andover, Mass., did actually supplement the deficiencies of their pocket-books by walking to New Haven, the aforesaid pocket-books being equal to the rest of the journey from that point.

About sixty delegates found their way to Philadelphia and organized on the morning of December 4th, in Adelphi Hall, the now famous convention. It was a notable gathering of apostolic spirits—"mainly composed of comparatively young men, some in middle age, and a few beyond that period." They had come together from ten of the twelve free States, which fact goes to show the rapid, the almost epidemic-like spread of Garrisonian Abolitionism through the North. The *Liberator* was then scarcely three years old, and its editor had not until the second day of the convention attained the great age of twenty-eight! The convention of 1787 did not comprise more genuine patriotism and wisdom than did this memorable assembly of American Abolitionists. It was from beginning to end an example of love to God and love to men, of fearless scorn of injustice and fearless devotion to liberty. Not one of those three score souls who made up the convention, who did not take his life in his hand by reason of the act. It was not the love of fame surely which brought them over so many hundreds of miles, which made so many of them endure real physical privation, which drew all by a common, an irresistible impulse to congregate for an unpopular purpose within reach of the teeth and the claws of an enraged public opinion.

The convention, as one man might have said with the single-minded Lundy, "My heart was deeply grieved at the gross abomination; I heard the wail of the captive; I felt his pang of distress; and the iron entered my soul." The iron of slavery had indeed entered the soul of every member of the convention. It was the divine pang and pity of it which collected from the East and from the West this remarkable body of reformers.

The story of how they had to find a president illustrates the contemporary distrust and antagonism, which the anti-slavery movement aroused among the men of standing and influence. Knowing in what bad odor they were held by the community, and anxious only to serve their cause in the most effective manner, the members of the convention hit upon the plan of asking some individual eminent for his respectability to preside over their deliberations, and thereby disarm the public suspicions and quiet the general apprehensions felt in respect of the incendiary character of their intention. So in pursuance of this plan six of their number were dispatched on the evening of December 3d to seek such a man. But the quest of the committee like that of Diogenes proved a failure. After two attempts and two repulses the committee were not disposed to invite the humiliation of a third refusal and must have listened with no little relief, to this blunt summary of the situation by Beriah Green, who was one of the six. "If there is not timber amongst ourselves," quoth Green, "big enough to make a president of, let us get along without one, or go home and stay there until we have grown up to be men." The next day Green was chosen, and established in a manner never to be forgotten by his associates that the convention did possess "timber big enough to make a president of."

Narrow as were the circumstances of many of the members, the convention was by no means destitute of men of wealth and business prominence. Such were the Winslows, Isaac and Nathan, of Maine, Arnold Buffum, of Massachusetts, and John Rankin and Lewis Tappan, of New York. Scholarship, talents, and eloquence abounded among the delegates. Here there was no lack, no poverty, but extraordinary sufficiency, almost to redundancy. The presence of the gentler sex was not wanting to lend grace and picturesqueness to the occasion. The beautiful and benignant countenance of Lucretia Mott shed over the proceedings the soft radiance of a pure and regnant womanhood ; while the handful of colored delegates with the elegant figure of Robert Purvis at their head, added pathos and picturesqueness to the *personnel* of the convention. Neither was the element of danger wanting to complete the historic scene. Its presence was grimly manifest in the official intimation that evening meetings of the convention could not be protected, by the demonstrations of popular ill-will which the delegates encountered on the streets, by the detachment of constabulary guarding the entrance to Adelphi Hall, and by the thrillingly significant precaution observed by the delegates of sitting with locked doors. Over the assembly it impended cruel and menacing like fate. Once securely locked within the hall, the Abolitionists discreetly abstained from leaving it at noon for dinner, well knowing how small a spark it takes to kindle a great fire. It was foolhardy to show themselves nnnecessarily to the excited crowds in the streets, and so mindful that true courage consisteth not in recklessness, they despatched one of their number for crackers and cheese, which they washed down with copious draughts of cold water. But they had that to eat and drink besides, whereof the spirits of mischief without could not conceive.

The grand achievement of the convention was, of course, the formation of the American Anti-Slavery Society, but the crown of the whole was unquestionably the Declaration of Sentiments. The composition of this instrument has an interesting history. It seems that the delegates considered that the remarkable character of the movement which they were launching upon the wide sea of national attention demanded of them an expression altogether worthy of so momentous an undertaking. The adoption of a constitution for this purpose was felt to be inadequate. A constitution was indispensable, but some other expression was necessary to give to their work its proper proportion and importance. Such a manifestation it was deemed meet to make in the form of a declaration of sentiments. A committee was accordingly appointed to draft the declaration. This committee named three of its number, consisting of Garrison, Whittier, and Samuel J. May to draw up the document. The sub-committee in turn deputed Garrison to do the business.

Mr. May has told in his *Recollections of the Anti-Slavery Conflict*, how he and Whittier left their friend at ten o'clock in the evening, agreeing to call at eight the following morning and how on their return at the appointed hour they found Garrison with shutters closed and lamps burning, penning the last paragraph of the admirable document. He has told how they three read it over together two or three times, making some slight alterations in it, and how at nine o'clock the draft was laid by them before the whole committee. The author of the recollections has left a graphic account of its effect upon the convention. "Never in my life," he says, "have I seen a deeper impression made by words than was made by that admirable document upon all who were present. After the voice of the reader had ceased there was silence for several minutes. Our hearts were in perfect unison. There was but one thought with us all. Either of the members could have told what the whole convention felt. We felt that the word had just been uttered which would be mighty, through God, to the pulling down of the strongholds of slavery." Such was the scene at the first reading of the Declaration of Sentiments, Dr. Atlee, the reader. The effect at its final reading was, if possible, even more dramatic and eloquent. Whittier has depicted this closing and thrilling scene. He has described how Samuel J. May read the declaration for the last time. "His sweet, persuasive voice faltered with the intensity of his emotions as he repeated the solemn pledges of the concluding paragraphs. After a season of silence, David Thurston of Maine, rose as his name was called by one of the secretaries and affixed his name to the document. One after another passed up to the platform, signed, and retired in silence. All felt the deep responsibility of the occasion—the shadow and forecast of a life-long struggle rested upon every countenance."

The effects, so electrical and impressive, which followed the reading of the declaration were not disproportioned to its merits, for it was an instrument of singular power, wisdom, and eloquence. Indeed, to this day, more than half a century after it was written it still has virtue to quicken the breath and stir the pulses of a sympathetic reader out of their normal time. A great passion for freedom and righteousness irradiates like a central light the whole memorable document. It begins by a happy reference to an earlier convention, held some fifty-seven years before in the same place, and which adopted a declaration holding "that all men are created equal; that they are endowed by their Creator with certain inalienable rights; that among these are life, LIBERTY, and the pursuit of happiness;" and how at the trumpet-call of its authors three millions of people rushed to arms "deeming it more glorious to die instantly as free men, than desirable to live one hour as slaves"; and how, though few in number and poor in resources those same people were rendered invincible by the conviction that truth, justice, and right were on their side. But the freedom won by the men of 1776 was incomplete without the freedom for which the men of 1833 were striving. The authors of the new declaration would not be inferior to the authors of the old "in purity of motive, in earnestness of zeal, in decision of purpose, intrepidity of action, in steadfastness of faith, in sincerity of spirit." Unlike the older actors, the younger had eschewed the sword, the spilling of human blood in defence of their principles. Theirs was a moral warfare, the grappling of truth with error, of the power of love with the inhumanities of the nation. Then it glances at the wrongs which the fathers suffered, and at the enormities which the slaves were enduring. The "fathers were never slaves, never bought and sold like cattle, never shut out from the light of knowledge and religion, never subjected to the lash of brutal taskmasters," but all these woes and more, an unimaginable mountain of agony and misery, was the appalling lot of the slaves in the Southern States. The guilt of this nation, which partners such a crime against human nature, "is unequaled by any other on earth," and therefore it is bound to instant repentance, and to the immediate restitution of justice to the oppressed.

The Declaration of Sentiments denies the right of man to hold property in a brother man, affirms the identity in principle between the African slave trade and American slavery, the imprescriptibility of the rights of the slaves to liberty, the nullity of all laws which run counter to human rights, and the grand doctrine of civil and political equality in the Republic, regardless of race and complexional differences. It boldly rejects the principle of compensated emancipation, because it involves a surrender of the position that man cannot hold property in man; because slavery is a crime, and the master is not wronged by emancipation but the slaves righted, restored to themselves; because immediate and general emancipation would only destroy nominal, not real, property, the labor of the slaves would still remain to the masters and doubled by the new motives which freedom infuses into the breasts of her children; and, finally because, if compensation is to be given at all it ought to be given to those who have been plundered of their rights. It spurns in one compact paragraph the pretensions of the colonization humbug as "delusive, cruel, and dangerous."

But lofty and uncompromising as were the moral principles and positions of the declaration, it nevertheless recognized with perspicuity of vision the Constitutional limitations of the Federal Government in relation to slavery. It frankly conceded that Congress had no right to meddle with the evil in any of the States. But wherever the national jurisdiction reached the general government was bound to interfere and suppress the traffic in human flesh. It was the duty of Congress, inasmuch as it possessed the power, to abolish slavery in the District of Columbia, the National Territories, along the coast and between the States. The free States are the *particeps criminis* of the slave States. They are living under a pledge of their tremendous physical force to rivet the manacles of chattel slavery upon millions in the South ; they are liable at any instant to be called on under the Constitution to suppress a general insurrection of the slaves. This relationship is criminal, "is full of danger, IT MUST BE BROKEN UP."

So much for the views and principles of the declaration, now for the designs and measures as enumerated therein : "We shall organize anti-slavery societies, if possible, in every city, town and village in our land.

"We shall send forth agents to lift up the voice of remonstrance, of warning, of entreaty, and of rebuke.

"We shall circulate, unsparingly and extensively, anti-slavery tracts and periodicals.

"We shall enlist the pulpit and the press in the cause of the suffering and the dumb.

"We shall aim at a purification of the churches from all participation in the guilt of slavery.

"We shall encourage the labor of freemen rather than that of slaves, by giving a preference to their productions ; and

"We shall spare no exertions nor means to bring the whole nation to speedy repentance."

The instrument closes by pledging the utmost of its signers to the overthrow of slavery—"come what may to our persons, our interests, or our reputations

—whether we live to witness the triumph of Liberty, Justice, and Humanity, or perish untimely as martyrs in this great, benevolent, and holy cause." Twin pledge it was to that ancestral, historic one made in 1776: "And for the support of this declaration, with a firm reliance on the protection of DIVINE PROVIDENCE, we mutually pledge to each other, our lives, our fortunes, and our sacred honor."

Whittier has predicted for the Declaration of Sentiments an enduring fame: "It will live," he declares, "as long as our national history." Samuel J. May was equally confident that this "Declaration of the Rights of Man," as he proudly cherished it, would "live a perpetual, impressive protest against every form of oppression, until it shall have given place to that brotherly kindness which all the children of the common Father owe to one another." As a particular act and parchment-roll of high thoughts and resolves, highly expressed, it will not, I think, attain to the immortality predicted for it. For as such it has in less than two generations passed almost entirely out of the knowledge and recollection of Americans. But in another sense it is destined to realize all that has been foreshadowed for it by its friends. Like elemental fire its influence will glow and flame at the center of our national life long after as a separate and sovereign entity it shall have been forgotten by the descendants of its illustrious author and signers.

The convention was in session three days, and its proceedings were filled with good resolutions and effective work. Arthur Tappan was elected President of the national organization, and William Green,

Jr., Treasurer. Elizur Wright, Jr., was chosen Secretary of Domestic Correspondence, William Lloyd Garrison Secretary of Foreign Correspondence, and Abraham L. Cox Recording Secretary. Besides these officers there were a Board of Management and a number of Vice-Presidents selected. For three days the hearts of the delegates burned within them toward white-browed Duty and the master, Justice, who stood in their midst and talked with divine accents to their spirits of how men were enslaved and cruelly oppressed by men, their own brothers, and how the cry of these bondmen came up to them for help. And with one accord there fell upon the delegates a pang and pity, an uplifting, impelling sense of 'woe unto us' if we withhold from our brethren in bonds the help required of us. This rising tide of emotion and enthusiasm gathering mass at each sitting of the convention, culminated during the several readings of the Declaration of Sentiments. And when on the third day Beriah Green brought the congress to a close in a valedictory address of apostolic power and grandeur, and with a prayer so sweet, so fervent, and strong as to melt all hearts, the pent-up waters of the reform was ready to hurl themselves into an agitation the like of which had never before, nor has since, been seen or felt in the Union. Thenceforth freedom's little ones were not without great allies, who were "exultations, agonies, and love, and man's unconquerable mind."

Everywhere the flood of Abolitionism burst upon the land, everywhere the moral deluge spread through the free States. Anti-slavery societies rose as it were, out of the ground, so rapid, so astonishing were their growth during the year following the formation of the national society. In nearly every free State they had appeared doubling and quadrupling in number, until new societies reached in that first year to upwards of forty. Anti-slavery agents and lecturers kept pace with the anti-slavery societies. They began to preach, to remonstrate, to warn, entreat, and rebuke until their voices sounded like the roar of many waters in the ears of the people. Wherever there was a school-house, a hall, or a church, there they were, ubiquitous, irrepressible, a cry in the wilderness of a nation's iniquity. Anti-slavery tracts and periodicals multiplied and started from New York and Boston in swarms, and clouds, the thunder of their wings were as the thunder of falling avelanches to the guilty conscience of the country. There was no State, city, town, or village in the Republic where their voice was not heard.

The Rev. Amos A Phelp's "Lectures on Slavery and Its Remedy;" "the Rev. J. D. Paxton's 'Letters on Slavery'; the Rev. S. J. May's letters to Andrew T. Judson, 'The Rights of Colored People to Education Vindicated'; Prof. Elizur Wright, Jr's, 'Sin of Slavery and Its Remedy;' Whittier's 'Justice and Expediency'; and, above all, Mrs. Lydia Maria Child's startling 'Appeal in favor of that class of Americans called Africans' were the more potent of the new crop of writings betokening the vigor of Mr. Garrison's Propagandism," says that storehouse of anti-slavery facts the "Life of Garrison" by his children. Swift poured the flood, widespread the inundation of anti-slavery publications. Money, although not commensurate with the vast wants of the crusade, came in in copious and generous streams. A marvelous munificence characterized the charity of wealthy Abolitionists. The poor gave freely of their mite, and the rich as freely of their thousands. Something of the state of simplicity and community of goods which marked the early disciples of Christianity seemed to have revived in the hearts of this band of American reformers. A spirit of renunciation, of self-sacrifice, of brotherly kindness, of passionate love of righteousness, of passionate hatred of wrong, of self-consecration to truth and of martyrdom lifted the reform to as high a moral level as had risen any movement for the betterment of mankind in any age of the world.

The resolutions of the signers of the Declaration of Sentiment, to enlist the pulpit in the cause of the suffering and dumb, and to attempt the purification of the churches from all participation in the guilt of slavery, encountered determined opposition from the pulpits and the churches themselves. The Abolitionists were grieved and indignant at the pro-slavery spirit which pulpits and churches displayed. But what happened was as we now look back at those proceedings, an inevitable occurrence, a foregone conclusion. The pulpits were only representative of the religion of the pews, and the pews were occupied by the same sort of humanity that toil and spin and haggle over dollars and cents six out of every seven days. They have their selfish and invested interests, fixed social notions, relationships, and prejudices, which an episode like Sunday, churches, and sermons do not seriously affect. Indeed, Sunday, churches, and sermons constitute an institution of modern civilization highly conservative of invested interests, fixed social notions, relationships, and prejudices. Who advances a new idea, a reformatory movement, disturbs the *status quo*, stirs up the human bees in that great hive called society, and that lesser one called the church, and he must needs expect to have the swarm about his head.

This was precisely what happened in the case of the anti-slavery movement. It threatened the then *status quo* of property rights, it attacked the fixed social notions, relationships, and prejudices of the South and of the North alike. The revolution which this new idea involved in the slave States, was of the most radical character, going down to a complete reconstruction of their entire social system. At once the human hornets were aroused, and in these circumstances, the innocent and the guilty were furiously beset. Because the new idea which disturbed the South had originated in the North, the wrath of the South rose hot against not the authors of the new idea alone but against the people of that section as well. But this sectional unpleasantness endangered the stability of the Union, and menaced with obstructions and diversions the golden stream of Northern traffic, dollars, and dividends. This was intolerable, and forthwith the Apiarian brotherhood of the free States put together their heads with those of the slave States to attack, sting, and utterly abolish the new idea, and the new idea's supporters. The Northern churches were, of course, in the Northern brotherhood. And when the new fanaticism threatened the financial stability of the pews, the pulpits instead of exerting themselves in behalf of the suffering and dumb slaves, exerted themselves to preserve the prosperity of the pews by frowning down the friends of the slaves. They were among the first to stone the new idea and its fiery prophets. "Away with them!" shouted in chorus pulpit and pews. Sad? yes, but alas! natural, too. These men were not better nor worse than the average man. They were the average men of their generation, selfish, narrow, material, encrusted in their prejudices like snails in their shells, struggling upward at a snail's pace to the larger life, with its added sweetness and humanities, but experiencing many a discomfiture by the way from those foul and triple fiends, the World, the Flesh, and the Devil.

Nowhere in the churches was their opposition to the Abolition movement more persistent and illiberal than in the theological seminaries, whence the pulpits drew their supplies of preachers. Like master, like servant, these institutions were indentured to the public, and reflected as in a mirror the body and pressure of its life and sentiment. That a stream cannot rise higher than its source, although a theological stream, found remarkable demonstration in the case of Lane Seminary. Here after the publication of the "Thoughts on Colonization," and the formation of the National Society, an earnest spirit of inquiry broke out among the students on the subject of slavery. It was at first encouraged by the President, Lyman Beecher, who offered to go in and discuss the question with his "boys." That eminent man did not long remain in this mind. The discussions which he so lightly allowed swept through the institution with the force of a great moral awakening. They were continued during nine evenings and turned the seminary at their close, so far as the students went, into an anti-slavery society. This is not the place to go at length into the history of that anti-slavery debate, which, in its consequences, proved one of the events of the anti-slavery conflict. Its leader was Theodore D. Weld, who was until Wendell Phillips appeared upon the scene, the great orator of the agitation.

Dr. Beecher had no notion of raising such a ghost when he said, "Go ahead, boys, I'll go in and discuss with you." It was such an apparition of independence and righteousness as neither the power of the trustees nor the authority of the faculty was ever able to dismiss. The virtue of a gag rule was tried to suppress Abolition among the students, but instead of suppressing Abolition, it well-nigh suppressed the seminary; for, rather than wear a gag on the obnoxious subject, the students—to between seventy and eighty, comprising nearly the whole muster-roll of the school—withdrew from an institution where the exercise of the right of free inquiry and free speech on a great moral question was denied and repressed. The same spirit of repression arose later in the Theological School at Andover, Mass. There the gag was effectively applied by the faculty, and all inquiry and discussion relating to slavery disappeared among the students. But the attempt to impose silence upon the students of Phillips's Academy near-by was followed by the secession of forty or fifty of the students.

Ah! the Abolitionists had undertaken to achieve the impossible, when they undertook to enlist the pulpit in the cause of the slaves, and to purify the churches from all participation in the guilt of slavery. For the average man, whether within or without the church, is not controlled in his conduct toward his brother man by the principles aud precepts of Jesus, but by the laws of social and individual selfishness. These selfish forces may at epochal moments align themselves with justice and liberty, and they not infrequently do, otherwise human progress must be at an end. In advancing themselves, they perforce advance justice and liberty. Thus do men love their neighbors as themselves, and move forward to fraternity and equality in kingdoms and commonwealths. The special province of moral reformers, like Garrison and the Abolitionists, seems to be to set these egoistic and altruistic elements of human society at war, the one against the other, thereby compelling its members and classes, willy nilly, to choose between the belligerents. Some will enlist on one side, some on the other, but in the furnace heat of the passions which ensues, an ancient evil, or a bad custom or institution, gets the vitality burned out of it, which in due time falls as slag out of the new order that arises at the close of the conflict.

CHAPTER X.

BETWEEN THE ACTS.

Mr. Garrison, in a private letter to a friend under date of September 12, 1834, summarises the doings of the preceding twelve months of his life, and makes mention of a fact which lends peculiar interest to that time: "It has been the most eventful year," he remarks, "in my history. I have been the occasion of many uproars, and a continual disturber of the public peace. As soon as I landed I turned the city of New York upside down. Five thousand people turned out to see me tarred and feathered, but were disappointed. There was also a small hubbub in Boston on my arrival. The excitement passed away, but invective and calumny still followed me. By dint of some industry and much persuasion, I succeeded in inducing the Abolitionists in New York to join our little band in Boston, in calling a national convention at Philadelphia. We met, and such a body of men, for zeal, firmness, integrity, benevolence, and moral greatness, the world has rarely seen in a single assembly. Inscribed upon a declaration which it was my exalted privilege to write, their names can perish only with the knowledge of the history of our times. A National Anti-Slavery Society was formed, which astonished the country by its novelty, and awed it by its boldness. In five months its first annual meeting was held in the identical city in which, only seven antecedent months, Abolitionists were in peril of their lives. In ability, interest, and solemnity it took precedence of all the great religious celebrations which took place at the same time. During the same month, a New England anti-slavery convention was held in Boston, and so judicious were its measures, so eloquent its appeals, so unequivocal its resolutions, that it at once gave shape and character to the anti-slavery cause in this section of the Union. In the midst of all these mighty movements, I have wooed "a fair ladye," and won her, have thrown aside celebacy, and jumped body and soul into matrimony, have sunk the character of bachelor in that of husband, have settled down into domestic quietude, and repudiated all my roving desires, and have found that which I have long been yearning to find, a home, a wife, and a beautiful retreat from a turbulent city."

Garrison does not exaggerate the importance of the initiatives and achievements of the year, or the part played by him in its history. His activity was indeed phenomenal, and the service rendered by him to the reform, was unrivaled. He was in incessant motion, originating, directing, inspiring the agitation in all portions of the North. What strikes one strongly in studying the pioneer is his sleeplessness, his indefatigableness, his persistency in pursuit of his object. Others may rest after a labor, may have done one, two, or three distinct tasks, but between Garrison's acts there is no hiatus, each follows each, and is joined to all like links in a chain. He never closed his eyes, nor folded his arms, but went forward from work to work with the consecutiveness of a law of nature.

But amid labors so strenuous and uninterrupted the leader found opportunity to woo and win "a fair ladye." She was a daughter of a veteran Abolitionist, George Benson, of Brooklyn, Conn., who with his sons George W. and Henry E. Benson, were among the stanchest of the reformer's followers and supporters. The young wife, before her marriage, was not less devoted to the cause than they. She was in closest sympathy with her husband's anti-slavery interests and purposes. Never had husband found wife better fitted to his needs, and the needs of his life work. So that it might be truly said that Garrison even when he went a-wooing forgot not his cause and that when he took a wife, he made at the same time a grand contribution to its ultimate triumph.

How did Helen Eliza Garrison serve the great cause? One who knew shall tell. He has told it in his own unequaled way. "That home," he says, "was a great help. Her husband's word and pen scattered his purpose far and wide; but the comrades that his ideas brought to his side her welcome melted into friends. No matter how various and discordant they were in many things—no matter how much there was to bear and overlook—her patience and her thanks for their sympathy in the great idea were always sufficient for the work also. . . . In that group of remarkable men and women which the anti-slavery movement drew together, she had her own niche—which no one else could have filled so perfectly or unconsciously as she did. . . . She forgot, omitted nothing. How much we all owe her!" These were words spoken by a friend, whose name will appear later on in this story; words spoken by him at the close of her beautiful life, as she lay dead in her coffin.

And here is another account of her written by the husband on the first anniversary of their marriage: "I did not marry her," he confides to her brother George, "expecting that she would assume a prominent station in the anti-slavery cause, but for domestic quietude and happiness. So completely absorbed am I in that cause, that it was undoubtedly wise in me to select as a partner one who, while her benevolent feelings were in union with mine, was less immediately and entirely connected with it. I knew she was naturally diffident, and distrustful of her own ability to do all that her heart might prompt. She is one of those who prefer to toil unseen—to give by stealth—and to sacrifice in seclusion. By her unwearied attention to my wants, her sympathetic regards, her perfect equanimity of mind, and her sweet and endearing manners; she is no trifling support to Abolitionism, inasmuch as she lightens my labors, and enables me to find exquisite delight in the family circle, as an offset to public adversity."

And here is a lovely bit of self-revelation made to her betrothed several months before they were wedded. "I am aware of the responsibility that will devolve upon me," she writes, "and how much my example will be copied among that class you have so long labored to elevate and enlighten. I have been considering how the colored people think of dress, and how much of their profits are expended for useless ornaments that foolishly tend to make a show and parade. As much stress will, of course, be laid on

Garrison's *wife* by that class, it behooves me to be very circumspect in all things, when called upon to fill so important a station."

The marriage occurred September 4, 1834, and the next day the pair set up housekeeping in "Freedom's Cottage," on Bower street, Roxbury. The young housekeepers were rich in every good thing except money; and of that commodity there was precious little that found its way into the family till. And money was indispensable even to a philanthropist, who cared as little for it as did Garrison. He had never in his twenty-eight years experienced the sensation which a bank account. however small, gives its possessor. He had been toiling during the last three years in a state of chronic self-forgetfulness, and of consequence in a state of chronic inpecuniosity. He had never been careful of what he got—was careful only of what he gave. For himself he was ready to subsist on bread and water and to labor more than fourteen hours at the case to make the issue of the *Liberator* possible. But surely he could not put "a fair ladye" on such limited commons even for the sake of his cause. The laborer is worthy of his hire, and an unworldly minded reformer ought to be supplied with the wherewithal needful to feed, clothe, and house himself and those dependent upon him. Some such thought shaped itself in Garrison's mind as his circumstances grew more and more straitened, and his future as the head of a family looked more and more ominous. Anxiety for the morrow pressed heavily upon him as his responsibilities as a breadwinner hugged closer and closer his everyday life. Poverty ceased to be the ordinary enemy of former years, whom he from the lookouts of the unconquerable mind used to laugh to scorn ; it had become instead a cruel foe who worried as by fire the peace of his soul.

There was the *Liberator?* The *Liberator* as a moral engine was a marvelous success; but the *Liberator* as a money-maker was a most dismal failure. If its owners had possessed only common aptitude for business the failure need not have been so complete, indeed the enterprise might have been crowned with a moderate degree of success. But never were two men more entirely lacking in the methods, which should enter into ventures of that character, than were Garrison and Knapp. Garrison was unfortunate in this respect but it seems that Knapp was more so. Neither took to book-keeping, and neither overcame his serious deficiency in this regard. The consequence was that the books kept themselves, and confusion grew upon confusion until the partners were quite confounded. Garrison naïvely confesses this fault of the firm to his brother-in-law thus: "Brother Knapp, you know, resembles me very closely in his habits of procrastination. Indeed I think he is rather worse than I am in this respect!"

The paper was issued originally without a single subscriber. At the end of the first volume the subscription list numbered five hundred names. In the course of the next two volumes this number was more than doubled, almost tripled, in fact. The subscription price was two dollars. The property would have begun from this point to make returns to its owners had they possessed the business training and instinct requisite to its successful management. But they were reformers, not money-getters, and instead of enjoying the profits they proceeded to use them up incontinently in their first enlargement of the paper. But while they had added to the cost of publication, they took no thought to augment the cost of subscription. The publishers gave more and the subscribers received more for the sum of two dollars. The pecuniary embarrassments of the *Liberator* increased, and so the partners' "bondage to penury" increased also. This growing pressure was finally relieved by "several generous donations," made for the support of the paper. At the beginning of the fourth volume, the publishers wisely or otherwisely, again enlarged their darling, and again neglected to raise the subscription rates at the same time.

Misfortunes never come without company, but alight in flocks, and a whole flock of misfortunes it was to the *Liberator* when Joshua Coffin, "that huge personification of good humor," was appointed canvassing agent for the paper. He was as wanting in business methods as his employers were. Confusion now gathered upon confusion around the devoted heads of the partners, was accelerated and became daily more and more portentous and inextricable. The delinquencies of subscribers grew more and more grave. On the three first volumes they were two thousand dollars in arrears to the paper. This was a large, a disastrous loss, but traceable, to no inconsiderable extent, doubtless, to the loose business methods of the reformer and his partner. The *Liberator* at the beginning of its fourth year was struggling in a deep hole of financial helplessness and chaos. Would it ever get out alive, or SHALL THE *LIBERATOR* DIE?" burst in a cry of anguish, almost despair, from its editor, so weak in thought of self, so supreme in thought of others.

This carelessness of what appertained to the things which concerned self, and devotion to the things which concerned his cause, finds apt and pathetic illustration in this letter to Samuel J. May in the summer of 1834, when his pecuniary embarrassments and burdens were never harder to carry:

"In reply to your favor of the 24th [July], my partner joins with me in consenting to print an edition of Miss Crandall's [defence] as large as the one proposed by you, at our own risk. As to the profits that may arise from the sale of the pamphlet, we do not expect to make any; on the contrary, we shall probably suffer some loss, in consequence of the difficulty of disposing of any publication, however interesting or valuable in itself. But a trial so important as Miss C.'s, involving such momentous consequences to a large portion of our countrymen, implicating so deeply the character of this great nation, ought not to go unpublished, and *shall* not while we have the necessary materials for printing it."

It is interesting to note that the weekly circulation of the *Liberator*, in the spring of 1834, was twenty-three hundred copies, and that this number was distributed in Philadelphia, four hundred; in New York, three hundred; in Boston, two hundred; in other parts of the free States eleven hundred; and that of the remaining three hundred, one-half was sent as exchange with other papers, and eighty of the other half were divided equally between England and Hayti, leaving seventy copies for gratuitous distribution. The colored subscribers to the paper were to the whites as three to one.

There were several suggestions by sundry friends looking to the release of the *Liberator* from its embarrassments, and, to the relief of its unselfish publishers, from the grinding poverty which its issue imposed upon them. The most hopeful and feasible of them was the scheme of which Garrison wrote his betrothed April 14, 1834: "I am happy to say," he pours into her ears, "that it is probable the managers of the New England Anti-Slavery Society will determine, to-morrow afternoon, to take all the pecuniary liabilities of the *Liberator* hereafter, and give me a regular salary for editing it, and friend Knapp a fair price for printing it. My salary will not be less than $800 per annum, and perhaps it will be fixed at a $1,000. . . . The new arrangement will go into effect on the 1st of July." But alas; the managers took no such action on the morrow, nor went the "new arrangement" into effect at the time anticipated. The editor was married in September, and two months later the eagerly expected relief was still delayed. This hope deferred must have caused the young husband meanwhile no little anxiety and heart sickness.

Love in a cottage is very pretty and romantic in novels, but love in a cottage actually thriving on "bread and water," was a sweet reality in the home of the young couple in Roxbury. "All the world loves a lover," says Emerson, but alas! there are exceptions to all rules, and all the world loved not Garrison in his newly found felicity as shall presently appear.

The pledge made by the reformer in the initial number of the *Liberator* to be "as harsh as truth," had been kept to the letter. To some minds there is nothing more difficult to understand and tolerate than is the use of harsh language toward individual wrongdoers. They appear to be much more solicitous to turn away the wrath of the wicked than to do away with their wickedness. Multitudes of such minds were offended at the tremendous severities of Garrison's speech. They were for peace at any cost, while Garrison was for truth at any cost. These pro-slavery critics were not necessarily wanting in good feelings to the slaves, or lacking in a sense of the justice of their cause. But the feelings and the sense were transitive to an abstract object, intransitive to that terrible reality, the American slave. The indignation of such people exceeded all bounds when contemplating wrongs in the abstract, iniquity in the abstract, while the genuine article in flesh and blood and habited in broadcloth and respectability provoked no indignation, provoked instead unbounded charity for the willing victims of ancestral transgressions. Upon the Southern slaveholder, as a creature of circumstances, these people expended all their sympathy while upon the Southern slave, who were to their view *the circumstances*, they looked with increasing disapprobation. Garrison's harsh language greatly shocked this class—excited their unbounded indignation against the reformer.

Besides this class there was another, composed of friends, whom Garrison's denunciatory style offended. To Charles Follen and Charles Stuart, and Lewis Tappan, this characteristic of the writings of the great agitator was a sore trial. To them and to others, too, his language seemed grossly intemperate and vituperative, and was deemed productive of harm to the movement. But Garrison defended his harsh language by pointing to the state of the country on the subject of slavery before he began to use it, and to the state of the country afterward. How utterly and morally dead the nation was before, how keenly and marvelously alive it became afterward. The blast which he had blown had jarred upon the senses of his slumbering countrymen he admitted, but he should not be blamed for that. What to his critics sounded harsh and abusive, was to him the trump of God. For, at the thunder-peal which the Almighty blew from the mouth of his servant, how, as by a miracle, the dead soul of the nation awoke to righteousness. He does not arrogate to himself infallibility, indeed he is sure that his language is not always happily chosen. Such errors, however, appear to him trivial, in view of indisputable and extraordinary results produced by the *Liberator*. He believes in marrying masculine truths to masculine words. He protests against his condemnation by comparison. "Every writer's style is his own—it may be smooth or rough, plain or obscure, simple or grand, feeble or strong," he contends, "but *principles* are immutable." By his principles, therefore he would, be judged. "Whittier, for instance,," he continues, "is highly poetical, exuberant, and beautiful. Stuart is solemn, pungent, and severe. Wright is a thorough logician, dextrous, transparent, straightforward. Beriah Green is manly, eloquent, vigorous, devotional. May is persuasive, zealous, overflowing with the milk of human kindness. Cox is diffusive, sanguine, magnificent, grand. Bourne thunders and lightens. Phelps is one great, clear, infallible argument—demonstration itself. Jocelyn is full of heavenly-mindedness, and feels and speaks and acts with a zeal according to knowledge. Follen is chaste, profound, and elaborately polished. Goodell is perceptive, analytical, expert, and solid. Child (David L.) is generously indignant, courageous, and demonstrative; his lady combines strength with beauty, argumentation with persuasiveness, greatness with humility. Birney is collected, courteous, dispassionate—his fearlessness excites admiration, his conscientiousness commands respect." Of these writers, which is acceptable to slaveholders or their apologists? Some have been cruelly treated and all been calumniated as "fanatics, disorganizers, and madmen." And why? "Certainly not for the *phraseology* which they use, but for the *principles* which they adopt."

From another quarter came presently notes of discord, aroused by Garrison's *hard language.* Sundry of the Unitarian clergy, under the lead of Rev. Henry Ware, Jr., took it into their heads that the editor of the *Liberator* and some others were outrageously abusing the Abolition cause, "mismanaging it by their unreasonable violence" of language. Wherefore those gentlemen interposed to rescue the great cause from harm by a brilliant scheme designed to secure moderation in this regard. This brilliant scheme was nothing less ubsurd than the establishment of a censorship over the *Liberator.* But as these solicitous souls had reckoned without their host, their amiable plan came to naught; but not, however, before adding a new element to the universal discord then fast swelling to a roar. To the storm of censure gathering about his head the reformer bowed not—neither swerved he to the right hand nor to the left—all the while deeming it, "with the apostle, a small thing to be judged by man's judgment." "I solicit no man's praise," he sternly replies to his critics, "I fear no men's censure.'

There was still another cause of offence given by Garrison to his countrymen. It was not his *hard language*, but a circumstance less tolerable, if that was possible, than even that rock of offence. It seems that when the editor of the *Liberator* was in England, and dining with Thomas Fowell Buxton, he was asked by the latter in what way the English Abolitionists could best assist the anti-slavery movement in America, and he had replied, "*By giving us George Thompson.*" This unexpected answer of the American appeared without doubt to the Englishman at the time somewhat extraordinary. He had his misgivings as to the wisdom, to say nothing of the propriety, of an international act of such importance and delicacy as the sending of George Thompson to America. He questioned whether the national self-love of the American people would not resent the arrival of an Englishman on such a mission among them and refuse him a fair hearing in consequence. But Garrison was confident that while Thompson's advent would stir up the pro-slavery bile of the North and all that, he would not be put to much if any greater disadvantage as a foreigner in speaking in New England on the subject of slavery, than were those Abolitionists who were to the manner born. As to his friend's personal safety in the East, Garrison was extremely optimistic, had not apparently the slightest apprehensions for him in this regard.

Well, after due deliberation, George Thompson consented to undertake the mission to America, and the English reformers to send him, though not all of them. For some there were like James Cropper, who were indisposed to promoting such a mission, or "paying agents to travel in the United States." It was natural enough for Mr. Garrison to prefer such a request after hearing George Thompson speak. For he was one of those electric speakers, who do with popular audiences what they will. In figure and voice and action, he was a born orator. His eloquence was graphic, picturesque, thrilling, and over English audiences it was irresistible. Garrison fancied that such eloquence would prove equally attractive to and irresistible over American audiences as well. But in this he was somewhat mistaken, for Thompson had to deal with an element in American audiences of which he had had no experience in England. What that element was he had occasion to surmise directly he arrived upon these shores. He reached New York just sixteeen days after the marriage of his friend, the editor of the *Liberator* to be immediately threatened with mob violence by the metropolitan press in case he ventured to "lecture in favor of immediate Abolition," and to be warned that: "If our people will not suffer our own citizens to tamper with the question of slavery, it is not to be supposed that they will tolerate the officious intermeddling of a foreign fanatic." Then as if by way of giving him a taste of the beak and talons of the American *amour propre*, he and his family were put out of the Atlantic Hotel in deference to the wish of an irate Southerner.

Thus introduced the English orator advanced speedily thereafter into closer acquaintance with the American public. He lectured in many parts of New England where that new element of rowdyism and virulence of which his English audiences had given him no previous experience, manifested its presence first in one way and then in others, putting him again and again in jeopardy of life and limb. At Augusta, Maine, his windows were broken, and he was warned out of the town. At Concord, New Hampshire, his speech was punctuated with missiles. At Lowell, Massachusetts, he narrowly escaped being struck on the head and killed by a brickbat. Indeed it was grimly apparent that the master of Freedom's Cottage would be obliged to revise his views as to the hazard, which his friend ran in speaking upon the subject of slavery in New England. To do so was weekly becoming for that friend an enterprise of great personal peril. But it added also to the fierce hatred with which the public now regarded Garrison. He was the author of all the mischief, the slavery agitation, the foreign emissary. He had even dared to inject the poison of Abolitionism into the politics of Boston and Massachusetts. This attempt on the part of the *Liberator* to establish an anti-slavery test of office was only another proof of the dangerous character of the new fanaticism and the Jacobinical designs of the Garrisonian fanatics, ergo, the importance of suppressing the incendiaries. Down with Thompson! Garrison must be destroyed! The

Union—it must and shall be preserved! All these the public excitement, which had risen everywhere to a tempest, had come more and more to mean. A tremendous crisis had come in the life of Garrison, and a great peril, eagle-like, with the stirred-up hate of a nation, was swooping upon him.

CHAPTER XI.

MISCHIEF LET LOOSE.

A WILD-CAT-LIKE creature was abroad. To it the Abolitionists were to be thrown. It was to destroy Garrison, make an end of Thompson, and suppress between its enormous jaws the grandest moral movement of the century. Besides doing up this modest little programme, the beast, O wonderful to say, was also to crown its performances by "saving" the Union. Rejoicing in the possession of such a conservative institution, the politicians, the press, and public opinion uncaged the monster, while from secure seats they watched the frightful scenes of fury and destruction enacted by it in the national arena.

These scenes began in the summer of 1834, and in the city of New York. They were ushered in by the breaking up of an anti-slavery celebration on the Fourth of July by the clack and roar of several hundred young rowdies, gathered for the purpose. Their success but whetted the appetite of the spirit of mischief for other ventures against the Abolitionists. As a consequence New York was in a more or less disturbed state from the fourth to the ninth of the month. The press of the city, with but a single exception (*The Evening Post*) meanwhile goaded the populace on by false and inflammatory representations touching the negroes and their friends, to the rioting which began in earnest on the evening of the ninth. That night a mob attacked Lewis Tappan's house on Rose street, breaking in the door, smashing blinds and windows, and playing havoc generally with the furniture. On the following evening the rioters assailed the store of Arthur Tappan, on Pearl street, demolishing almost every pane of glass in the front of the building. On the same evening the mob paid its respects to Rev. Dr. Cox, by breaking windows both at his house and at his church. The negro quarters in the neighborhood of Five Points, and their houses in other parts of the city, were raided on the night of the 11th, and much damage done by the lawless hordes which for nearly a week wreaked their wrath upon the property of the negroes and their anti-slavery friends.

After this brave beginning, the wild-cat-like spirit continued, these ferocious demonstrations in New Jersey, Pennsylvania, Ohio, Michigan, Connecticut, Maine, and New Hampshire. The slavery agitation had increased apace. It had broken out in Congress on the presentation of anti-slavery petitions. The fire thus kindled spread through the country. Southern excitement became intense, amounted almost to panic. The activity of the anti-slavery press, the stream of anti-slavery publications, which had, indeed, increased with singular rapidity, was exaggerated by the Southern imagination, struck it with a sort of terror. There were meetings held in many parts of the South, tremendous scenes enacted there. In Charleston, South Carolina, the post-office was broken open by an aristocratic mob, under the lead of the famous Robert Y. Hayne, and a bonfire made of the Abolition mail-matter which it contained. As this Southern excitement advanced, a passionate fear for the stability of the Union arose in the heart of the North. Abolition and the Abolitionists had produced these sectional disturbances. Abolition and the Abolitionists were, therefore, enemies of the "glorious Union." Northern excitement kept pace with Southern excitement until, in the summer of 1835, a reign of terror was widely established over both sections. To Garrison, from his *Liberator* outlook, all seemed "Consternation and perplexity, for perilous times have come." They had, indeed, come in New York, as witness this from the pen of Lydia Maria Child, who was at the time (August 15) in Brooklyn. Says she:

"I have not ventured into the city, nor does one of us dare to go to church to-day, so great is the excitement here. You can form no conception of it. 'Tis like the time of the French Revolution, when no man dared trust his neighbor. Private assassins from New Orleans are lurking at the corners of the streets to stab Arthur Tappan, and very large sums are offered for any one who will convey Mr. Thompson into the slave States. . . . There are several thousand Southerners now in the city, and I am afraid there are not seven hundred among them who have the slightest fear of God before their eyes. Mr. Wright [Elizur] was yesterday barricading his doors and windows with strong bars and planks an inch thick. Violence in some form seems to be generally expected."

Great meetings to put the Abolitionists down afforded vents during this memorable year to the pent-up excitement of the free States. New York had had its great meeting, and had put the Abolitionists down with pro-slavery resolutions and torrents of pro-slavery eloquence. Boston, too, had to have her great meeting and her cataracts of pro-slavery oratory to reassure the South of the sympathy and support of "the great body of the people of the Northern States." The toils seemed everywhere closing around the Abolitionists. The huge head of the asp of public opinion, the press of the land was everywhere busy, day and night, smearing with a thick and virulent saliva of lies the brave little band and its leader. Anti-slavery publications, calculated to inflame the minds of the slaves against their masters, and intended to instigate the slaves to servile insurrections, had been distributed broadcast through the South by the emissaries of anti-slavery societies. The Abolitionists advocated the emancipation of the slaves in the South by Congress, intermarriages between the two races, the dissolution of the Union, etc. All of which outrageous misrepresentations were designed to render the movement utterly odious to the public, and the public so much the more furious for its suppression.

It was in the midst of such intense and widespread excitement that Boston called its meeting to abolish the Abolitionists. It was the month of August, and the heat of men's passions was as great as the heat of the August sun. The moral atmosphere of the city was so charged with inflammable gases that the slightest spark would have sufficed to produce an explosion. The Abolitionists felt this and carried themselves the while with unusual circumspection. They deemed it prudent to publish an address to neutralize the falsehoods with which they were assailed by their enemies. The address drawn up by Garrison for the purpose was thonght "too fiery for the present time," by his more cautious followers and was rejected. The *Liberator* office had already been threatened in consequence of a fiery article by the editor, denouncing the use of Faneuil Hall for the approaching pro-slavery meeting. It seemed to the unawed and indignant champion of liberty that it were "better that the winds should scatter it in fragments over the whole earth—better that an earthquake should engulf it—than that it should be used for so unhallowed and detestable a purpose!" The anti-abolition feeling of the town had become so bitter and intense that Henry E. Benson, then clerk in the anti-slavery office, writing on the 19th of the month, believed that there were persons in Boston, who would assassinate George Thompson in broad daylight, and doubted whether Garrison or Samuel J. May would be safe in Faneuil Hall on the day of the meeting, and what seemed still more significant of the inflamed state of the public mind, was the confidence with which he predicted that a mob would follow the meeting. The wild-cat-like spirit was in the air—in the seething heart of the populace.

The meeting was held August 21st, in the old cradle of liberty. To its call alone fifteen hundred names were appended. It was a Boston audience both as to character and numbers, an altogether imposing affair, over whom the mayor of the city presided and before whom two of the most consummate orators of the commonwealth fulmined against the Abolitionists.

One of their hearers, a young attorney of twenty-four, who listened to Peleg Sprague and Harrison Gray Otis that day, described sixteen years afterward the latter and the effects produced by him on that audience. Our young attorney vividly recalled how "'Abolitionist' was linked with contempt, in the silver tones of Otis, and all the charms that a divine eloquence and most felicitous diction could throw around a bad cause were given it; the excited multitude seemed actually ready to leap up beneath the magic of his speech. It would be something, if one must die, to die by such a hand—a hand somewhat worthy and able to stifle anti-slavery, if it could be stifled. The orator was worthy of the gigantic task attempted; and thousands crowded before him, every one of their hearts melted by that eloquence, beneath which Massachusetts had bowed, not unworthily, for more than thirty years."

Here is a specimen of the sort of goading which the wild-cat-like spirit of the city got from the orators. It is taken from the speech of Peleg Sprague. The orator is paying his respects to George Thompson, "an avowed *emissary*," "*a professed agitator*," who "comes here from the dark and corrupt institutions of Europe to enlighten *us* upon the rights of man and the moral duties of our own condition. Received by our hospitality, he stands here upon our soil, protected by our laws, and hurls firebrands, arrows, and death into the habitations of our neighbors and friends, and brothers; and when he shall have kindled a conflagration which is sweeping in desolation over our land, he has only to embark for his own country, and there look serenely back with indifference or exultation upon the widespread ruin by which *our* cities are wrapt in flames, and *our* garments rolled in blood."

The great meeting was soon a thing of the past but not so its effects. The echoes of Otis and Sprague did did not cease at its close. They thrilled in the air, they thrilled long afterward in the blood of the people. When the multitude dispersed Mischief went out into the streets of the city with them. Wherever afterward they gathered Mischief made one in their midst. Mischief was let loose, Mischief was afoot in the town. The old town was no place for the foreign emissary, neither was it a safe place for the arch-agitator. On the day after the meeting, Garrison and his young wife accordingly retreated to her father's home at Brooklyn, Conn., where the husband needed not to be jostling elbows with Mistress Mischief, and her *pals*.

Garrison's answer to the speeches of Otis and Sprague was in his sternest vein. He is sure after reading them that, "there is more guilt attaching to the people of the free States from the continuance of slavery, than those in the slave States." At least he is ready to affirm upon the authority of Orator Sprague, "that New England is as really a slaveholding section of the republic as Georgia or South Carolina." Sprague, he finds, "in amicable companionship and popular repute with thieves and adulterers; with slaveholders, slavedealers, and slavedestroyers; . . . with the disturbers of the public peace; with the robbers of the public mail; with ruffians who insult, pollute, and lacerate helpless women; and with conspirators against the lives and liberties of New England citizens."

To Otis who was then nearly seventy years of age Garrison addressed his rebuke in tones of singular solemnity. It seemed to him that the aged statesman had transgressed against liberty "under circumstances of peculiar criminality." "Yet at this solemn period," the reprobation of the prophet ran, "you have not scrupled, nay, you have been ambitious, to lead and address an excited multitude, in vindication of all imaginable wickedness, embodied in one great system of crime and blood—to pander to the lusts and desires of the robbers of God and his poor—to consign over to the tender mercies of cruel taskmasters, multitudes of guiltless men, women, and children—and to denounce as an 'unlawful and dangerous association' a society whose only object is to bring this nation to repentance, through the truth as it is in Jesus."

These audacious and iconoclastic performances of the reformer were not exactly adapted to turn from him the wrath of the idol worshipers. They more likely added fuel to the hot anger burning in Boston against him. Three weeks passed after his departure from the city, and his friends did not deem it safe for him to return. Toward the end of the fourth week of his enforced absence, against which he was chafing not a little, an incident happened in Boston which warned him to let patience have its perfect work. It was on the night of September 17th that the dispositions of the city toward him found grim expression in a gallows erected in front of his house at 23 Brighton street. This ghastly reminder that the fellow-citizens of the editor of the *Liberator* continued to take a lively interest in him, "was made in real workmanship style, of *maple joist* five inches through, eight or nine feet high, for the accommodation of two persons." Garrison and Thompson were the two persons for whom these brave accommodations were prepared. But as neither they nor their friends were in a mood to have trial made of them, the intended occupants consented to give Boston a wide berth, and to be somewhat particular that they did not turn in with her while the homicidal fit lasted.

This editing his paper at long range, and this thought of life and safety Garrison did not at all relish. They grew more and more irksome to his fearless and earnest spirit. For his was a "pine-and-fagot" Abolitionism that knew not the fear of men or their wrath. But now he must needs have a care for the peace of mind of his young wife, who was, within a few months, to give birth to a child. And her anxiety for him was very great. Neither was the anxiety of devoted friends and followers to be lightly disregarded. All of which detained the leader in Brooklyn until the 25th of the month, when the danger signals seemed to have disappeared. Whereupon he set out immediately for his post in Boston to be at the head of his forces. He found the city in one of those strange pauses of popular excitement, which might signify the ebb of the tide or only the retreat of the billows. He was not inclined to let the anti-Abolition agitation subside so soon, before it had carried on its flood Abolition principles to wider fields and more abundant harvests in the republic. Anxious lest the cat-like temper of the populace was falling into indifference and apathy, he and his disciples took occasion to prod it into renewed wakefulness and activity. The instruments used for this purpose were anti-slavery meetings and the sharp goad of his *Liberator* editorials. The city was possessed with the demon of slavery, and its foaming at the mouth was the best of all signs that the Abolition exorcism was working effectively. So, in between the glittering teeth and the terrible paws was thrust the maddening goad, and up sprang the mighty beast horrible to behold.

One of these meetings was the anniversary of the formation of the Boston Female Anti-Slavery Society which fell on October 14th. The ladies issued their notice, engaged a hall, and invited George Thompson to address them. Now the foreign emissary was particularly exasperating to Boston sensibility on the subject of slavery. He was the veritable red rag to the pro-slavery bull. The public announcement, therefore, that he was to speak in the city threw the public mind into violent agitation. The *Gazette* and the *Courier* augmented the excitement by the recklessness with which they denounced the proposed meeting, the former promising to Thompson a lynching, while the latter endeavored to involve his associates who were to the "manner born" in the popular outbreak, which was confidently predicted in case the "foreign vagrant" wagged his tongue at the time appointed.

Notwithstanding the rage of press and people the meeting was postponed through no willingness on the part of the ladies, but because of the panic of the owners of the hall lest their property should be damaged or destroyed in case of a riot. The ladies, thereupon, appointed three o'clock in the afternoon of October 21st as the time, and the hall adjoining the Anti-Slavery Office, at 46 Washington street, as the place where they would hold their adjourned meeting. This time they made no mention of Mr. Thompson's addressing them, merely announcing several addresses. In fact, an address from Mr. Thompson, in view of the squally outlook, was not deemed expedient. To provide against accidents and disasters, he left the city on the day before the meeting. But this his enemies did not know. They confidently expected that he was to be one of the speakers. An inflammatory handbill distributed on the streets at noon of the 21st seemed to leave no doubt of this circumstance in the pro-slavery portion of the city.

The handbill referred to ran as follows:

THOMPSON,

THE ABOLITIONIST!!!

That infamous foreign scoundrel, THOMPSON, will hold forth *this afternoon* at the *Liberator* office, No. 48 Washington street. The present is a fair opportunity for the friends of the Union to *snake Thompson out!* It will be a contest between the Abolitionists and the friends of the Union. A purse of $100 has been raised by a number of patriotic citizens to reward the individual who shall first lay violent hands on Thompson, so that he may be brought to the tar-kettle before dark. Friends of the Union, be vigilant!

Boston, Wednesday, 12 o'clock.

That Wednesday forenoon Garrison spent at the anti-slavery office, little dreaming of the peril which was to overtake him in that very spot in the afternoon. He went home to an early dinner, since his wife was a member of the society, and he himself was set down for an address. As he wended his way homeward, Mischief and her gang were afoot distributing the aforesaid handbills "in the insurance offices, the reading-rooms, all along State street, in the hotels, bar-rooms, etc.," and scattering it "among mechanics at the North End, who were mightily taken with it." Garrison returned about a half hour before the time appointed for the meeting. He found a small crowd of about a hundred individuals collected in front of the building where the hall was situated, and on ascending to the hall more of the same sort, mostly young men, choking the access to it. They were noisy, and Garrison pushed his way through them with difficulty. As he entered the place of meeting and took his seat among the ladies, twenty had already arrived, the gang of young rowdies recognized him and evinced this by the exclamation: "That's Garrison!" The full significance of the crowd just without the hall did not seem to have occurred to the man whom they had identified. He did not know that they were the foam blown from the mouth of a great mob at the moment filling the streets in the neighborhood of the building where he sat with such serenity of spirit. His wife who had followed him from their home saw what Garrison did not see. The crowd of a hundred had swelled to thousands. It lay in a huge irregular cross, jammed in between the buildings on Washington street, the head lowering in front of the anti-slavery office, the foot reaching to the site where stood Joy building, now occupied by the Rogers, the right arm stretching along Court street to the Court House, and the left encircling the old State

House, City Hall and Post-office then, in a gigantic embrace. All hope of urging her way through that dense mass was abandoned by Mrs. Garrison, and a friend, Mr. John E. Fuller, escorted her to his home, where she passed the night.

Meantime the atmosphere upstairs at the hall began to betoken a fast approaching storm. The noises ominously increased on the landing just outside. The door of the hall was swung wide open and the entrance filled with rioters. Garrison, all unconscious of danger, walked over to these persons and remonstrated in his grave way with them in regard to the disturbance which they were producing, winding up with a characteristic bit of pleasantry: "Gentlemen," said he, "perhaps you are not aware that this is a meeting of the Boston *Female* Anti-Slavery Society, called and intended exclusively for *ladies*, and those only who have been invited to address them. Understanding this fact you will not be so rude and indecorous as to thrust your presence upon this meeting." But he added, "If, *gentlemen*, any of you are *ladies* in disguise—why only apprise me of the fact, give me your names, and I will introduee you to the rest of your sex, and you can take seats among them accordingly." The power of benignity over malignity lasted a few moments after this little speech, when the situation changed rapidly from bad to worse. "The tumult continually increased," says an eye-witness, "with horrible execrations, howling, stamping, and finally shrieking with rage. They seemed not to dare to enter, notwithstanding their fury, but mounted on each other's shoulders, so that a row of hostile heads appeared over the slight partition, of half the height of the wall which divides the society's rooms from the landing place. We requested them to allow the door to be shut; but they could not decide as to whether the request should be granted, and the door was opened and shut with violence, till it hung useless from its hinges."

Garrison thinking that his absence might quiet these perturbed spirits and so enable the ladies to hold their meeting without further molestation volunteered at this juncture to the president of the society to retire from the hall unless she desired him to remain. She did not wish him to stay but urged him to go at once not only for the peace of the meeting but for his own safety. Garrison thereupon left the hall meaning at the time to leave the building as well, but egress by the way of the landing and the stairs, he directly perceived was impossible, and did what seemed the next best thing, entered the anti-slavery office, separated from the hall by a board partition. Charles C. Burleigh accompanied him within this retreat. The door between the hall and the office was securely locked, and Garrison with that marvelous serenity of mind, which was a part of him, busied himself immediately with writing to a friend an account of the scenes which were enacting in the next room.

The tempest had begun in the streets also. The mob from its five thousand throats were howling "Thompson! Thompson!" The mayor of the city, Theodore Lyman, appeared upon the scene, and announced to the gentlemen of property and standing, who were thus exercising their vocal organs, that

Mr. Thompson was not at the meeting, was not in the city. But the mayor was a modern Canute before the sea of human passion, which was rushing in over law and authority. He besought the rioters to disperse, but he might as well have besought the waves breaking on Nastasket Beach to disperse. Higher, higher rose the voices ; fiercer, fiercer waxed the multitude; more and more frightful became the uproar. The long-pent-up excitement of the city and its hatred of Abolitionists had broken loose at last and the deluge had come. The mayor tossed upon the human inundation as a twig on a mountain stream, and with him for the nonce struggled helplessly the police power of the town also.

Upstairs in the hall the society and its president are quite as powerless as the mayor and the police below. Miss Mary S. Parker, the president, is struggling with the customary opening exercises. She has called the meeting to order, read to the ladies some passages from the Bible, and has lifted up her voice in prayer to the All Wise and Merciful One "for direction and succor, and the forgiveness of enemies and revilers." It is a wonderful scene, a marvelous example of Christian heroism, for in the midst of the hisses and threats and curses of the rioters, the prayer of the brave woman rose clear and untremulous. But now the rioters have thrown themselves against the partition between the landing-place and the hall. They are trying to break it down; now, they have partially succeeded. In another moment they have thrown themselves against the door of the office where Garrison is locked. The lower panel is dashed in. Through the opening they have caught sight of their object, Garrison, serenely writing at his desk. "There he is! That's Garrison! Out with the scoundrel!" and other such words of recognition and execration, burst from one and another of the mob. The shattering of the partition, the noise of splitting and ripping boards, the sharp crash caused by the shivering of the office door, the loud and angry outcries of the rioters warn the serene occupant of the office that his position has become one of extreme peril. But he does not become excited. His composure does not forsake him. Instead of attempting to escape, he simply turns to his friend, Burleigh, with the words, "You may as well open the door, and let them come in and do their worst." But fortunately, Burleigh was in no such extremely non-resistant mood.

The advent of the mayor and the constables upon the scene at this point rescued Garrison from immediately falling into the hands of the mob, who were cleared out of the hall and from the stairway. Now the voice of the mayor was heard urging the ladies to go home as it was dangerous to remain; and now the voice of Maria Weston Chapman, replying: "If this is the last bulwark of freedom, we may as well die here as anywhere." The ladies finally decided to retire, and their exit diverted, while the operation lasted, the attention of the huge, cat-like creature from their object in the anti-slavery office. When the passing of the ladies had ceased, the old fury of the mob against Garrison returned. "Out with him!" "Lynch him!" rose in wild uproar from thousands in the streets. But again the attention of the huge, cat-like creature was diverted from its object in the second story of the building before which it was lashing itself into frenzy. This time it was the anti-slavery sign which hung from the rooms of the society over the sidewalk. The mob had caught sight of it, and directly set up a yell for it. The sensation of utter helplessness in the presence of the multitude seemed at this juncture to return to the chief magistrate of the city. It was impossible to control the cataract-like passions of the rioters. He heard their awful roar for the sign. The din had risen to terrific proportions. The thought of what might happen next appalled him. The mob might begin to bombard the sign with brickbats, and from the sign pass to the building, and from the building to the constables, and then—but the mayor glanced not beyond, for he had determined to appease the fury of the mob by throwing down to it the hateful sign. A constable detached it, and hurled it down to the rioters in the street. But by the act the mayor had signified that the rule of law had collapsed, and the rule of the mob had really begun. When the rioters had wreaked their wrath upon the emblem of freedom, they were in the mood for more violence. The appetite for destruction, it was seen, had not been glutted; only whetted. Garrison's situation was now extremely critical. He could no longer remain where he was, for the mob would invade the building and hunt him like hounds from cellar to garret. He must leave the building without delay. To escape from the front was out of the question. A way of escape must, therefore, be found in the rear. All of these considerations the mayor and Garrison's friends urged upon him. The good man fell in with this counsel, and, with a faithful friend, proceeded to the rear of the building, where from a window he dropped to a shed, but in doing so was very nearly precipitated to the ground. After picking himself up he passed into a carpenter's shop, meaning to let himself down into Wilson's Lane, now Devonshire street, but the myriad-eyed mob, which was searching every portion of the building for their game, espied him at this point, and with that set up a great shout. The workmen came to the aid of the fugitive by closing the door of the carpenter's shop in the face of his pursuers. The situation seemed desperate. Retreat from the front was cut off; escape from the rear anticipated and foiled. Garrison perceived the futility of any further attempts to elude the mob, and proposed in his calm way to deliver himself up to them. But his faithful Achates, John Reid Campbell, advised him that it was his duty to avoid the mob as long as it was possible to do so. Garrison thereupon made a final effort to get away. He retreated up stairs, where his friend and a lad got him into a corner of the room and tried to conceal his whereabouts by piling some boards in front of him. But, by that time, the rioters had entered the building, and within a few moments had broken into the room where Garrison was in hiding. They found Mr. Reid, and demanded of him where Garrison was. But Reid firmly refused to tell. They then led him to a window, and exhibited him to the mob in the Lane, advising them that it was not Garrison, but Garrison's and Thompson's friend, who knows where Garrison is, but refuses to tell. A shout of fierce exultation from below greeted this announcement. Almost immediately afterward, Garrison was discovered and dragged furiously to the window, with the intention of hurling him thence to the pavement. Some of the rioters were for doing this, while others were for milder measures. "Don't let us kill him outright!" they begged. So his persecutors relented, coiled a rope around his body instead, and bade him descend to the street. The great man was never greater than at that moment. With extraordinary meekness and benignity he saluted his enemies in the street. From the window he bowed to the multitude who were thirsting for his destruction, requesting them to wait patiently, for he was coming to them. Then he stepped intrepidly down the ladder raised for the purpose, and into the seething sea of human passion.

Garrison must now have been speedily torn to pieces had he not been quickly seized by two or three powerful men, who were determined to save him from falling into the hands of the mob. They were men of great muscular strength, but the muscular strength of two or three giants would have proven utterly unequal to the rescue, and this Mr. Garrison's deliverers evidently appreciated. For while they employed their powerful arms, they also employed stratagem as well to effect their purpose. They shouted anon as they fought their way through the excited throng, "He is an American! He shan't be hurt!" and other such words which divided the mind of the mob, arousing among some sympathy for the good man. By this means he was with difficulty got out of Wilson's lane into State street, in the rear of the old State House. The champion was now on historic ground,

ground consecrated by the blood of Crispus Attucks and his fellow-martyrs sixty-five years before. His hat was lost, much of his clothing was stripped from his body, he was without his customary glasses, and was therefore practically blind. He could hear the awful clamor, the mighty uproar of the mob, but he could not distinguish them one from another, friend from foe. Nevertheless he "walked with head erect, calm countenance flashing eyes like a martyr going to the stake, full of faith and manly hope" according to the testimony of an eye-witness. Garrison himself has thrown light on the state of his mind during the ordeal. "The promises of God," he afterward remembered, sustained his soul, "so that it was not only divested of fear, but ready to sing aloud for joy."

The news now reached the ears of the mayor that Garrison was in the hands of the mob. Thereupon the feeble but kindly magistrate began to act afresh the rôle of the twig in the mountain stream. He and his constables struggled helplessly in the human current rushing and raging around City Hall, the head and seat of municipal law and authority. Without the aid of private citizens Garrison must inevitably have perished in the commotions which presently reached their climax in violence and terror. He was in the rear of City Hall when the mayor caught up to him and his would-be rescuers. The mayor perceived the extremity of the situation, and said to the Faneuil Hall giants who had hold of Garrison, "Take him into my office," which was altogether more easily said than done. For the rioters have raised the cry "to the Frog Pond with him!" Which order will be carried out, that of the magistrate or that of the mob?

These were horrible moments while the two hung trembling in the balance. But other private citizens coming to the assistance of the mayor struck the scales for the moment in his favor, and Garrison was finally hustled, and thrust by main force into the south door of the City Hall and carried up to the mayor's room. But the mob had immediately effected an entrance into the building through the north door and filled the lower hall. The mayor now addressed the pack, strove manfully in his feeble way to prevail upon the human wolves to observe order, to sustain the law and the honor of the city, he even intimated to them that he was ready to lay down his life on the spot to maintain the law and preserve order. Then he got out on the ledge over the south door and spoke in a similar strain to the mob on the street. But alas! he knew not the secret for reversing the Circean spell by which gentlemen of property and standing in the community had been suddenly transformed into a wolfish rabble.

The increasing tumult without soon warned the authorities that what advantage the mayor may have obtained in the contest with the mob was only temporary and that their position was momentarily becoming more perilous and less tenable. It was impossible to say to what extreme of violence a multitude so infuriated would not go to get their prey. It seemed to the now thoroughly alarmed mayor that the mob might in their frenzy attack the City Hall to effect their purpose. There was one building in the city, which the guardians of the law evidently agreed could resist the rage of the populace, and that building was the jail. To this last stronghold of Puritan civilization the authorities and the powers that were, fell back as a dernier resort to save Garrison's life. But even in this utmost pitch and extremity, when law was trampled in the streets, when authority was a reed shaken in a storm, when anarchy had drowned order in the bosom of the town, the Anglo-Saxon passion for legal forms asserted itself. The good man, hunted for his life, must forsooth be got into the only refuge which promised him security from his pursuers by a regular judicial commitment as a disturber of the peace. Is there anything at once so pathetic and farcical in the Universal history of mobs?

Pathetic and farcical to be sure, but it was also well meant, and therefore we will not stop to quarrel with men who were equal to the perpetration of a legal fiction so full of the comedy and tragedy of civilized society. But enough — the municipal wiseacres having put their heads together and evolved the brilliant plan of committing the prophet as a disturber of the peace, immediately set about its execution, which developed in the sequence into a bird of altogether another color. For a more perilous and desperate device to preserve Garrison's life could not well have been hit upon. How was he ever to be got out of the building and through that sea of ferocious faces surging and foaming around it. First then by disguising his identity by sundry changes in his apparel. He obtained a pair of trousers from one kindly soul, another gave him a coat, a third lent him a stock, a fourth furnished him a cap. A hack was summoned and stationed at the south door, a posse of constables drew up and made an open way from the door to it. Another hack was placed in readiness at the north door. The hack at the south door was only a ruse to throw the mob off the scent of their prey, while he was got out of the north door and smuggled into the other hack. Up to this point, the plan worked well, but the instant after Garrison had been smuggled into the hack he was identified by the mob, and then ensued a scene which defies description ; no writer however skillful, may hope to reproduce it. The rioters rushed madly upon the vehicle with the cry: "Cut the traces! Cut the reins!" They flung themselves upon the horses, hung upon the wheels, dashed open the doors, the driver the while belaboring their heads right and left with a powerful whip, which he also laid vigorously on the backs of his horses. For a moment it looked as if a catastrophe was unavoidable, but the next saw the startled horses plunging at break-neck speed with the hack up Court street and the mob pursuing it with yells of baffled rage. Then began a thrilling, a tremendous race for life and Leverett street jail. The vehicle flew along Court street to Bodoin square, but the rioters, with fell purpose flew hardly less swiftly in its track. Indeed the pursuit of the pack was so close that the hackman did not dare to drive directly to the jail but reached it by a detour through Cambridge and Blossom streets. Even then the mob pressed upon the heels of the horses as they drew up before the portals of the old prison, which shut not an instant too soon upon the editor of the *Liberator*, who was saved from a frightful fate to use a Biblical phrase but by the skin of his teeth.

Here the reformer safe from the wrath of his foes, was locked in a cell; and here, during the evening, with no abatement of his customary cheerfulness and serenity of spirit, he received several of his anxious friends, Whittier among them, whom through the grated bars he playfully accosted thus: "You see my accommodations are so limited, that I cannot ask you to spend the night with me." That night in his prison cell, and on his rude prison bed, he slept the sleep of the just man, sweet and long:

> "When peace within the bosom reigns,
> And conscience gives th' approving voice;
> Though bound the human form in chains,
> Yet can the soul aloud rejoice.
>
> "'Tis true, my footsteps are confined—
> I cannot range beyond this cell—
> But what can circumscribe my mind,
> To chain the winds attempt as well!"

The above stanzas he wrote the next morning on the walls of his cell. Besides this one he made two other inscriptions there, to stand as memorabilia of the black drama enacted in Boston on the afternoon of October 21, 1835.

After being put through the solemn farce of an examination in a court, extemporized in the jail, Garrison was discharged from arrest as a disturber of the peace! But the authorities, dreading a repetition of the scenes of the day before, prayed him to leave the city for a few days, which he did, a deputy sheriff driving him to Canton, where he boarded the train from Boston to Providence, containing his wife, and together they went thence to her father's at Brooklyn, Conn. The apprehensions of the authorities in respect of the danger of a fresh attack upon him were unquestionably well founded, inasmuch as diligent search was made for him in all of the outgoing stages and cars from the city that morning.

In this wise did pro-slavery, patriotic Boston translate into *works* her sympathy for the South.

CHAPTER XII.

FLOTSAM AND JETSAM.

THE results of the storm became immediately manifest in several ways. Such a commotion did not leave things in precisely the state in which they were on the morning of the memorable day on which it struck the city. The moral landscape and geography of the community had sensibly changed at its close. The full extent of the alteration wrought could not at once be seen, nor was it at once felt. But that there were deep and abiding changes made by it in the court of public opinion in Boston and Massachusetts on the subject of slavery there is little doubt. It disgusted and alarmed many individuals who had hitherto acted in unison with the social, business, and political elements, which were at the bottom of the riot. Francis Jackson, for instance, had been one of the fifteen hundred signers of the call for the great Faneuil Hall meeting of the 21st of August. But on the afternoon of the 21st of October he threw his house open to the Boston Female Anti-Slavery Society, after its meeting had been broken up by the mob. It seemed to him then that it was no longer a mere struggle for the freedom of the slave, but for the right of free speech and free discussion as well. Dr. Henry I. Bowditch, a young man, in 1835, eminent professor and physician subsequently, dates from that afternoon of mob violence his conversion to Abolitionism.

In that selfsame hour seeds of resistance to slavery were sown in two minds of the first order in the city and State. Wendell Phillips was a spectator in the streets that day, and the father of Charles Sumner, the sheriff at the time, fought bravely to save Garrison from falling into the hands of the mob The great riot gave those young men their first summons to enter the service of freedom. It was not long afterward probably that they both began to read the *Liberator*. From that event many intelligent and conservative people associated slavery with lynch law and outrage upon the rights of free speech and popular assembly.

This anti-slavery reaction of the community received practical demonstration in the immediate increase of subscribers to the *Liberator*. Twelve new names were added to the subscription list in one day. It received significant illustration also in Garrison's nomination to the legislature. In this way did between seventy and eighty citizens testify their sympathy for him and their reprobation of mob rule. In yet another way was its influence felt, and this was in the renewed zeal and activity which it instantly produced on the part of the Abolitionists themselves. It operated upon the movement as a powerful stimulus to fresh sacrifices and unwearied exertions. George W. Benson, Garrison's brother-in-law, led off bravely in this respect, as the following extract from a letter written by him in Boston, two days after the riot, to Garrison, at Brooklyn, well illustrates. He had come up to the city from Providence the night before, in quest of his sister and her husband. Not finding them, he turned to the cause which had been so ruthlessly attacked, and this is the sort of care which he bestowed upon it. He got Burleigh to write a general relation of the mob for publication in the *Liberator*, and Whittier to indite another, with an appeal to the public, the same to be published immediately, and of which he ordered three thousand copies for himself.

"I further ordered," he writes, "one thousand copies of A. Grimke's letter, with your introductory remarks, and your address published in the *Liberator* several weeks since, with your name appended, and Whittier's poetry on the times, in a pamphlet form. I urged all our friends to redouble their exertions. They seemed well disposed to accept the advice, as nothing will now avail but thorough measures. *Liberty or Death!*"

This is a fair specimen of the indomitable, indefatigable spirit which was born of the attempt to put Abolitionism down by lawlessness and violence. Indeed, the "Broad-Cloth Mob," viewed in the light of the important consequences which followed it, was equal to a hundred anti-slavery meetings, or a dozen issues of the *Liberator*.

It is a curious and remarkable circumstance that, on the very day of the Boston mob, there occurred one in Utica, N. Y., which was followed by somewhat similar results. An anti-slavery convention was attacked and broken up by a mob of "gentlemen of property and standing in the community," under the active leadership of a member of Congress. Here there was an apparent defeat for the Abolitionists, but the consequences which followed the outrage proved it a blessing in disguise. For the cause made many gains thereby, and conspicuously among them was Gerrit Smith, ever afterward one of its most eloquent and munificent supporters. If anti-slavery meetings made converts by tens, anti-slavery mobs made them by hundreds. The enemies of freedom builded better than they knew or intended, and Garrison had the weightiest of reasons for feeling thankful to them for the involuntary, yet vast aid and comfort which their pro-slavery virulence and violence were bringing him and the anti-slavery movement throughout the free States. Example: in 1835–36, the great mob year, as many as three hundred and twenty-eight societies were organized in the North for the immediate abolition of slavery.

The mob did likewise help towards a satisfactory solution of the riddle propounded by Garrison: "Shall the *Liberator* die?" The fresh access of anti-slavery strength, both in respect of zeal and numbers, begotten by it, exerted no slight influence on the longevity of the *Liberator*. Poor the paper continued, and embarrassed the editor for many a month thereafter, but as an anti-slavery instrument its survival may be said from that proceeding to have become a necessity. To allow the *Liberator* to die at this juncture would have been such a confession of having been put down, such an ignominious surrender to the mobocrats as the Abolitionists of Boston would have scorned to make. "I trust," wrote Samuel E. Sewall, "there will not be even one week's interruption in the publication of the *Liberator*." *Ex uno disce omnes.* He but voiced the sentiment of the editor's disciples and associates in the city, in the State, and in New England as well.

Besides these larger consequences there were others of a more personal and less welcome character. The individual suffers but the cause goes forward. Property-holders in Boston after the riot were not at all disposed to incur the risk of renting property to such disturbers of the peace as Garrison and the *Liberator*. The owner of his home on Brighton street was thrown into such alarm for the safety of his property, if Garrison continued to occupy it, that he requested the cancellation of the lease and the vacation of the premises. Garrison and his friends, all things considered, decided that it was the part of wisdom to accede to the request—although this breaking up of his home was a sore trial to the young husband in more ways than one.

The landlord of the building where was located the *Liberator* office promptly notified the publishers to remove the paper not many mornings after the mob. This was particularly hard luck, inasmuch as the most dilligent quest for another local habitation for the paper, failed of success. No one was willing to imperil his property by letting a part of it to such a popularly odious enterprise. So that not only had the household furniture of the editor to be stored, but the office effects of the paper as well. The inextinguishable pluck and zeal of Garrison and his Boston coadjutors never showed to better advantage than when without a place to print the *Liberator*, the paper was "set up in driblets" in other offices at extraordinary expense, and sent out week after week to tell the tale of the mob, and to preach with undiminished power the gospel of universal emancipation.

But more afflictive to the feelings of the reformer than the loss of his home, or that of the office of the *Liberator*, was the loss of his friend, George Thompson. It seemed to him when the English orator departed that "the paragon of modern eloquence," and "the benefactor of two nations," had left these shores. Garrison's grief was as poignant as his humiliation was painful. George Thompson had come hither only as a friend of America, and America had pursued him with the most relentless malice. The greatest precautions were taken after the "Broadcloth Mob" to ensure his safety. The place of his concealment was kept a secret and committed only to a few tried friends. There is no doubt that had these precautions not been observed and his hiding place been discovered by the ruffians of the city, his life would have been attempted. Indeed it is almost as certain that had he ventured to show himself in public he would have been murdered in broad daylight in any of the large towns and cities of Massachusetts. His mission was clearly at an end unless he was determined to invite martyrdom. In these circumstances there was nothing to do but to smuggle him out of the country at the first opportunity. On Sunday, November 8, the anxiously looked-for moment came when George Thompson was put upon a packet, in which he sailed for St. Johns, New Brunswick, whence he subsequently took passage for England. Garrison was inconsolable. "Who now shall go forth to argue our cause in public," he sadly asked, "with subtle sophists and insolent scoffers?" little dreaming that there was then approaching him out of the all-hail hereafter a greater in these identical respects than George Thompson, indisputably great as he was.

It was a blessed refuge to Garrison, the Benson homestead of Brooklyn, termed Friendship's Valley. Hunted as a partridge by his enemies here he found the quiet, and sympathy, and the right royal welcome and affection for which his heart panted amidst the dust, and din, and dangers of the crusade against slavery. But grateful as were the domestic sweets of Friendship's Valley, his was altogether too militant and masterful a spirit to yield himself without a struggle to the repose which it offered. He did not at all relish the idea of being a forced exile from Boston, of being obliged to edit the *Liberator* at such long range. But his friends urged him to submit to the one, and do the other, both on grounds of economy and common prudence. He was almost super-anxious lest it be said that the fear of the mob drove him out of Boston, and that the fear of it kept him out. This super-anxiety in that regard his friends to a certain degree shared with him. It was a phase of Abolition grit. Danger attracted this new species of reformers as a magnet draws iron. Instead of running away from it, they were, with one accord, forever rushing into it. And the leader in Brooklyn was for rushing back to Boston, where, if one chanced to sow the wind in the morning, he might be morally certain of reaping the whirlwind in the afternoon.

Two weeks after he had been secretly conveyed to Canton by Deputy Sheriff Parkman, being the day of his discharge from Leverett street jail, he was back again in Boston. The popular excitement had subsided. He showed himself freely in the streets and was nowhere molested. One day, however, while at the anti-slavery office on Washington street, he witnessed what was perhaps a final manifestation of the cat-like spirit of the great mob. A procession passed by with band and music, bearing aloft a large board on which were represented George Thompson and a black woman with this significant allusion to the riot, made as if addressed to himself by his dusky companion in disgrace: "When are we going to have another meeting, Brother Thompson?" The cat-like creature had lapsed into a playful mood, but its playfulness would have quickly given place to an altogether different fit did it but know that Garrison was watching it from the window of the very room where a few weeks before he had nearly fallen into its clutches.

Garrison remained in Boston two weeks, going about the city, wherever and whenever business or duty called him in a perfectly fearless way. He left on the afternoon of November 18th. On that same afternoon the Boston Female Anti-Slavery Society held a memorable meeting at the house of Francis Jackson. It was then that Harriet Martineau, another foreign emissary, avowed her entire agreement with the principles of the Abolitionists, which subjected her to social ostracism, and to unlimited abuse from the pro-slavery press of the city.

The new hatred of slavery which the mob had aroused in Boston found heroic expression in a letter of Francis Jackson's replying to a vote of thanks of the Massachusetts Anti-Slavery Society to him for his hospitality to the ladies after their meeting was broken up by the mob. Mr. Jackson in his answer points with emphasis to the fact that his hospitality had a double aim, one was the accommodation of the ladies, the other the preservation of the right of free discussion. In his regard a foundation principle of free institutions had been assailed. "Happily," he shrewdly observed, "one point seems already to be gaining universal assent, that slavery cannot long survive free discussion. Hence the efforts of the friends, and apologists of slavery to break down this right. And hence the immense stake which the enemies of slavery hold, in behalf of freedom and mankind, in its preservation. The contest is, therefore, substantially between liberty and slavery.

"As slavery cannot exist with free discussion, so neither can liberty breathe without it. Losing this, we, too, shall be no longer free men indeed, but little, if at all, superior to the millions we now seek to emancipate." This apprehension and spirit of resistance, voiced by Francis Jackson, was Garrison's new ally, which, phœnix-like, was born out of the ashes of that terrific attempt of his enemies to effect his destruction, known as the "Broad-Cloth Mob."

CHAPTER XIII.

THE BAROMETER CONTINUES TO FALL.

HAVING made trial of the strong arm of the mob as an instrument for putting down the Abolitionists, and been quite confounded by its unexpected energy and unmanageableness, Boston was well disposed to lay the weapon aside as much too dangerous for use. For the wild-cat-like creature might take it into its head, when once it had got a taste of blood, to suppress some other isms in the community besides Abolitionism. No, no, the gentlemen of property and standing in the community had too much at stake to expose their property and their persons to the perils of any further experiments in that direction, even for the sake of expressing their sympathy for their dear brethren in the South, or of saving the dear Union into the bargain. Another method more in accord with the genius of their high state of civilization, they opined, might be invented to put the agitation and the agitators of the slavery question down. The politicians thereupon proceeded to make this perfectly wonderful invention. Not the strong arm of the mob, quoth these wiseacres, but the strong arm of the law it shall be. And the strong arm of the law they forthwith determined to make it.

Massachusetts was hearkening with a sort of fascination to the song of the slave syren. And no wonder.

For the song of the slave syren was swelling and clashing the while with passionate and imperious energy. South Carolina had led off in this kind of music. In December following the Boston mob Governor McDuffie, pitched the key of the Southern concert in his message to the legislature descriptive of anti-slavery publications, and denunciatory of the anti-slavery agitation. The Abolitionists were, to his mind, "enemies of the human race," and the movement for immediate emancipation ought to be made a felony punishable "by death without benefit of clergy." He boldly denied that slavery was a political evil, and vaunted it instead as "*the corner stone of our republican edifice.*" The legislature upon the receipt of this extraordinary message proceeded to demand of the free States the suppression, by effective legislation, of anti-slavery societies and their incendiary publications. The burden of this demand was directly caught up by North Carolina, Alabama, Virginia, and Georgia. But there were some things which even a pro-slavery North could not do to oblige the South. Neither party, much as both desired it, dared to undertake the violation by law of the great right of free speech and of the freedom of the press. Not so, however, was it with sundry party leaders, notably the governors of New York and Massachusetts, who were for trying the strong arm of the law as an instrument for suppressing Abolitionism. Edward Everett was so affected by the increasing Southern excitement and his fears for the safety of the dear Union that he must needs deliver himself in his annual message upon the Abolition agitation. He was of the opinion that the Abolitionists were guilty of an offence against Massachusetts which might be "prosecuted as a misdemeanor at common law." He evidently did not consider that in the then present state of political parties and of public opinion any repressive legislation upon the subject could be got through the legislature, and hence the immense utility of the old machinery of the common law, as an instrument for putting down the agitation. But in order to get this machinery into operation, careful preparation was necessary. Proof must not be wanting as to the dangerous and unpatriotic character and tendency of the movement to be repressed. There should be the most authoritative utterance upon this point to warrant the effective intervention of the Courts and Grand Juries of the commonwealth in the prosecution of the Abolitionists, as disturbers of the peace. Ergo the Governor's deliverance in his annual message against them. Now, if the legislature could be brought to deliver itself in tones not less certain, the third coördinate branch of the State government might catch its cue and act with energy in suppressing the disturbers of the peace of the commonwealth and of the dear Union as well. This was the scheme, the conspiracy which was in a state of incubation in Massachusetts in the year 1836. The pro-slavery portion of Governor Everett's message, together with the Southern demands for repressive legislation against the Abolitionists were referred to a joint legislative committee for consideration and report. The chairman of the committee was George Lunt, of Newburyport, a bitter pro-slavery politician, who saw no sign, received no light which did not come out of the South.

The Abolitionists perceived the gravity of the new danger which threatened them, and rallied promptly to avert it. They shrewdly guessed that the object of the committee would not be the enactment of any new law against themselves but the adoption of condemnatory resolutions instead. This course they rightly dreaded more than the other, and to defeat it the managers of the Massachusetts Anti-slavery Society requested a public hearing of the committee, which was granted. On March 4th Garrison and many of the anti-slavery leaders appeared before the committee, with a carefully planned programme of procedure. To each of the selected speakers was assigned a distinct phase of the great subject of discussion before the committee. Samuel J. May was appointed to open with an exposition of the anti-slavery movement and of the object and motives of its founders; Garrison to follow with an exhibition of the pacific character of the agitation as contained in official publications whereby forgiveness, submission, and non-resistance were steadily inculcated; Ellis Gray Loring was next to demonstrate the perfectly constitutional character of the agitation. The Abolitionists had in no wise contravened the National or the State Constitution, either in letter or spirit, and so on through the programme. It was thus that the Abolitionists dexterously killed two birds with one stone; for at the same time that they made their defence before the committeee, they managed to present their cause to the attention of the public as well. Appearing before the committee to prevent hostile action on the part of the legislature against their movement, they skillfully turned the occasion into the most notable meeting for agitating the subject of slavery in the State during the year.

The pro-slavery malignity of the chairman helped not a little to bring this result to pass. He again and again interrupted the speakers with the greatest insolence of behavior. Garrison, for a wonder, was allowed to finish his remarks without interruption. Here is a specimen of the way in which Paul addressed himself to King Agrippa's master—public opinion:

"Sir," spoke he to the committee, "we loudly boast of our free country, and of the union of these States, yet I have no country! As a New Englander and as an Abolitionist I am excluded by a bloody proscription from one-half of the national territory, and so is every man who is known to regard slavery with abhorrence. Where is our Union? . . . The right of free and safe locomotion from one part of the land to the other is denied to us, except on peril of our lives. . . . Therefore it is, I assert, that the Union is now virtually dissolved. . . . Look at McDuffie's sanguinary message! Read Calhoun's Report to the U. S. Senate, authorizing every postmaster in the South to plunder the mail of such Northern letters or newspapers as he may choose to think incendiary! Sir, the alternative presented to the people of New England is this: they must either submit to be gagged and fettered by Southern taskmasters, or labor unceasingly for the removal of slavery from our country."

This was a capital stroke, a bold and brilliant adaptation of the history of the times to the advancement of the anti-slavery movement in New England.

Missing Garrison, the anger of the chairman fell upon Goodell and Prof. Follen, like a tiger's whelp. Follen was remarking upon the Faneuil Hall meeting, how it had rendered the Abolitionists odious in Boston, and how, in consequence, the mob had followed the meeting.

"Now, gentlemen," the great scholar continued, "may we most reasonably anticipate that similar consequences would follow the expression by the legislature of a similar condemnation? Would not the mob again undertake to execute the informal sentence of the General Court? Would it not let loose again its bloodhounds upon us?"

At this point Mr. Lunt peremptorily stopped the speaker, exclaiming:

"Stop, sir! You may not pursue this course of remark. It is insulting to this committee and the legislature which they represent."

The Abolitionists, after this insult, determined to withdraw from the hearing, and appeal to the legislature to be heard, not as a favor but of right. A new hearing was, therefore, ordered, and the reformers appeared a second time before the committee. But the scenes of the first were repeated at the second hearing. The chairman was intolerably insolent to the speakers. His violent behavior to William Goodell, who was paying his respects to the Southern documents lying on the table of the committee, terminated the second hearing. These documents Mr. Goodell described as fetters for Northern freemen, and boldly interrogated the chairman in respect of them thus:

"Mr. Chairman, are you prepared to attempt putting

them on?" But the chairman was in no mood to listen to the question. His insolence reached a climax as he exclaimed passionately to Mr. Goodell, "Stop, sir! Sit down, sir! The committee will hear no more of this." But the temper of the Abolitionists had risen also, as had also risen the temper of the great audience of citizens who were present at the hearing which was had in the hall of the House of Representatives. "Freemen we came," retorted Goodell, "and as freemen we shall go away." Scarcely had these words died upon the ears when there rose sharply from the auditory, the stern protest "Let us go quickly, lest we be made slaves."

The attempt to suppress the Abolitionists was a failure. It but stimulated the agitation and deepened the popular interest in the subject. Strong allies within and without the legislature were enlisted on the side of freedom. The turning of the tide of public sentiment in the grand old State had come. Slowly did it rise for awhile, but from that event it never ceased to flow in and with increasing volume. The condemnatory report of the insolent chairman proved as innocuous as the baying of dogs at the moon. The legislature refused to indorse it and the pro-slavery resolutions attached to it. They were both ignominiously laid upon the table, and what is more to the purpose as a straw to show the drift of popular opinion on the slavery question in Massachusetts, their author failed of a renomination as Senator at the hands of his dissatisfied constituents.

The conflic was raging not alone in Massachusetts but all through the free States. In Congress the battle was assuming an intensely bitter character.

Here the South was the agitator. Here she kept the political waters in a state of violent ebullition. As the discord grew, sectionalism threw darkening and portentous shadows over the face of the Union. The South was insisting in all stages of passion that the tide of Abolition be checked in the North, that the flood of incendiary publications be suppressed at their sources in the free States. The Southern slave-holding President had suggested the suppression of these by Congress. He would "prohibit, under severe penalties, the circulation in the Southern States, through the mail, of incendiary publications intended to instigate the slaves to insurrection." But when Webster and a few Northern leaders objected to such a proceeding as unconstitutional and in derogation of the freedom of the press, the South treated the objection as inimical to Southern interest and security. Thereupon the Southern excitement increased all the faster. The slave-power was not disposed to accept anything short of complete submission on the part of the North. And this the North could not well yield. While the slave-holding States were clamoring for the suppression of Abolitionism in the free States, Abolitionism was giving evidences of extraordinary expansion, and activity. It had risen well above the zero point in politics. It was gaining numbers and it was gaining votes. A new element had appeared at the polls and both of the old parties began to exhibit a certain degree of impressibility to the latest attraction. The slave-power with quick instinct recognized in the new comer a dangerous rival, and schemed for its destruction. Southern jealousy took on the character of insanity. Neither Northern Whigs nor Northern Democrats were permitted to show any regard for the rival. They were to snub and utterly abolish her, otherwise they should be snubbed and utterly abolished by the slave-power. They could not with impunity give to Abolitionism the scantiest attention or courtesy. Not even a gallant like John Quincy Adams, who was able to see nothing attractive in the little band of reformers. They seemed to him, in fact, "a small, shallow, and enthusiastic party preaching the abolition of slavery upon the principles of extreme democracy." If Mr. Adams had little love for the South, he had none whatever for the Abolitionists. By no stretch of the imagination could he have been suspected of any sentimental attachment to the Abolition movement. For his unvarying attitude towards it was one of grim contempt. But if the old Roman had no love for the Abolitionists, he did have a deep-seated attachment and reverence for certain ancient rights appertaining to free institutions, which nothing was able to shake. Among these was the great right of petition, viewed by the ex-President as a right of human nature. For a dozen years he stood in Congress its sleepless sentinel. And herein did he perform for freedom most valiant service. It made no difference to the dauntless old man whether he approved of the prayer of a petition or not, if it was sent to him he presented it to the House all the same. He presented petitions for the abolition of slavery in the District of Columbia, and one, at least, against it, petitions from black and white, bond and free, with superb fidelity to the precious right which he championed.

This characteristic of the aged statesman kept the Southern members in a state of chronic apprehension and excitement. They bullied him, they raged like so many wild animals against him, they attempted to crush him with votes of censure and expulsion all to no purpose. Then they applied the gag: "That all petitions, memorials, and papers touching the abolition of slavery, or the buying, selling, or transferring slaves, in any State, or district, or territory of the United States, be laid on the table without being debated, printed, read, or referred, and that no action be taken thereon." Mr. Adam's denunciation of this action as a violation of the Constitution, of the right of the people to petition, and of the right to freedom of speech in Congress, found wide echo through the North. The violence, intolerence. and tyranny of the South were disgusting many of the most intelligent and influential minds in the non-slave-holding States, and driving them into more or less close affiliation with the anti-slavery movement.

And so it was wherever one turned there were conflict and uproar. Everywhere contrary ideas, interests, institutions, tendencies, were colliding with inextinguishable rage. All the opposites and irreconcilables in a people's life had risen and clashed together in a death struggle for mastery. Freedom and slavery, civilization and barbarism had found an Armageddon in the moral consciousness of the Republic. Now the combatants rallied and the battle thickened at one point, now around another. At Washington the tide rolls in with resounding fury about the right of petition and the freedom of debate, then through the free States it surges and beats around the right of free speech and the freedom of the press. Storm clouds are flying from the East and from the West, flying out of the North and out of the South. Everywhere the chaos of the winds has burst, and the anarchy of the "live thunder."

Benton with his customary optimism from a Southern standpoint, rejoiced in the year 1836 that the people of the Northern States had "chased off the foreign emissaries, silenced the gabbling tongues of female dupes, and dispersed the assemblies, whether fanatical, visionary, or incendiary, of all that congregated to preach against evils that afflicted others, not them, and to propose remedies to aggravate the disease which they pretended to cure." Calhoun's pessimism was clearer eyed. The great nullifier perceived at once the insuppressible nature of the Abolition movement and early predicted that the spirit then abroad in the North would not "die away of itself without a shock or convulsion." Yes, it was as he had prophesied, the anti-slavery reform was, at the very moment of Benton's groundless jubilation, rising and spreading with astonishing progress through the free States. It was gaining footholds in the pulpit, the school, and the press. It was a stalwart sower, scattering broadcast as he walked over the fields of the then coming generation truths and antipathies of social principles, which were to make peace impossible between the slave-holding and the non-slave-holding halves of the Union.

In the year 1836 the anti-slavery leaven or residuum for instance, was sufficiently potent to preserve the statutes of the free States, free from repressive laws directed against the Abolitionists. This was much but there was undoubtedly another phase of the agitation, a phase which struck the shallow eye of Benton, and led him into false conclusions. It was not clear sailing for the reform. It was truly a period of stress and storm. Sometimes the reform was in a trough of the sea of public opinion, sometimes on the crest of a billow, and then again on the bosom of a giant ground swell. In Boston in this selfsame year which witnessed Benton's exultation over the fall of Abolitionism, the Massachusetts Anti-Slavery Society was not able to obtain the use of hall or church for its annual meeting, and was in consequence forced into insufficient accommodations at its rooms on Washington street. The succeeding year the society was obliged, from inability to obtain the use of either hall or church in the city, to occupy for its annual meeting the loft over the stable connected with the Marlborough Hotel. It is a long way from this rude meeting-house to the hall of the House of Representatives, but in this storm and stress period the distance was traversed in a few brief hours. The society applied in its exigency for the use of the hall for an evening meeting, and the application was granted by the members. It was a *jeu d'esprit* of Henry B. Stanton, "That when Boston votes we go into a stable, but when the State votes we go into the State House." It was even so, for the incident served to reveal what was true everywhere through the free States that the anti-slavery reform was making fastest progress among people away from the great centres of population. It found ready access to the simple American folk in villages, in the smaller towns, and in the rural districts of New England and the North. And already from these independent and uncorrupted sons and daughters of freedom had started the deep ground swell which was to lift the level of Northern public opinion on the question of slavery.

This Walpurgis period of the movement culminated on November 7, 1837, in a terrible tragedy. The place was a little Illinois town, Alton, just over the Mississippi River from St. Louis, and the victim was Elijah P. Lovejoy. He was a minister of the Presbyterian Church, and the editor of a weekly religious newspaper, first published in St. Louis and removed by him later to Alton. His sin was that he did not hold his peace on the subject of slavery in the columns of his paper. He was warned "to pass over in silence everything connected" with that question. But he had no choice, he had to cry aloud against iniquities, which, as a Christian minister and a Christian editor, he dared not ignore. His troubles with the people of St. Louis took in the spring of 1836 a sanguinary turn, when he denounced the lynching of a negro by a St. Louis mob, perpetrated under circumstances of peculiar atrocity. In consequence of his outspoken condemnation of the horror, his office was broken into and destroyed by a mob. Lovejoy thereupon removed his paper to Alton, but the wild-cat-like spirit pursued him across the river and destroyed his press. He replaced his broken press with a new one, only to have his property a second time destroyed. He replaced the second with a third press, but a third time the mob destroyed his property. Then he bought a fourth press, and resolved to defend it with his life. Pierced by bullets he fell, resisting the attack of a mob bent on the destruction of his rights. Lovejoy died a martyr to free speech and the freedom of the press.

The tidings of this tragedy stirred the free States to unwonted depths. The murder of an able and singularly noble man by a mob was indeed horrible enough, but the blow which took his life was aimed at the right of free speech and the freedom of the press. He was struck down in the exercise of his liberties as a citizen of the town where he met death, and of the State and country to which he belonged. What brave man and good in the North who might not meet a similar fate for daring to denounce evils approved by the community in which his lot was cast? Who was safe? Whose turn would it be next to pay with his life for attempts to vindicate the birthright of his citizenship? What had Lovejoy done, what had he written, that thousands of people who did not agree with Garrison would not have done and have written under like circumstances? He was not a disciple of Garrison, he did not accept the doctrine of immediate emancipation, and yet a pro-slavery mob had murdered him. Yes, who was safe? Who was to be the next? A great horror transfixed the North, and bitter uncertainty, and tremendous dread of approaching perils to its liberties.

Ah! had not Garrison spoken much plain truth at the public hearing of the Massachusetts Anti-Slavery Society before the insolent chairman and his committee when he said: "The liberties of the people of the free States are identified with those of the slave population. If it were not so, there would be no hope, in my breast, of peaceful deliverance of the latter class from their bondage. Our liberties are bound together by a ligament as vital as that which unites the Siamese twins. The blow which cuts them asunder, will inevitably destroy them both. Let the freedom of speech and of the press be abridged or destroyed, and the nation itself will be in bondage; let it remain untrammeled, and Southern slavery must speedily come to an end." The tragedy at Alton afforded startling illustration of the soundness of this remark. Classes like individuals gain wisdom only by experience; and the murder of Lovejoy was one of those terrific experiences which furrow themselves in the soul of a people in frightful memories and apprehensions which do not disappear but remain after long lapse of years.

Twelve days after the murder—it was before the development of the telegraph and rapid postal facilities—the news reached Boston. It produced the most profound sensation. Many of the leading citizens felt straightway that if the rights assailed in the person of Lovejoy were to be preserved to themselves and their section, immediate action was required. A great meeting was proposed, and Faneuil Hall applied for. The application was denied by the municipal authorities on the plea that its use for such a purpose might provoke a mob. The city was, however, dealing now not with the despised Abolitionists, but with men of property and standing in the community and was soon brought to its senses by the indignant eloquence of Dr. Channing, appealing to the better self of Boston in this strain: "Has it come to this? Has Boston fallen so low? May not its citizens be trusted to come together to express the great principles of liberty for which their forefathers died? Are our fellow-citizens to be murdered in the act of defending their property and of assuming the right of free discussion? And is it unsafe in this metropolis to express abhorrence of the deed?"

A second application for the hall was granted, and a meeting, which is an historical event in the annals of the old town, was held December 8, 1837—a meeting memorable as an uprising, not of the Abolitionists, but of the conservatism and respectability of the city in behalf of the outraged liberties of white men. Ever memorable, too, for that marvelous speech of Wendell Phillips, which placed him instantly in the front rank of minds with a genius for eloquence, lifted him at once as an anti-slavery instrument and leader close beside William Lloyd Garrison. The wild-cat-like spirit which had hunted Thompson out of the country and Lovejoy to death, had more than made good the immense deficit of services thus created through the introduction upon the national stage of the reform of this consummate and incomparable orator.

The assassination of Lovejoy was an imposing object lesson to the North, but it was not the last. Other and terrible illustrations of the triumph of mobs followed it, notably the burning of Pennsylvania Hall in Philadelphia on the evening of May 17, 1838. As the murder of Lovejoy formed the culmination of outrages directed against the rights of person, the burning of Pennsylvania Hall furnished the climax of outrages committed against the rights of property. The friends of the slave and of free discussion in Philadelphia feeling the need of a place where they might assemble for the exercise of the right of free speech in a city which denied to them the use of its halls and meeting-houses, determined to erect for themselves such a place. At a cost of forty thousand dollars they built Pennsylvania Hall and devoted it to "Free Discussion, Virtue, Liberty, and Independence."

Two days after the dedicatory exercises were had the hall was occupied by the annual convention of American Anti-Slavery Women. On the evening of May 16th, Garrison, Maria Weston Chapman, Angelina Grimké Weld and others addressed the convention in the new temple of freedom. The scenes of that evening have been graphically described by the first speaker as follows: "The floor of the hall was densely crowded with women, some of the noblest specimens of our race, a large proportion of whom were Quakers. The side aisles and spacious galleries were as thickly filled with men. Nearly three thousand people were in the hall. There seemed to be no visible symptoms of a riot. When I rose to speak I was greeted with applause by the immense assembly, and also several times in the course of my remarks. As soon, however, as I had concluded my address, a furious mob broke into the hall, yelling and shouting as if the very fiends of the pit had suddenly broken loose. The audience rose in some confusion, and would undoubtedly have been broken up, had it not been for the admirable self-possession of some individuals, particularly the women. The mobocrats finding that they could not succeed in their purpose, retreated into the streets, and, surrounding the building, began to dash in the windows with stones and brick-bats. It was under these appalling circumstances that Mrs. Chapman rose for the first time in her life, to address a promiscuous assembly of men and women—and she acquitted herself nobly. She spoke about ten minutes, and was succeeded by A. E. G. Weld, who occupied nearly an hour. As the tumult from without increased, and the brick-bats fell thick and fast (no one, however, being injured) her eloquence kindled, her eye flashed, and her cheeks glowed, as she devoutly thanked the Lord that the stupid repose of that city had at length been disturbed by the force of truth. When she sat down, Esther Moore (a Friend) made a few remarks, then Lucretia Mott, and finally Abby Kelley, a noble young woman from Lynn.

"The meeting broke up about 10 o'clock, and we all got safely home. The next day the street was thronged with profane ruffians and curious spectators—the women, however, holding their meetings in the hall all day, till towards evening. It was given out by the mob that the hall would be burnt to the ground that night. We were to have a meeting in the evening, but it was impossible to execute our purpose. The mayor induced the manager to give the keys of the building into his hands. He then locked the doors, and made a brief speech to the mob, assuring them that he had the keys, and that there would be no meeting, and requesting them to retire. He then went home, but the mob were bent on the destruction of the hall. They had now increased to several thousands, and soon got into the hall by dashing open the doors with their axes. They then set fire to this huge building, and in the course of an hour it was a solid mass of flame. The bells of the city were rung, and several engines rallied; but no water was permitted to be thrown upon the building. The light of the fire must have been seen â great distance."

At midnight Garrison was spirited out of the city, and conveyed in a covered carriage by a friend to Bristol, about twenty miles, where in the morning he took the steamboat for Boston. The light of that fire was visible a great distance in more senses than one. The burning of Pennsylvania Hall proved a public enlightener. After that occurrence the gentlemen of property scattered through the free States devoted themselves less to the violent suppression of Abolitionism and more to the forcible suppression, upon occasion, of the alarming manifestations of popular lawlessness, which found significant demonstration just a week later in the city of Boston.

Mr. Garrison has preserved for us an instructive account of this affair, too, and here is the story as told by him to his brother-in-law, George W. Benson, in a letter dated May 25th: "The spirit of mobocracy, like the pestilence, is contagious; and Boston is once more ready tc reënact the riotous scenes of 1835. The Marlboro' Chapel, having just been completed, and standing in relation to our cause just as did Pennsylvania Hall, is an object of pro-slavery malevolence. Ever since my return, threats have been given out that the chapel should share the fate of the hall. Last evening was the time for its dedication; and, so threatening was the aspect of things, four companies of light infantry were ordered to be in readiness, each being provided with 100 *ball* cartridges, to rush to the scene of riot on the tolling of the bells. The Lancers, a powerful body of horsemen, were also in readiness. During the day placards were posted at the corners of the streets, denouncing the Abolitionists, and calling upon the citizens to rally at the chapel in the evening, in order to put them down. An immense concourse of people assembled, a large proportion doubtless from motives of curiosity, and not a few of them with evil designs; but owing to the strong military preparations, the multitude refrained entirely from any overt acts of violence. They did not disperse till after 10 o'clock, and during the evening shouted and yelled like a troop of wild savages. Some ten or twelve were seized and carried to the watch-house, and this morning fined for their disorderly conduct."

The frightful excesses of the Walpurgis period of the agitation reacted through the free States to an extraordinary extent in favor of Abolition. The greater the horror committed by the wild-cat-like spirit, the greater the help which the reform derived therefrom. The destruction of property, and the destruction of life instead of putting down the hated Abolitionists aroused in the public mind apprehensions and antagonisms in respect of mobs, which proved, immediately and ultimately, of immense advantage to freedom. This revulsion on the part of the North from lawless attempts to abolish Abolitionism, affected almost unavoidably, and in the beginning of it almost unconsciously, the friendly dispositions of that section toward slavery, the root and mainspring of these attempts. Blows aimed at the agent were sure, regardless of the actor's intention, to glance and strike the principal. In spite of mobs then, and to a remarkable degree because of mobs, Abolitionism had become a powerful motor in revolutionizing public opinion in the free States on the subject of slavery.

CHAPTER XIV.

BROTHERLY LOVE FAILS, AND IDEAS ABOUND.

During those strenuous, unresting years, included between 1829 and 1836, Garrison had leaned on his health as upon a strong staff. It sustained him without a break through that period, great as was the strain to which it was subjected. But early in the latter year the prop gave way, and the pioneer was prostrated by a severe fit of sickness. It lasted off and on for quite two years. His activity the first year was seriously crippled, though at no time, owing to his indomitable will, could he be said to have been rendered completely *hors de combat*. Almost the whole of 1836 he spent with his wife's family in Brooklyn, where his first child was born. This new mouth brought with it fresh cares of a domestic character. He experienced losses also. Death removed his aged father-in-law in the last month of 1836, and four weeks later Henry E. Benson, his brother-in-law. Their taking off was a sad blow to the reformer and to the reform. That of the younger man cast a gloom over anti-slavery circles in New England ; for at the time of his death he was the secretary and general agent of the Massachusetts Society, and although not twenty-three, had displayed uncommon capacity for affairs. The business ability which he brought into his office was of the greatest value where there was such a distinct deficiency in that respect among his coadjutors, and the loss of it seemed irreparable.

Afflicted as he was, the leader was nevertheless cheered by the extraordinary progress of the movement started by him. The growth and activity of Abolitionism were indeed altogether phenomenal. In February, 1837, Ellis Gray Loring estimated that there were then eight hundred anti-slavery societies in the United States, that an anti-slavery society had been formed in the North every day for the last two years, and that in the single State of Ohio there were three hundred societies, one of which had a membership of four thousand names. The moral agitation was at its height. The National Society had hit upon a capital device for increasing the effectiveness of its agents and lecturers. This was to bring them together in New York for a few weeks' study of the slavery question under the direction of such masters as Theodore D. Weld, Beriah Green, Charles Stuart, and others. All possible phases of the great subject, such as, What is slavery? What is immediate emancipation? The consequences of emancipation to the South, etc., etc., pro-slavery objections and arguments were stated and answered. The agents and lecturers went forth from the convention bristling with facts, and glowing with enthusiasm to renew the crusade against slavery. Garrison, broken in health as he was, went on from Boston to attend this school of his disciples. He spoke briefly but repeatedly to them upon the all-absorbing topic which had brought them together. "It was a happy circumstance, too," he wrote, "that I was present with them, and that they had an opportunity to become *personally* acquainted with me; for, as I am a great stumbling-block in the way of the people, or, rather, of some people, it would be somewhat disastrous to our cause if any of our agents, through the influence of popular sentiment, should be led to cherish prejudices against me."

In February, 1837, the Massachusetts Anti-Slavery Society came to the rescue of the *Liberator* from its financial embarrassments and hand-to-mouth existence by assuming the responsibility of its publication. The arrangement did not in any respect compromise Mr. Garrison's editorial independence, but lifted from him and his friend Knapp in his own language, "a heavy burden, which has long crushed us to the earth." The arrangement, nevertheless, continued but a year when it was voluntarily set aside by Mr. Garrison for causes of which we must now give an account.

In the letter from which we have quoted above, touching his visit to the Convention of Anti-Slavery Agents, Garrison alludes to one of these causes. He says: "I was most kindly received by all, and treated as a brother, notwithstanding the wide difference of opinion between us on some religious points, *especially the Sabbath question.*" The italics are our own. Until within a few years he had been one of the strictest of Sabbath observers. Although never formally connected with any church, he had been a narrow and even an intolerant believer in the creed and observances of New England orthodoxy. Words failed him in 1828 to express his abhorrence of a meeting of professed infidels: "It is impossible," he exclaimed with the ardor of a bigot, "to estimate the depravity and wickedness of those who, at the present day, reject the Gospel of Jesus Christ," etc. A year and a half later while editing the *Genius* in Baltimore, he held uncompromisingly to the stern Sabbatical notions of the Puritans. A fête given to Lafayette in France on Sunday seemed to him an act of sheer religious desecration. The carrying of passengers and the mails on the Sabbath provoked his energetic reprobation. He was in all points of New England Puritanism, orthodox of the orthodox.

Subsequently he began to see things in a different light. As the area of his experience extended it came to him that living was more than believing, that it was not every one who professed faith in Jesus had love for him in the heart; and that there were many whom his own illiberalism had rated as depraved and wicked on mere points of doctrine, who, nevertheless, shamed by the blamelessness and nobility of their conduct multitudes of ardent Christians of the lip-service sort. Indeed this contradiction between creed and conduct struck him with considerable force in the midst of his harsh judgments against unbelief and unbelievers. "There are, in fact," he had remarked a year or two after he had attained his majority, "few *reasoning* Christians; the majority of them are swayed more by the usages of the world than by any definite perception of what constitutes duty—so far, we mean, as relates to the subjugation of vices which are incorporated, as it were, into the existence of society; else why is it that intemperance, and slavery, and war, have not ere this in a measure been driven from our land?"

As the months of his earnest young life passed him by, they showed him as they went how horrible a thing was faith without works. "By their fruits ye shall know them," the Master had said, and more and more as he saw how many and great were the social evils to be reformed, and in what dire need stood his country of righteous action, did he come to put increasing emphasis on conduct, as the one thing needful to rid the land of the triple curse of slavery, intemperance, and war. As he mused upon these giant evils, and the desolation which they were singly and together causing in the world, and upon the universal apathy of the churches in respect of them, it seemed to him that the current religion was an offence and an abomination. And in his prophetic rage he denounced it as "a religion which quadrates with the natural depravity of the heart, giving license to sin, restraining no lust, mortifying not the body, engendering selfishness, and cruelty!—a religion which walks in silver slippers, on a carpeted floor, having thrown off the burden of the cross and changed the garments of humiliation for the splendid vestments of pride! a religion which has no courage, no faithfulness, no self-denial, deeming it better to give heed unto men than unto God!" This was in the autumn of 1829, but though he was thus violently denunciatory of contemporary religion, the severity of his judgment against the skepticism of the times had not been materially modified. He still regarded the unbeliever with narrow distrust and dislike. When, after his discharge from Baltimore jail, he was engaged in delivering his message on the subject of slavery, and was seeking an opportunity to make what he knew known to the people of Boston, he was forced, after vainly advertising for a hall or meeting-house in which to give his three lectures, to accept the offer of Abner Kneeland's Society of Infidels of the use of their hall for that purpose. The spirit of these people, branded by the community as blasphemers, and by himself, too, in all probability, Garrison saw to be as admirable as the spirit displayed by the churches of the city toward him and his cause was unworthy and sinful. But, grateful as he was for the hospitality of the infidels, he, nevertheless, rather bluntly informed them that he had no sympathy with their religious notions, and that he looked for the abolition of slavery to evangelicism, and to it alone.

A few years in the university of experience, where he learned that conduct is better than creeds, and living more than believing, served to emancipate him from illiberal prejudices and narrow sectarianism. He came to see, "that in Christ Jesus all stated observances are so many self-imposed and unnecessary yokes; and that prayer and worship are all embodied in that pure, meek, child-like state of heart which affectionately and reverently breathes but one petition—'Thy will be done on earth as it is in heaven.' Religion . . . is nothing but love—perfect love toward God and toward man—without formality, without hypocrisy, without partiality—depending upon no outward form to preserve its vitality or prove its existence."

This important change in Mr. Garrison's religious convictions became widely known in the summer of 1836 through certain editorial strictures of his upon a speech of Dr. Lyman Beecher, at Pittsburgh, on the subject of the Sabbath. The good doctor was cold enough on the question of slavery, which involved not only the desecration of the Sabbath, but of the souls and bodies of millions of human beings. If Christianity was truly of divine origin, and Garrison devoutly believed that it was, it would approve its divinity by its manner of dealing with the vices and evils which were dragging and chaining the feet of men to the gates of hell. If it parleyed with iniquity, if it passed its victims by on the other side, if it did not war incessantly and energetically to put down sin, to destroy wickedness, it was of the earth, earthy, and its expounders were dumb dogs where they should bark the loudest and bite the hardest; and Dr. Beecher appeared to him one of these dumb dogs, who, when he opened his mouth at all, was almost sure to open it at the men who were trying through evil report and good to express in their lives the spirit of Him who so loved the world that He gave His Son to die to redeem it. He bayed loud enough at the Abolitionists but not at the abomination which they were attacking. He was content to leave it to the tender mercies of two hundred years. No such liberal disposition of the question of the Sabbath was he willing to allow. He waxed eloquent in its behalf. His enthusiasm took to itself wings and made a great display of ecclesiastical zeal beautiful to behold. "The Sabbath," quoth the teacher who endeavored to muzzle the students of Lane Seminary on the subject of slavery, whose ultimate extinction his prophetic soul quiescently committed to the operation of two centuries; "the Sabbath," quoth he, "is the *great sun of the moral world*." Out upon you, said Garrison, the LORD GOD is the *great sun of the moral world*, not the Sabbath. It is not one, but every day of the week which is His, and which men should be taught to observe as holy days. It is not regard for the forms of religion but for the spirit, which is essential to righteousness. What is the command, 'Remember the Sabbath day to keep it holy,' but one of ten commandments? Is the violation of the fourth any worse than the violation of the third or fifth, or sixth? Nowhere is it so taught in the Bible. Yet, what is slavery but a breaking and treading down of the whole ten, what but a vast system of adultery, robbery, and murder, the daily and yearly infraction on an appalling scale not alone of the spirit but of the letter of the decalogue?

Mr. Garrison then passed to criticisms of a more special character touching the observance of the day thus: "These remarks are made not to encourage men to do wrong at any time, but to controvert a pernicious and superstitious notion, and one that is very prevalent, that extraordinary and supernatural visitations of divine indignation upon certain transgressors (of the Sabbath particularly and almost exclusively) are poured out now as in the days of Moses and the prophets. Whatever claim the Sabbath may have to a strict religious observance, we are confident it cannot be strengthened, but must necessarily be weakened, by all such attempts to enforce or prove its sanctity." This pious but rational handling of the Sabbath question gave instant offence to the orthodox readers of the *Liberator*. For it was enough in those days to convict the editor of rank heresy. From one and another of his subscribers remonstrances came pouring in upon him. A young theological student at Yale ordered his paper stopped in consequence of the anti-Sabbatarian views of the editor. A Unitarian minister at Harvard, Mass., was greatly cut up by reason thereof, and suddenly saw what before he did not suspect. "I had supposed you," he wrote in his new estate, "a very pious person, and that a large proportion of the Abolitionists were religious persons. . . . I have thought of you as another Wilberforce—but would Wilberforce have spoken thus of the day on which the Son of God rose from the dead?" Garrison's query in reply—"Would Wilberforce have denied the identity of Christ with the Father?"—was a palpable hit. But as he himself justly remarked, "Such questions are not arguments, but fallacies unworthy of a liberal mind." Nevertheless, so long as men are attached to the leading strings of sentiment rather than to those of reason, such questions will possess tremendous destructive force, as Mr. Garrison, in his own case, presently perceived. He understood the importance of not arousing against him "denominational feelings or peculiarities," and so had steered the *Liberator* clear of the rocks of sectarianism. But when he took up in its columns the Sabbath question he ran his paper directly among the breakers of a religious controversy. He saw how it was with him at once, saw that he had stirred up against him all that religious feeling which was crystallized around the first day of the week, and that he could not hope to escape without serious losses in one way or another. "It is pretty certain," he writes Samuel J. May in September, 1836, "that the *Liberator* will sustain a serious loss in its subscriptions at the close of the present volume; and all appeals for aid in its behalf will be less likely to prevail than formerly. I am conscious that a mighty sectarian conspiracy is forming to crush me, and it will probably succeed to some extent."

This controversy over the Sabbath proved the thin edge of differences and dissensions, which, as they went deeper and deeper, were finally to rend asunder the erstwhile united Abolition movement. The period was remarkable for the variety and force of new ideas, which were coming into being, or passing into general circulation. And to all of them it seems that Garrison was peculiarly receptive. He took them all in and planted them in soil of extraordinary fertility. It was immediately observed that it was not only one unpopular notion which he had adopted, but a whole headful of them. And every one of these new ideas was a sort of rebel-reformer, a genuine man of war. They had come as a protest against the then existing beliefs and order of things, come as their enemies and destroyers. Each one of them was in a sense a stirrer-up of sedition against old and regnant relations and facts, political, moral, and religious. Whoever espoused them as his own, espoused as his own also the antagonisms, political, moral, and religious which they would excite in the public mind. All of which was directly illustrated in the experience of the editor of the *Liberator*. Each of these new notions presently appeared in the paper along with Abolitionism. What was his intention timid people began to inquire? Did he design to carry them along with the Abolition movement? Suspicious minds fancied they saw "in Mr. Garrison, a decided wish, nay, a firm resolve, in laboring to overthrow slavery, to overthrow the Christian Sabbath and the Christian ministry. His doctrine is that every day is a Sabbath, and every man his own minister. There are no Christian ordinances, there is no visible church." His no-government and non-resistant ideas excited yet further the apprehensions of some of his associates for the safety of that portion of the present order to which they clung. As developed by Garrison they seemed to deny the right of the people "to frame a government of laws to protect themselves against those who would injure them, and that man can apply physical force to man rightfully under no circumstances, and not even the parent can apply the rod to the child, and not be, in the sight of God, a trespasser and a tyrant."

Garrison embraced besides Perfectionism, a sort of political, moral, and religious Come-outerism, and faith in "universal emancipation from sin." His description of himself abont this time as "an Ishmaelitish editor" is not bad, nor his quotation of "Woe is me my mother! for I was born a man of strife" as applicable to the growing belligerency of his relations with the anti-slavery brethren in consequence of the new ideas and isms, which were taking possession of his mind and occupying the columns of the *Liberator*.

Among the strife-producers during this period of the anti-slavery agitation, the woman's question played a principal part. Upon this as upon the Sabbath question, Garrison's early position was one of extreme conservatism. As late as 1830, he shared the common opinions in regard to woman's sphere, and was strongly opposed to her stepping outside of it into that occupied by man. A petition of seven hundred women of Pittsburgh, Pa., to Congress in behalf of the Indians gave his masculine prejudices a great shock. "This is, in our opinion," he declared, "an uncalled for interference, though made with holiest intentions. We should be sorry to have this practice become general. There would then be no question agitated in Congress without eliciting the informal and contrariant opinions of the softer sex." This toplofty sentiment accorded well with the customary assumption and swagger of one of the lords of creation. For the young reformer was evidently a firm believer in the divine right of his sex to rule in the world of politics. But as he grew taller and broader the horizon of woman widened, and her sphere embraced every duty, responsibility, and right for which her gifts and education fitted her. The hard and fast lines of sex disappeared from his geography of the soul. He perceived for a truth that in humanity there was neither male nor female, but that man and woman were one in work and destiny—equals in bearing the world's burden, equals in building the world's glory. He heard in his heart the injunction of the eternal wisdom saying: "Whom God hath joined together let no man put asunder;" and straightway disposed his opinions and prejudices, his thoughts and purposes in cordial obedience therewith. He saw at once the immense value of woman's influence in the temperance movement, he saw no less quickly her importance in the anti-slavery reform, and he had appealed to her for help in the work of both, and she had justified his appeal and proven herself the most devoted of coadjutors.

In the beginning of the movement against slavery the line of demarcation between the sexes was strictly observed in the formation of societies. The men had theirs, the women theirs. Each, sexually considered, were very exclusive affairs. It did not seem to have occurred to the founders of the New England Anti-Slavery Society, or of the national organization to admit women to membership in them, nor did it seem to enter the mind of any woman to prefer a request to be admitted into them. Anti-slavery women organized themselves into female anti-slavery societies, did their work apart from the men, who plainly regarded themselves as the principals in the contest, and women as their moral seconds. The first shock, which this arrangement, so accordant with the oak-and-ivy notion of the masculine half of mankind, received, came when representatives of the gentler sex dropped the secondary rôle assigned women in the conflict, and began to enact that of a star. The advent of the sisters Grimké upon the anti-slavery stage as public speakers, marked the advent of the idea of women's rights, of their equality with men in the struggle with slavery.

At the start these ladies delivered their message to women only, but by-and-bye as the fame of their eloquence spread men began to appear among their auditories. Soon they were thrilling packed halls and meeting-houses in different parts of the country, comprised of men and women. The lesson which their triumph enforced of women's fitness to enact the rôle of principals in the conflict with slavery was not lost upon the sex. Women went, saw, and conquered their prejudices against the idea of equality; likewise, many men. The good seed of universal liberty and equality fell into fruitful soil and germinated in due time within the heart of the moral movement against slavery.

The more that Sarah and Angelina Grimké reflected upon the sorry position to which men had assigned women in Church and State the more keenly did they feel its injustice and degradation. They beat with their revolutionary idea of equality against the iron bars of the cage-like sphere in which they were born, and within which they were doomed to live and die by the law of masculine might. At heart they were rebels against the foundation principle of masculine supremacy on which society and government rested. While pleading for the freedom of the slaves, the sense of their own bondage and that of their sisters rose up before them and revealed itself in bitter questionings. "Are we aliens," asked Angelina, "because we are women? Are we bereft of citizenship because we are the *mothers, wives, and daughters* of a mighty people? Have *women* no country—no interests staked on the public weal—no partnership in a nation's guilt or shame?" This discontent with the existing social establishment in its relation to women received sympathetic responses from many friends to whom the sisters communicated the contagion of their unrest and dissatisfaction. Angelina records that, "At friend Chapman's, where we spent a social evening, I had a long talk with the brethren on the rights of women, and found a very general sentiment prevailing that it is time our fetters were broken. L. M. Child and Maria Chapman strongly supported this view ; indeed very many seem to think a new order of things is very desirable in this respect."

This prevalence of a sentiment favorable to women's rights, which Angelina observed in Mrs. Chapman's parlors possessed no general significence. For true to the character of new ideas, this particular new idea did not bring peace but a sword. It set Abolition brethren against Abolition brethren, and blew into a flame the differences of leaders among themselves. But the first irruption of strife which it caused proceeded from without, came from the church or rather from the clergy of the Orthodox Congregational churches of Massachusetts. This clerical opposition to the idea of women's rights found expression in the celebrated "Pastoral Letter," issued by the General Association of Ministers of that denomination to the churches of the same in the summer of 1837. This ecclesiastical bull had two distinct purposes to accomplish ; first, to discourage the agitation of the slavery question by excluding anti-slavery agents from lecturing upon that subject in the churches ; and, second, to suppress the agitation of the woman's question by setting the seal of the disapproval of the clergy to the appearance of women in their new and revolutionary rôle of public speakers and teachers on the burning subjects of the times. The reverend authors threw up their hands and eyes in holy horror at the "widespread and permanent injury" which seemed to them to threaten "the female character." They scorned the new-fangled notion of woman's independence, and asked for nothing better than the Pauline definition of her "appropriate duties and influence." "The power of women," quoth they, "is in her dependence. . . . . When she assumes the place and tone of man as a public reformer, our care and protection of her seem unnecessary ; we put ourselves in self-defence against her, she yields the power which God has given her for protection, and her character becomes unnatural!"

These Congregational ministers were not the only representatives of the lordly sex to whom the idea of women's equality was repellent. Anti-slavery brethren, too, were flinging themselves into all postures of self-defence against the dangerous innovation, which the sisters Grimké were letting into the social establishment, by itinerating "in the character of public lecturers and teachers." Amos A. Phelps was quite as strongly opposed to women preachers, to women assuming the "place and tone of man as a public reformer," as Nehemiah Adams himself. He remonstrated with them against their continued assumption of the character of public lecturers and teachers, but to no purpose. Sarah and Angelina were uncompromising, refused to yield one iota of their rights as "moral and responsible beings." They firmly declined to make their Quakerism and not their womenhood their warrant for "exercising the rights and performing the duties" of rational and responsible beings, for the sake of quieting tender consciences, like that of Phelps, among the anti-slavery brethren. They were in earnest and demanded to know "whether there is such a thing as male and female virtues, male and female duties." Angelina writes: "My opinion is that there is no difference, and that this false idea has run the ploughshare of ruin over the whole field of morality. My idea is that whatever is morally right for a man to do is morally right for a woman to do. I recognize no rights but human rights. . . . I am persuaded that woman is not to be, as she has been, a mere second-hand agent in the regeneration of a fallen world, but the acknowledged equal and co-worker with man in this glorious work."

The debate on the subject threatened for a short season to push the woman's question to the level of the slavery question. The contention became acrimonius, and the alienation of friendships was widespread. John G. Whittier and Theodore D. Weld, who were both avowed believers in the idea of women's rights, nevertheless, felt that the agitation of the subject, under the circumstances, was a grave blunder. "No moral enterprise, when prosecuted with ability and any sort of energy, *ever* failed under heaven," wrote Weld to Sarah and Angelina, "so long as its conductors pushed the *main* principle, and did not strike off until they reached the summit level. On the other hand, every reform that ever foundered in mid-sea, was capsized by one of these gusty side-winds." Both Weld and Whittier endeavored to dissuade the sisters from mooting the question of women's rights at all, and to urge them to devote their voice and pen to the "*main* principle" exclusively. But Angelina confesses that "our judgment is not convinced, and we hardly know what to do about it, for we have just as high an opinion of Brother Garrison's views, and *he* says '*go on.*'" The influence of Weld and Whittier finally prevailed with

"Carolina's high-souled daughters," and they refrained from further agitation of the subject of Women's rights lest they should thereby injure the cause of the slave.

But the leaven of equality was not so effectually disposed of. It had secured permanent lodgment in the anti-slavery body, and the fermentation started by it, went briskly on. Such progress did the principle of women's rights make among the Eastern Abolitionists, especially among those of Massachusetts, that in the spring of 1838 the New England Anti-Slavery Society voted to admit women to equal membership with men. This radical action was followed by a clerical secession from the society, which made a stir at the time. For among the seceding members was no less a personage than Amos A. Phelps, who was the general agent of the Massachusetts Society, and therefore one of Garrison's stanchest supporters. The reform instituted by the New England Society, in respect of the character of its membership, was quickly adopted by the Massachusetts Society and by several local organizations, all of which set the ball of discord spinning among the brethren at a great rate. But by this time all the new ideas, Sabbatical, no-government, perfectionist, non-resistance, as well as women's rights, were within the anti-slavery arena, and fencing and fighting for a chance to live, with the old ideas and the old order.

Garrison championed all of the new ideas, and in doing so arrayed against himself all of the special champions of the existing establishments. In his reduced physical state, the reformer was not equal to the tremendous concussions of this "era of activity," as Emerson named it. At moments he appeared bewildered amid the loud, fierce clamor of contending ideas, each asserting in turn its moral primacy. For an instant the vision of the great soul grew dim, the great heart seemed to have lost its bearings. All of the new ideas thawed and melted into each other, dissolved into one vague and grand solidarity of reforms. The voice of the whole was urging him amid the gathering moral confusion to declare himself for all truth, and he hearkened irresolute, with divided mind. "I feel somewhat at a loss to know what to do"—he confesses at this juncture to George W. Benson, "whether to go into all the principles of holy reform and make the Abolition cause subordinate, or whether still to persevere in the *one* beaten track as hitherto. Circumstances hereafter must determine this matter." That was written in August, 1837; a couple of months later circumstances had not determined the matter, it would seem, from the following extract from a letter to his brother-in-law: "It is not my intention at present to alter either the general character or course of the *Liberator*. My work in the anti-slavery cause is not wholly done; as soon as it is, I shall know it, and shall be prepared, I trust, to enter upon a mightier work of reform."

Meanwhile the relations between the editor of the *Liberator* and the managers of the national organization were becoming decidedly strained. For it seemed to them that Garrison had changed the anti-slavery character of his paper by the course which he had taken in regard to the new ideas which were finding their way into its columns to the manifest harm of the main principle of immediate emancipation. This incipient estrangement between the pioneer and the executive committee of the national society was greatly aggravated by an occurrence, which, at the time, was elevated to an importance that it did not deserve. This occurrence was what is known in anti-slavery annals as the "Clerical Appeal." Five clergymen, who were obviously unfriendly to Garrison, and distrustful of the religious and social heresies which they either saw or fancied that they saw in the *Liberator*, and withal jealous lest the severities of the paper against particular pro-slavery ministers should diminish the influence and sacred character of their order, published, in August of 1837, in the *New England Spectator* an acrid arraignment of editor and paper, upon five several charges, designed to bring Garrisonism to the block and speedy death. This document was followed by two other appeals by way of supplement and rejoinder from the same source, an "Andover Appeal" from kindred spirits and a bitter, personal letter from one of the "seventy agents," all of them having a common motive and purpose, viz., sectarian distrust and dislike of Garrison, and desire to reduce his anti-slavery influence to a nullity.

In his diseased and suffering bodily condition, Garrison naturally enough fell into the error of exaggerating the gravity of these attacks upon himself. Insignificant in an historical sense, they really were an episode, an unpleasant one to be sure for the time being, but no more. To Garrison, however, they appeared in a wholly different light. It seemed a rebellion on a pretty grand scale, which called for all his strength, all the batteries of the friends of freedom, all his terrible and unsparing severities of speech to quell it. All his artillery he posted promptly in positions commanding the camp of the mutineers, and began to pour, as only he could, broadside after broadside into the works of the wretched little camp of rebels. He could hardly have expended more energy and ammunition in attacking a strategical point of Southern slavery, than was expended in punishing a handful of deserters and insurgents. But, alas! he was not satisfied to draw upon his own resources for crushing the clerical sedition, he demanded reinforcements from the central authorities in New York as well. And then began a contention between him and the Executive Committee of the National Society, which issued only in ill.

Garrison considered it the duty of the Executive Committee to disapprove officially of the action of the Massachusetts recalcitrants, and also the duty of its organ, the *Emancipator*, to rebuke the authors of the "appeals." Not so, replied Lewis Tappan and Elizur Wright, your request is unreasonable. If you choose to make a mountain out of a molehill, you choose to make a mistake which the Executive Committee will not repeat. Your troubles are wholly local, of no general importance whatever. "What! Shall a whole army stop its aggressive movements into the territories of its enemies to charge bayonets on five soldiers, subalterns, company, or even staff officers, because they stray into a field to pick berries, throw stones or write an 'appeal?' To be frank with you we shall make bold to say that we do not approve of the appeal, it is very censurable, its spirit is bad, but neither do we approve of your action in the premises, it is also very censurable and its spirit is bad. What then? shall the Executive Committee condemn the authors of the appeal and not condemn the editor of the *Liberator* also? If strict military justice were done should not both parties be cashiered? Let the Sabbath and the theoretic theology of the priesthood alone for the present." "I could have wished, yes, I have wished from the bottom of my soul," it is Wright who now holds the pen, "that yon could conduct that dear paper, the *Liberator*, in the singleness of purpose of its first years, without traveling off from the ground of our true, noble, heart-stirring Declaration of Sentiments—without breathing sentiments which are novel and shocking to the community, and which seem to me to have no logical sequence from the principles on which we are associated as Abolitionists. I cannot but regard the taking hold of one great moral enterprise while another is in hand and but half achieved, as an outrage upon common-sense, somewhat like that of the dog crossing the river with his meat. But you have seen fit to introduce to the public some novel views—I refer especially to your sentiments on government and religious perfection—and they have produced the effect which was to have been expected. And now considering what stuff human nature is made of, is it to be wondered at that some honest-hearted, thorough-going Abolitionists should have lost their equanimity? As you well know I am comparatively no bigot to any creed, political or theological, yet to tell the plain truth, I look upon your notions of government and religious perfection as downright fanaticism—as harmless as they are absurd. I would not care a pin's head if they were preached to all Christendom ; for it is not in the human mind (except in a peculiar and, as I think, diseased state) to believe them."

Barring the extreme plainness of speech with which Wright and Tappan gave their advice to Mr. Garrison, it was in the main singularly sound and wise. But the pioneer did not so regard it. He was possessed with his idea of the importance of chastising the clerical critics, and of the duty of the Executive Committee and of the *Emancipator* to back him in the undertaking. His temper was, under all circumstances, masterful and peremptory. It was never more masterful and peremptory than in its manage ment of this business. The very reasonable course of the Board at New York suggested to his mind a predominance of " sectarianism at headquarters," seemed to him "criminal and extraordinary." As the Executive Committee and its organ would not rebuke the schismatics, he was moved to rebuke the Executive Committee and its organ for their " blind and temporizing policy." And so matters within the movement against slavery went, with increasing momentum, from bad to worse.

The break in the anti-slavery ranks widened as new causes of controversy arose between the management in Boston and the management at New York. The Massachusetts Abolitionists had stood stanchly by Garrison against the clerical schismatics. They also inclined to his side in his trouble with the national board. Instead of one common center of activity and leadership the anti-slavery reform began now to develop two centers of activity and leadership. Garrison and the *Liberator* formed the moral nucleus at one end, the Executive Committee and the *Emancipator* the moral nucleus at the other. Much of the energies of the two sides were in those circumstances, absorbed in stimulating and completing the processes which were to ultimate in the organic division of the body of the movement against slavery. When men once begin to quarrel they will not stop for lack of subjects to dispute over. There will be no lack, for before one disputed point is settled another has arisen. It is the old story of the box of evils. Beginnings must be avoided, else if one evil escapes, others will follow. The anti-slavery Pandora had let out one little imp of discord and many big and little imps were incontinently following.

Against all of the new ideas except one, viz., the idea of anti-slavery political action, the New York leadership, speaking broadly, had opposed itself. But as if by some strange perversity of fate, this particular new idea was the only one of the new ideas to which the Boston leadership did not take kindly. It became in time as the very apple of the eye to the management of the National Society. And the more ardently it was cherished by them, the more hateful did it become with the Boston Board. It was the only one of the new ideas which had any logical sequence from the Abolition cause. In a country where the principle of popular suffrage obtains, all successful moral movements must sometime ultimate in political action. There is no other way of fixing in laws the changes in public sentiment wrought during this period of agitation. The idea of political action was therefore a perfectly natural growth from the moral movement against slavery. The only reasonable objection to it would be one which went to show that it had arrived out of due course, that its appearance at any given time was marked by prematurity in respect of the reasons, so to speak, of the reform. For every movement against a great social wrong as was the anti-slavery movement must have its John-the-Baptist stage, its period of popular awakening to the nature and enormity of sin and the duty of immediate repentance.

The anti-slavery enterprise was at the time of the controversy between the New York and the Boston Boards in this first stage of its growth. It had not yet progressed naturally out of it into its next phase of political agitation. True there were tendencies more or less strong to enter the second stage of its development, but they seem irregular, personal, and forced. The time had not come for the adoption of the principle of associated political action against slavery. But the deep underlying motive of the advocates of the third-party idea was none the less a grand one, viz., "to have a free Northern nucleus," as Elizur Wright put it, "a standard flung to the breeze—something around which to rally." Garrison probed to the quick the question in a passage of an address to the Abolitionists, which is here given: "Abolitionists! you are now feared and respected by all political parties, not because of the number of votes you can throw, so much as in view of the moral integrity and sacred regard to principle which you have exhibited to the country. It is the religious aspect of your enterprise which impresses and overawes men of every sect and party. Hitherto you have seemed to be actuated by no hope of preferment or love of power, and therefore have established, even in the minds of your enemies, confidence in your disinterestedness. If you shall now array yourselves as a political party, and hold out mercenary rewards to induce men to rally under your standard, there is reason to fear that you will be regarded as those who have made the anti-slavery cause a hobby to ride into office, however plausible or sound may be your pretexts for such a course. You cannot, you ought not, to expect that the political action of the State will move faster than the religious action of the Church, in favor of the abolition of slavery; and it is a fact not less encouraging than undeniable, that both the Whig and Democratic parties have consulted the wishes of Abolitionists even beyond the measure of their real political strength. More you cannot expect under any circumstances."

Hotly around this point raged the strife among brethren. Actuated by the noblest motives were both sides in the main, yet, both sides displayed in the maintenance of their respective positions an amount of weak human nature, which proves that perfection is not attainable even by the most disinterested of men. Harsh and abusive language good men uttered against good men. Distrust, suspicion, anger, and alienation took possession of the thoughts of the grandest souls. Saints and heroes beseemed themselves like very ordinary folk, who, when they come to differences, come directly afterward to high words and thumping blows. The love of David and Jonathan which once united Garrison and Phelps, has died. Garrison and Stanton meet and only exchange civilities. They, too, have become completely alienated, and so on down the long list of the "goodliest fellowship . . . whereof this land holds record." To a sweet and gentle spirit like Samuel J. May, the acrimony and scenes of strife among his old associates was unspeakably painful. Writing to Garrison from South Scituate, May 1, 1839, he touches thus upon this head: "I now think I shall not go to New York next week. In the first place, I cannot afford the expense . . . But I confess, I do not lament my inability to go so much as I should do if the prospect of an agreeable meeting was fairer. I am apprehensive that it will be not so much an anti-slavery as anti-Garrison and anti-Phelps meeting, or anti-board-of-managers and anti-executive committee meeting. Division has done its work, I fear, effectually. The two parties seem to me to misunderstand, and therefore sadly misrepresent one another. I am not satisfied with the course you and your partisans have pursued. It appears to me not consistent with the non-resistant, patient, long-suffering spirit of the Gospel. And I do not believe that either the cause of the slave, or the cause of peace and righteousness has been advanced."

The situation was further complicated by the discovery of a fresh bone of contention. As if to give just a shade of sordidness to the strife there must needs arise a money difficulty between the two rival boards of leaders. This is how our recent band of brothers happened to stumble upon their new apple of discord. Soon after the formation of the National Society an arrangement was made with each of the State societies whereby they agreed to operate financially their respective territories and to turn into the national treasury the several sums which at the annual meeting they obligated themselves to contribute to the general work. This arrangement was intended to avoid the expense, conflict, and confusion consequent upon the employment of two sets of agents to work the same territory. Matters went on quite smoothly under this plan between the Massachusetts Board and the National Board until the beginning of the year 1839, when the former fell into arrears in the payment of its instalments to the latter. Money from one cause or another, was hard to get at by the Massachusetts Board, and the treasury in New York was in an extremely low state. The relations between the two boards were, as we have seen, much strained and neither side was in the mood to cover with charity the shortcomings of the other. Perhaps the board at New York was too exacting, perhaps the board at Boston was not sufficiently zealous, under the circumstances. But what were the real irritating causes which kept the two boards at loggerheads over the matter need not here be determined. This fact is clear that the arrangement was rescinded by the New York management, and their agents thrown into Massachusetts. This action only added fuel to a fire which was fast assuming the proportions of a conflagration. All the anti-Garrisonians formed themselves into a new anti-slavery society, and the National Board, as if to burn its bridges, and to make reconciliation impossible, established a new paper in Boston in opposition to the *Liberator*. The work of division was ended. There was no longer any vital connection between the two warring members of the anti-slavery reform.

To tear the dead tissues asunder which still joined them, all that was wanted was anothar sharp shock, and this came at the annual meeting of the National Society in 1840 over the woman's question. The issue, "Shall a woman serve with men on a committee?" was precipitated upon the convention by the appointment of that brilliant young Quakeress, Abby Kelley, on the business committee with ten men. The convention confirmed her appointment by about a hundred majority in a total vote of 1,008. Whereupon those opposed to this determination of the question, withdrew from the convention and organized the American and Foreign Anti-Slavery Society. Garrison had triumphed and he was immensely elated with his victory. His moral leadership was definitely established, never again to be disputed by his disciples and followers.

CHAPTER XV.

RANDOM SHOTS.

THE division of the anti-slavery organization into two distinct societies did not immediately terminate the war between them. From New York and the American society the contest over the woman's qnestion was almost directly shifted after the triumph of the Garrisonians in the convention, to London and the World's Convention, which was held in the month of June of the year 1840. To this anti-slavery congress both of the rival anti-slavery organizations in America elected delegates. These delegates, chosen by the older society and by its auxiliaries of the States of Massachusetts and Pennsylvania, were composed of women and men. Lucretia Mott was not only chosen by the National Society, but by the Pennsylvania Society as well. The Massachusetts Society selected Lydia Maria Child, Maria Weston Chapman, and Ann Green Phillips together with their husbands among its list of delegates. England at this time was much more conservative on the woman's question than America. The managers of the World's Convention did not take kindly to the notion of women members, and signified to the American societies who had placed women among their delegates that the company of the women was not expected. Those societies, however, made no alteration in deference to this notice, in the character of their delegations, but stood stoutly by their principle of "the EQUAL BROTHERHOOD of the entire HUMAN FAMILY without distinction of color, sex, or clime."

A contest over the admission of women to membership in the World's Convention was therefore a foregone conclusion. The convention, notwithstanding a brilliant fight under the lead of Wendell Phillips in behalf of their admission, refused to admit the women delegates. The women delegates instead of having seats on the floor were forced in consequence of this decision to look on from the galleries. Garrison, who with Charles Lenox Remond, Nathaniel P. Rogers, and William Adams, was late in arriving in England, finding, on reaching London the women excluded from the convention and sitting as spectators in the galleries, determined to take his place among them, deeming that the act of the convention which discredited the credentials of Lucretia Mott and her sister delegates, had discredited his own also. Remond, Rogers, and Adams followed his example and took their places with the rejected women delegates likewise. The convention was scandalized at such proceedings, and did its best to draw Garrison and his associates from the ladies in the galleries to the men on the floor, but without avail. There they remained an eloquent protest against the masculine narrowness of the convention. Defeated in New York, the delegates of the new American and Foreign Anti-Slavery Society triumphed over their victors in London. But their achievements in the World's Convention, in this regard, was not of a sort to entitle them to point with any special pride in after years ; and, as a matter of fact, not one of them would have probably cared to have their success alluded to in any sketch of their lives for the perusal of posterity.

Garrison and his associates were the recipients of the most cordial and flattering attention from the English Abolitionists. He was quite lionized, in fact, at breakfasts, fêtes, and soirées. The Duchess of Sunderland paid him marked attention and desired his portrait, which was done for Her Grace by the celebrated artist, Benjamin Robert Haydon, who executed besides a large painting of the convention, in which he grouped the most distinguished members with reference to the seats actually occupied by them during its sessions. Of course to leave Garrison out of such a picture would almost seem like the play of "Hamlet" with *Hamlet* omitted, a blunder which the artist was by no means disposed to make. Garrison was accordingly invited to sit to him for his portrait. Haydon, who it seems was a student of human nature as well as of the human form, made the discovery of a fact which at first surprised and angered him. In making his groupings of heads he decided to place together the Rev. John Scoble, George Thompson and Charles Lenox Remond. When Scoble sat to him, Haydon told him of his design in this regard. But, remarked Haydon, Scoble "sophisticated immediately on the propriety of placing the negro in the distance, as it would have much greater effect." The painter now applied his test to Thompson who "saw no objection." Thompson did not bear the test to Haydon's satisfaction, who observed that "A man who wishes to place the negro on a level must no longer regard him as having been a slave, and feel annoyed at sitting by his side." But when the artist approached Garrison on the subject it was wholly different. "I asked him," Haydon records with obvious pleasure, "and he met me at once directly."

Thompson was not altogether satisfactory to Garrison either during this visit as the following extract from one of his letters to his wife evinces: "Dear Thompson has not been strengthened to do battle for us, as I had confidently hoped he would be. He is placed in a difficult position, and seems disposed to take the ground of non-committal, publicly, respecting the controversy which is going on in the United States."

Garrison, Rogers, and Remond in the company of Thompson made a delightful trip into Scotland at this time. Everywhere the American Abolitionists were met with distinguished attentions. "Though I like England much, on many accounts," Garrison writes home in high spirits, "I can truly say that I like Scotland better." An instance, which may be coupled with that one furnished by Haydon, occurred during this Scottish tour, and illustrates strongly the kind of stuff of which he was made. On his way to the great public reception tendered the American delegates by the Glasgow Emancipation Society, a placard with the caption, "*Have we no white slaves?*" was put into his hands. Upon acquainting himself with its contents he determined to read it to the meeting, and to make it the text of remarks when he was called upon to address the meeting. He was presently announced and the immense audience greeted him with every manifestation of pleasure and enthusiasm, with loud cheering and waving of handkerchiefs.

Nevertheless he held to his purpose to speak upon the subject of the placard, unwelcome though it should prove to his hearers. "After reading the interrogation, I said in reply: 'No—broad as is the empire, and extensive as are the possessions of Great Britain, not a single *white* SLAVE can be found in them all;' and I then went on to show the wide difference that exists between the condition of human beings who are held and treated as chattels personal, and that of those who are only suffering from certain forms of political injustice or governmental oppression . . . . . 'But,' I said, 'although it is not true that England has any *white* slaves, either at home or abroad, is it not true that there are thousands of her population, both at home and abroad, who are deprived of their just rights, who are grievously oppressed, who are dying even in the midst of abundance, of actual starvation? YES!' and I expressly called upon British Abolitionists to prove themselves the true friends of suffering humanity abroad, by showing that they were the best friend of suffering humanity at home." Truth, justice, duty, always overrode with him the proprieties, however sacredly esteemed by others. Of a piece with this fact of the placard of the *white slave* was his custom in refusing the wine proffered by some of his British friends to their guests. He was not content with a simple refusal and the implied rebuke which it involved, he must needs couple his declaration with an express rebuke to host and hostess for tempting men into the downward way to drunkenness.

While in attendance upon the sessions of the World's Convention Garrison received tidings, of the birth of his third child. The second, whom he named for himself, was born in 1838. The third, who was also a son, the fond father named after Wendell Phillips. Three children and a wife did not tend to a solution of the always difficult problem of family maintenance. The pressure of their needs upon the husband sometimes, simple as indeed they were owing to the good sense and prudence of Mrs. Garrison, seemed to exceed the weight of the atmospheric column to the square inch. The fight for bread was one of the bitterest battles of the reformer's life. The arrangement made in 1837, whereby the Massachusetts Anti-Slavery Society assumed the responsibility of the publication of the *Liberator*, Garrison rescinded at the beginning of 1838, for the sake of giving himself greater freedom in the advocacy in its columns of the several other reforms in which he had enlisted, besides Abolitionism. But Garrison and the paper were now widely recognized as anti-slavery essentials and indispensables. Many of the leaders of the movement perceived, as Gerrit Smith expressed it in a letter enclosing fifty dollars for the editor, that "Among the many things in which the Abolitionists of our country should be agreed, are the two following: (1) The *Liberator* must be sustained; (2) its editor must be kept above want; not only, nor mainly, for his own or his family's happiness; but that, having his own mind unembarrassed by the cares of griping poverty, he may be a more effective advocate of the cause of the Saviour's enslaved poor." A new arrangement, in accordance with this suggestion for the support of the paper and the preservation of the editor from want, was made in 1839, and its performance taken in charge by a committee of gentlemen, who undertook to raise the necessary funds for those objects. Thus it was that Garrison, through the wise and generous provision of friends, was enabled to augment the happiness of an increasing family, and at the same time add to his own effectiveness as an anti-slavery instrument.

Garrison found occasion soon after his return from the World's Convention for the employment of all his added effectiveness for continuing the moral movement against slavery. For what with the strife and schism in the anti-slavery ranks, followed by the excitements of the long Presidential canvass of 1840, wherein the great body of the Abolitionists developed an uncontrollable impulse to political action, some through the medium of the new Liberty party which had nominated James G. Birney for the Presidency, while others reverted to the two old parties with which they had formerly acted—what with all these causes the pure moral movement started by Garrison was in grave danger of getting abolished or at least of being reduced to a nullity in its influence upon public opinion. John A. Collins, the able and resourceful general agent of the Massachusetts Anti-Slavery Society, wrote in the deepest anxiety to Garrison from New Bedford, September 1, 1840, on this head. Says he: "I really wish you understood perfectly the exact position the friends of the old organization hold to the two great political parties, and how generally they have been caught up in the whirlwind of political enthusiasm. Could you but go where I have been, and have seen and heard what I have seen and heard; could you see men—aye, and women, too—who have been and still are your warmest advocates, who have eschewed sectarianism, and lost their caste in the circle in which they moved, for their strong adherence to your views and measures, declare that they would sooner forego their Abolitionism than their party. . . . Now, these are not the views of here and there a straggling Abolitionist, but of seven-tenths of all the voting Abolitionists of the State. . . . They are entirely unconscious of the demoralizing influence of their course. They need light, warning, entreaty, and rebuke." Besides this demoralization of the Abolitionists, as described by Collins, the parent society at New York fell into bad financial straits. It was absolutely without funds, and without any means of supplying the lack. What should it do in its extremity but appeal to the Massachusetts Society which was already heavily burdened by its own load, the *Liberator*. The new organ of the national organization, *The Anti-Slavery Standard*, surely must not be allowed to fail for want of funds in this emergency. The Boston management rose to the occasion. Collins was sent to England in quest of contributions from the Abolitionists of Great Britain. But, great as was the need of money, the relief which it might afford would only prove temporory unless there could be effected a thorough antislavery revival. This was vital. And therefore to this end Garrison now bent his remarkable energies.

Agents, during this period when money was scarce, were necessarily few. But the pioneer proved a host in himself. Resigning the editorial charge of the *Liberator* into the capable hands of Edmund Quincy,

Garrison itinerated in the rôle of an anti-slavery lecturer in Massachusetts, Connecticut, and New Hampshire, reviving everywhere the languishing interest of his disciples. On the return of Collins in the summer of 1841, revival meetings and conventions started up with increased activity, the fruits of which were of a most cheering character. At Nantucket, Garrison made a big catch in his anti-slavery net. It was Frederick Douglass, young, callow, and awkward, but with his splendid and inimitable gifts flashing through all as he, for the first time in his life, addressed an audience of white people. Garrison, with the instinct of leadership, saw at once the value of the runaway slave's oratorical possibilities in their relations to the anti-slavery movement. It was at his instance that Collins added Douglass to the band of anti-slavery agents. The new agent has preserved his recollections of the pioneer's speech on that eventful evening in Nantucket. Says he: "Mr. Garrison followed me, taking me as his text; and now, whether I had made an eloquent plea in behalf of freedom or not, his was one never to be forgotten. Those who had heard him oftenest, and had known him longest, were astonished at his masterly effort. For the time he possessed that almost fabulous inspiration, often referred to but seldom attained, in which a public meeting is transformed, as it were, into a single individuality, the orator swaying a thousand heads and hearts at once, and by the simple majesty of his all-controlling thought, converting his hearers into the express image of his own soul. That night there were, at least, a thousand Garrisonians in Nantucket!"

Here is another picture of Garrison in the lecture-field. It is from the pen of N. P. Rogers, with whom he was making a week's tour among the White Mountains, interspersing the same with anti-slavery meetings. At Plymouth, failing to procure the use of a church for their purpose, they fell back upon the temple not made with hands.

"Semi-circular seats, backed against a line of magnificent trees to accommodate, we should judge, from two to three hundred," Rogers narrates, "were filled, principally with women, and the men who could not find seats stood on the green sward on either hand; and, at length, when wearied with standing, seated themselves on the ground. Garrison, mounted on a rude platform in front, lifted up his voice and spoke to them in prophet tones and surpassing eloquence, from half-past three till I saw the rays of the setting sun playing through the trees on his head. . . . They (the auditory) heeded it not any more than he, but remained till he ended, apparently indisposed to move, though some came from six, eight, and even twelve miles distance." So bravely prospered the revival agitation, under the vigorous preaching of the indomitable pioneer.

In the midst of the growing activities of the revival season of the anti-slavery movement, Garrison had some personal experiences of a distressing nature. One of these was the case of his quondam friend and partner in the publication of the *Liberator*, Isaac Knapp. He, poor fellow, was no longer the publisher of the paper. His wretched business management of his department tended to keep the *Liberator* in a state of chronic financial embarrassment. When the committee, who assumed charge of the finances of the paper, took hold of the problem. they determined to let Knapp go. He was paid $150 or $175 as a *quid pro quo* for his interest in the *Liberator*. Unfortunate in the business of a publisher, he was yet more unfortunate in another respect. He had become a victim of intemperance. His inebriety increased upon him, accelerated, no doubt, by his business failure. Notwithstanding Garrison's strong and tender friendship for Knapp, the broken man came to regard him as an enemy, and showed in many ways his jealousy and hatred of his old friend and partner. Very painful was this experience to the pioneer.

An experience which touched Garrison more nearly arose out of the sad case of his brother James, who, the reader will recall, ran away from his mother in Baltimore and went to sea. He ultimately enlisted in the United States Navy, and what with the brutalities which he suffered at the hands of his superiors, by way of discipline, and with those of his own uncontrolled passions and appetites, he was, when recovered by his brother William, a total moral and physical wreck. But the prodigal was gathered to the reformer's heart, and taken to his home where in memory of a mother long dead, whose darling was James, he was nursed and watched over with deep and pious love. There were sad lapses of the profligate man even in the sanctuary of his brother's home. The craving for liquor was omnipotent in the wretched creature, and he was attacked by uncontrollable desire for drink. But William's patience was infinite, and his yearning and pity at such times were as sweet and strong as a mother's. Death rung the curtain down in the fall of 1842, on this miserable life with its sorry and pathetic scenes.

About this time a trial of a different sort fell to the lot of Garrison to endure. The tongue of detraction was never more busy with his alleged infidel doctrines or to more damaging effect. Collins, in England, seeking to obtain contributions for the support of the agitation in America found Garrison's infidelity the *great lion* in the way of success. Even the good dispositions of the venerable Clarkson were affected by the injurious reports in this regard, circulated in England mainly by Nathaniel Colver, a narrow and violent sectary of the Baptist denomination of the United States. It was, of course, painful to Garrison to feel that he had become a rock of offence in the path of the great movement, which he had started and to which he was devoting himself so energetically. To Elizabeth Pease, one of the noblest of the English Abolitionists, and one of his stanchest transatlantic friends, he defended himself against the false and cruel statements touching his religious beliefs. "I esteem the Holy Scriptures," he wrote her, "above all other books in the universe, and always appeal to 'the law and the testimony' to prove all my peculiar doctrines." His religious sentiments and Sabbatical views are almost if not quite identical with those held by the Quakers. "I believe in an indwelling Christ," he goes on to furnish a summary of his confession of faith, "and in His righteousness alone; I glory in nothing here below, save in Christ and in Him crucified; I believe all the works of the devil are to be destroyed, and Our Lord is to reign from sea to sea, even to the ends of the earth; and I profess to have passed from death unto life, and know by happy experience, that there is no condemnation to them who are in Christ Jesus, who walk not after the flesh, but after the spirit." These were the pioneer's articles of faith. Their extreme simplicity and theological conservatism it would seem ought to have satisfied the evangelicals of all denominations. They were in essentials thoroughly orthodox. But in the composition of the shibboleths of beliefs non-essentials as well as essentials enter, the former to the latter in the proportion of two to one. It is not surprising, therefore, that Garrison's essentials proved unequal to the test set up by sectarianism, inasmuch as his spiritual life dropped the aspirate of the non-essentials of religious forms and observances.

But the good man had his compensation as well as his trials. Such of a very noble kind was the great Irish address brought over from Ireland by Remond in December 1841. It was signed by Daniel O'Connell, Father Mathew, and sixty thousand Roman Catholics of Ireland, who called upon the Irish Roman Catholics of America to make the cause of the slaves of the United States their cause. Large expectations of Irish assistance in the anti-slavery agitation were excited in the bosoms of Abolitionists by this imposing appeal. Garrison shared the high hopes of its beneficent influence upon the Ireland of America, with many others. Alas! for the "best laid schemes of mice and men," for the new Ireland was not populated with saints, but a fiercely human race who had come to their new home to better their own condition, not that of the negro. Hardly had they touched these shores before they were Americanized in the colorphobia sense, out-Heroded Herod in hatred of the colored people and their anti-slavery friends. Indeed, it was quite one thing to preach Abolitionism with three thousand miles of sea-wall between one and his audience, and quite another to rise and do the preaching with no sea-wall to guard the preacher from the popular consequences of his preaching, as Father Mathew quickly perceived and reduced to practice eight years later, when he made his memorable visit to this country. In vain was the monster document unrolled in Faneuil Hall, and many Abolitionists with Irish blood were put forward to sweep the chords of Erin's heart, and to conjure by their eloquence the disciples of St. Patrick to rally under the banner of freedom. There was no response, except the response of bitter foes. Erin's harp vibrated to no breeze which did not come out of the South. The slave-power had been erected into patron saint by the new Ireland in America, and the new Ireland in America was very well content with his saintship's patronage and service. Thus it happened that the great expectations, which were excited by the Irish address, were never realized. But the pioneer had other fish in his net, had, in fact, meanwhile, got himself in readiness for a launch into a new and startling agitation. As to just what this new and startling agitation was we must refer the reader to the next chapter.

CHAPTER XVI.

THE PIONEER MAKES A NEW AND STARTLING DEPARTURE.

WHEN Garrison hoisted the banner of immediate emancipation he was over-confident of success through the instrumentality of the church. It did not enter his heart to conceive that after he had delivered his message touching the barbarism of slavery that a church calling itself Christian, or that a ministry arrogating to itself the character of the Christ, could possibly say him nay. But he learned sadly enough the utter folly of such expectations. For from pew and pulpit the first stones were hurled against him, and the most cruel and persistent opposition and persecution issued. Then as the movement which he had started advanced, he saw how it was, why the church had played him false and the cause of freedom. It was because the poison of slavery which the evil one had injected into the nation's arteries had corrupted the springs of justice and mercy in that body. The Church was not free, it, too, was in bonds to slavery, how then could it help to free the slaves? That was the reason that pulpit and pew cried out against him and persecuted him. It was not they but the slave despotism, which ruled them, which wrought its fell purpose within them.

If the reformer cast his eyes about him for other help it was the same; the slime of the serpent was upon State as well as Church. Both of the two great political parties were bound hands and feet, and given over to the will of the slave tyranny. In all departments of Government, State and National, the positive, all-powerful principle was slavery. Its dread *nolo me tangere* had forced Congress into the denial of the right of petition, and into the imposition of a gag upon its own freedom of debate. It was the grand President-maker, and the judiciary bent without a blush to do its service. What, then, in these circumstances could the friends of freedom hope to achieve? The nation had been caught in the snare of slavery, and was in Church and State helpless in the vast spider-like web of wrong. The more the reformer pondered the problem, the more hopeless did success look under a Constitution which united right and wrong, freedom and slavery. As his reflections deepened, the conviction forced its way into his mind that the Union was the strong tower of the slave-power, which could never be destroyed until the fortress which protected it was first utterly demolished. In the spring of 1842 the pioneer was prepared to strike into this new path to effect his purpose.

"We must dissolve all connection with those murderers of fathers," he wrote his brother-in-law, "and murderers of mothers, and murderers of liberty, and traffickers of human flesh, and blasphemers against the Almighty at the South. What have we in common with them? What have we gained? What have we not lost by our alliance with them? Are not their principles, their pursuits, their policies, their interests, their designs, their feelings, utterly diverse from ours? Why, then, be subject to their dominion? Why not have the Union dissolved in form as it is in fact, especially if the form gives ample protection to the slave system, by securing for it all the physical force of the North? It is not treason against the cause of liberty to cry, "Down with every slave-holding Union!" Therefore, I raise that cry. And O that I had a voice louder than a thousand thunders, that it might shake the land and electrify the dead—the dead in sin, I mean—those slain by the hand of slavery."

A few weeks later the first peal of this thunder broke upon the startled ears of the country through the columns of the *Liberator*. The May meeting of the American Anti-Slavery Society was drawing near, and the reformer, now entirely ready to enter upon an agitation looking to the dissolution of the Union, suggested "the duty of making the REPEAL OF THE UNION between the North and the South the grand rallying point until it be accomplished, or slavery cease to pollute our soil. We are for throwing all the means, energies, actions, purposes, and appliances of the genuine friends of liberty and republicanism into this one channel," he goes on to announce, "and for measuring the humanity, patriotism, and piety of every man by this one standard. This question can no longer be avoided, and a right decision of it will settle the controversy between freedom and slavery.' The stern message of Isaiah to the Jews, beginning, "Hear the word of the Lord, ye scornful men that rule this people. Because ye have said, We have made a covenant with DEATH and with HELL are we at agreement," seemed to the American Isaiah to describe exactly the character of the National Constitution. "Slavery is a combination of DEATH and HELL," he declares, with righteous wrath, "and with it the North have made a covenant, and are at agreement. As an element of the Government it is omnipotent, omniscient, omnipresent. As a component part of the Union, it is necessarily a national interest. Divorced from Northern protection, it dies; with that protection it enlarges its boundaries, multiplies its victims, and extends its ravages."

The announcement of this new radicalism caused a sensation. Many genuine Garrisonian Abolitionists recoiled from a policy of disunion. Lydia Maria Child and James S. Gibbon of the Executive Committee of the National Society hastened to disavow for the society all responsibility for the disunion sentiment of the editor of the *Liberator*. His new departure seemed to them "foreign to the purpose for which it was organized." Like all new ideas, it was a sword-bearer, and proved a decided disturber of the peace. The Union-loving portion of the free States had never taken to the Abolition movement, for the reason that it tended to disturb the stability of their idol. But now the popular hatred of Abolitionism was intensified by the avowal of a distinct purpose on the part of its leader to labor for the separation of the sections. The press of the North made the most of this design to render altogether odious the small band of moral reformers, to reduce to a nullity their influence upon public opinion.

Notwithstanding its rejection by James Gibbons and Lydia Maria Child the new idea of the dissolution of the Union, as an anti-slavery object, found instant favor with many of the leading Abolitionists, like Wendell Phillips, Edmund Quincy, Parker Pillsbury, Stephen S. Foster and Abby Kelley. At the anniversary meeting of the American Society in 1842, the subject was mooted, and, although there was no official action taken, yet it was apparent that a majority of the delegates were favorable to its adoption as the sentiment of the society.

The ultimate object of Garrison was the abolition of slavery. Disunion led directly to this goal, therefore he planted his feet in that way. But while he shot the agitation at a distant mark, he did not mean to miss less remote results. There was remarkable method in his madness. He agitated the question of the dissolution of the Union "in order that the people of the North might be induced to reflect upon their debasement, guilt, and danger in continuing in partnership with heaven-daring oppressors, and thus be led to repentance."

The Massachusetts Anti-Slavery Society at its annual meeting in January, 1843 "dissolved the Union," wrote Quincy to R. D. Webb, "by a handsome vote, after a warm debate. The question was afterward reconsidered and passed in another shape, being wrapped up by Garrison in some of his favorite Old Testament Hebraisms by way of vehicle, as the apothecaries say." This is the final shape which Garrison's "favorite Old Testament Hebraisms" gave to the action of the society:

"*Resolved*, That the compact which exists between the North and the South is a covenant with death and an agreement with hell—involving both parties in atrocious criminality—and should be immediately annulled."

At its tenth anniversary, in 1844, the American Society resolved likewise that there should be no Union with slaveholders; and in May of the same year the New England Society voted by a large majority to dissolve the 'covenant with death, and the agreement with hell.' Almost the whole number of the Garrisonian Abolitionists had by this time placed upon their banner of immediate emancipation the revolutionary legend "No Union with slaveholders." *Cathago est delenda* were now ever on the lips of the pioneer. 'The Union it must and shall be destroyed' became the beginning, the middle, and the end of all his utterances on the slavery question.

The attitude of the anti-slavery disunionists to the Government which they were seeking to overthrow was clearly stated by Francis Jackson in a letter returning to the Governor of Massachusetts his commission as a justice of the peace. Says he, "To me it appears that the vices of slavery, introduced into the constitution of our body politic by a few slight punctures, has now so pervaded and poisoned the whole system of our National Government that literally there is no health in it. The only remedy that I can see for the disease is to be found in the *dissolution of the patient*. . . . Henceforth it (the Constitution) is dead to me, and I to it. I withdraw all profession of allegiance to it, and all my voluntary efforts to sustain it. The burdens that it lays upon me, while it is held up by others, I shall endeavor to bear patiently, yet acting with reference to a higher law, and distinctly declaring that, while I retain my own liberty, I will be a party to no compact which helps to rob any other man of his."

The Abolition agitation for the dissolution of the Union was assisted not a little by sundry occurrences of national importance. The increasing arrogance and violence of the South in Congress on all matters relating to the subject of slavery was one of these occurrences. Freedom of debate and the right of petition, Southern intolerance had rendered well nigh worthless in the National Legislature. In this way the North, during several months in every year, was forced to look at the reverse and the obverse faces of the Union. These object-lessons taught many minds, no doubt, to count the cost which the preservation of the Union entailed upon the free States—"to reflect upon their debasement, guilt, and danger" in their partnership with slaveholders. Another circumstance which induced tø this kind of reflection was the case of George Latimer, who was seized as a fugitive slave in Boston in the autumn of 1842. From beginning to end the Latimer case revealed how completely had Massachusetts tied her own hands as a party to the original compact with slavery whose will was the supreme law of the land. In obedience to this supreme law Chief-Justice Shaw refused to the captive the writ of *habeas corpus*, and Judge Story granted the owner possession of the fugitive, and time to procure evidence of his ownership. But worse still Massachusetts officials and one of her jails were employed to aid in the return of a man to slavery. This degradation aroused the greatest indignation in the State and led to the enactment of a law prohibiting its officials from taking part in the return of fugitive slaves, and the use of its jails and prisons for their detention. The passage of this personal liberty measure served to increase the activity of the anti-Union working forces in the South

Then, again, the serious difficulty between Massachusetts and two of the slave States in regard to their treatment of her colored seamen aided Garrison in his agitation for the dissolution of the Union by the keen sense of insult and injury which the trouble begat and left upon the popular mind. Colored men in Massachusetts enjoyed a fair degree of equality before her laws, were endowed with the right to vote, and were, barring the prejudice against color, treated by the commonwealth as citizens. They were employed in the merchant service of her interstate trade. But at two of the Southern ports where her vessels entered, the colored seamen were seized by the local police and confined in houses of detention until the vessels to which they belonged were ready to depart, when they were released and allowed to join the vessels. This was a most outrageous proceeding, outrageous to the colored men who were thus deprived of their liberty, outrageous also to the owners of the vessels who were deprived of the service of their employés. Of what avail was the constitutional guaranty that "the citizens of each State shall be entitled to all the privileges and immunities of citizens in the several States, many men began to question? The South was evidently disposed to support only that portion of the national compact which sustained the slave system, all the rest upon occasion it trampled on and nullified. This lesson was enforced anew upon

Massachusetts by the affair of her colored seamen. Unable to obtain redress of the wrong done her citizens, the State appointed agents to go to Charleston and New Orleans and test the constitutionality of the State laws under which the local authorities had acted. But South Carolina and Louisiana, especially the former, to whom Samuel Hoar was accredited, evinced themselves quite equal to the exigency to which the presence of the Massachusetts agents gave rise. To cut a long story short, these gentlemen, honored citizens of a sister State, and covered with the ægis of the Constitution, found that they could make no success of the business which they had in hand, found indeed that as soon as that business was made public that they stood in imminent peril of their lives. Whereupon, wisely conceiving discretion to be the better part of valor, they beat a hasty retreat back to their native air. The Massachusetts agents were driven out of Charleston and New Orleans. Where was the sacred and glorious union between Massachusetts and South Carolina and Louisiana that such things were possible—were constantly occurring? The circumstance made a strong impression on the State whose rights were thus grossly violated. It helped to convert Massachusetts to its later opposition to slavery, and to make its public sentiment more tolerant of the Garrisonian opposition to the covenant with death and the agreement with hell.

To the agitation growing out of the scheme for the annexation of Texas must, however, be ascribed the premium among all the anti-Union working facts and forces of the first few years after Garrison and his coadjutors had raised the cry of "No union with slaveholders." This agitation renewed the intensity and sectionalism of the then almost forgotten struggle over the admission of Missouri nearly a quarter of a century before, and which was concluded by the Missouri compromise. This settlement was at the time considered quite satisfactory to the South. But Calhoun took an altogether different view of the matter twenty years later. The arrangement by which the South was excluded from the upper portion of the Louisiana Territory he came to regard as a cardinal blunder on the part of his section. The fact is that within those two decades the slave-holding had been completely outstripped by the non-slave-holding States in wealth, population, and social growth. The latter had obtained over the former States an indisputable supremacy in those respects. Would not the political balance settle also in the natural order of things in the Northern half of the Union unless it could be kept where it then was to the south of Mason and Dixon's line by an artificial political make-weight. This artificial political make-weight was nothing less than the acquisition of new slave territory to supply the demand for new slave States. Texas, with the territorial dimensions of an empire, answered the agrarian needs of the slave system. And the South, under the leadership of Calhoun, determined to make good their fancied loss in the settlement of the Missouri controversy by annexing Texas.

But all the smouldering dread of slave domination, all the passionate opposition to the extension of slavery, to the acquisition of new slave territory and the admission of new slave States, awoke hotly in the heart of the North. "No more slave territory."

"No more slave States," resounded during this crisis, through the free States. "Texas or disunion," was the counter cry which reverberated through the slave States. Even Dr. Channing, who had no love for Garrison or his anti-slavery ultraism, was so wrought upon by the scheme for the annexation of Texas as to profess his preference for the dissolution of the Union, "rather than receive Texas into the Confederacy." "This measure, besides entailing on us evils of all sorts," the doctor boldly pointed out, "would have for its chief end to bring the whole country under the slave-power, to make the general Government the agent of slavery; and this we are bound to resist at all hazards. The free States should declare that the very act of admitting Texas will be construed as a dissolution of the Union."

The Northern blood was at fever heat, and an unwonted defiance of consequences, a fierce contempt of ancient political bugaboos marked the utterances of men erstwhile timid of speech upon all questions relating to slavery. In the anti-Texas convention held in Faneuil Hall January 29, 1845, all this timidity disappeared in the presence of the new peril. It was not a convention of Abolitionists, although Garrison was a member, but of politicians, mostly of the Whig party. "The anti-slavery spirit of the convention," wrote Edmund Quincy to R. D. Webb, "was surprising. The address and the speeches of the gentlemen, not Abolitionists, were such as caused Garrison to be mobbed ten years ago, and such as we thought thorough three or four years ago. There were no qualifications, or excuses, or *twaddle*."

Garrison flung himself into the anti-Texas movement with all his customary force and fire. Elected a delegate to the Faneuil Hall Convention by the influence of Francis Jackson, he took a leading part in its proceedings, "created the most stir in the whole matter," Wendell Phillips thought. Charles Sumner, who heard him speak for the first time, was struck with his "natural eloquence," and described his words as falling "in fiery rain." Again at a mass meeting for Middlesex County, held at Concord, to consider the aggressions of the slave-power, did the words of the pioneer fall "in fiery rain." Apprehensive that the performance of Massachusetts, when the emergency arose, would fall far short of her protestations, he exclaimed, "I have nothing to say, sir, nothing. I am tired of words, tired of hearing strong things said, where there is no heart to carry them out. When we are prepared to state the whole truth, and die for it, if necessary—when, like our fathers, we are prepared to take our ground, and not shrink from it, counting not our lives dear unto us—when we are prepared to let all earthly hopes go back to the board—*then* let us say so ; *till* then, the less we say the better, in such an emergency as this. 'But who are we, will men ask.' that talk of such things ? 'Are we enough to make a revolution?' No, sir ; but we are enough to *begin* one, and, once begun, it never can be turned back. I am for revolution were I utterly alone. I am there because I *must* be there. I *must* cleave to the right. I cannot choose but obey the voice of God.

". . . Do not tell me of our past Union, and for how many years we have been one. We were only one while we were ready to hunt, shoot down, and deliver up the slave, and allow the slave-power to form an oligarchy on the floor of Congress! The moment we say no to this, the Union ceases—the Government falls."

The Texan struggle terminated in the usual way, in the triumph of the slave-power. Texas was annexed and admitted into the sisterhood of States, giving to the Southern section increased slave representation in both branches of Congress, and thereby aiding to fasten, what at the moment appeared to be its permanent domination in national affairs. As Garrison had apprehended, the performance of the North fell far short of its protestations when the crisis came. It swallowed all its brave words, and collapsed into feeble and disheartened submission to its jubilant and hitherto invincible antagonist. The whole North except the small and irrepressible band of Garrisonian Abolitionists were cast down by the revulsive wave of this disastrous event. Writing to his friend Webb, Garrison discourses thus upon the great defeat: "Apparently the slave-holding power has never been so strong, has never seemed to be so invincible, has never held such complete mastery over the whole, has never so sucessfully hurled defiance at the Eternal and Just One, as at the present time; and yet never has it in reality been so weak, never has it had so many uncompromising assailants, never has it been so filled with doubt and consternation, never has it been so near its downfall, as at this moment. Upon the face of it, this statement looks absurdly paradoxical; but it is true, nevertheless. We are groping in thick darkness; but it is that darkest hour which is said to precede the dawn of day."

CHAPTER XVII.

AS IN A LOOKING GLASS.

GARRISON was the most dogmatic, as he was the most earnest of men. It was almost next to impossible for him to understand that his way was not the only way to attain a given end. A position reached by him, he was curiously apt to look upon as a sort of *ultima thule* of human endeavor in that direction of the moral universe. And, notwithstanding instances of honest self-depreciation, there, nevertheless, hung around his personality an air and assumption of moral infallibility, as a reformer. His was not a tolerant mind. Differences with him he was prone to treat as gross departures from principle,.as evidences of faithlessness to freedom. He fell upon the men who did not see eye to eye with him with tomahawk and scalping knife. He was strangely deficient in a sense of proportion in such matters. His terrible severities of speech, he visited upon the slave-power and the Liberty party alike. And although a non-resistent, in that he eschewed the use of physical force, yet there never was born among the sons of men a more militant soul in the use of moral force, in the quickness with which he would whip out the rapiers, or hurl the bolts and bombs of his mother tongue at opponents. The pioneer must have been an unconscious believer in the annihilation of the wicked, as he must have been an unconscious believer in the wickedness of all opposition to his idea of right and duty. This, of course, must be taken only as a broad description of the reformer's character. He was a man, one of the grandest America has given to the world, but still a man with his tendon of Achilles, like the rest of his kind.

His narrow intolerance of the idea of anti-slavery political action, and his fierce and unjust censure of the champions of that idea, well illustrate the trait in point. Birney and Whittier, and Wright and Gerrit Smith, and Joshua Leavitt, he apparently quite forgot, were actuated by motives singularly noble, were in their way as true to their convictions as he was to his. No, there was but one right way, and in that way stood the feet of the pioneer. His way led directly, unerringly, to the land of freedom. All other ways, and especially the Liberty party way, twisted, doubled upon themselves, branched into labyrinths of folly and self-seeking. "Ho! all ye that desire the freedom of the slave, who would labor for liberty, follow me and I will show you the only true way," was the tone which the editor of the *Liberator* held to men, who were battering with might and main to breach the walls of the Southern Bastile. They were plainly not against the slave, although opposed to Mr. Garrison, narrowly, unjustly opposed to him, without doubt, but working strenuously according to their lights for the destruction of a common enemy and tyrant. This was the test, which Garrison should have taken as conclusive. The leaders of the Liberty party, though personally opposed to him and to his line of action, were, nevertheless, friends of the slaves, and ought to have been so accounted and treated by the man who more than any other was devoted to the abolition of slavery.

But the whole mental and moral frame of the man precluded such liberality of treatment of opponents. They had rejected his way, which was the only true way, and were, therefore, anathema maranatha. When a moral idea which has been the subject of wide-spread agitation, and has thereby gained a numerous following, reaches out, as reach out it must, sooner or later, for incorporation into law, it will, in a republic like ours, do so naturally and necessarily through political action—along the lines of an organized party movement. The Liberty party formation was the product of this strong tendency in America. Premature it possibly was, but none the less perfectly natural. Now every political party, that is worthy of the name, is a compound rather than a simple fact, consisteth of a bundle of ideas rather than a single idea. Parties depend upon the people for success, upon the people not of one interest but of many interests and of diversities of views upon public questions. One plank is not broad enough to accommodate their differences and multiplicity of desires. There must be a platform built of many planks to support the number of votes requisite to victory at the polls. There will always be one idea or interest of the many ideas or interests, that will dominate the organization, be erected into a paramount issue upon which the party throws itself upon the country, but the secondary ideas or interests must be there all the same to give strength and support to the main idea and interest.

Besides this peculiarity in the composition of the great political parties in America, there is another not less distinct and marked, and that is the Constitutional limitations of the Federal political power. Every party which looks for ultimate success at the polls must observe strictly these limitations in its aims and issues. Accordingly when the moral movement against slavery sought a political expression of the idea of Abolition it was constrained within the metes and bounds set up by the National Constitution. Slavery within the States lay outside of the political boundaries of the general Government. Slavery within the States, therefore, the more sagacious of the Liberty party leaders placed not among its bundle of ideas, into its platform of national issues. But it was otherwise with slavery in the District of Columbia, in the national territories, under the national flag on the high seas, for it lay within the constitutional reach of the federal political power, and its abolition was demanded in the Third party platform. These leaders were confident that the existence of slavery depended upon its connection with the National Government. Their aim was to destroy the evil by cutting this connection through which it drew its blood and nerve supplies. They planted themselves upon the anti-slavery character of the Constitution, believing that it "does not sanction nor nationalize slavery but condemns and localizes it."

This last position of the Liberty party leaders struck Garrison as a kind of mental and moral enormity. At it and its authors, the anti-slavery Jupiter, launched his bolts, fast and furious. Here is a specimen of his chain lightning: "We have a very poor opinion of the intelligence of any man, and very great distrust of his candor or honesty, who tries to make it appear that no pro-slavery compromise was made between the North and the South, at the adoption of the Constitution. We cherish feelings of profound contempt for the quibbling spirit of criticism which is endeavoring to explain away the meaning of language, the design of which as a matter of practice, and the adoption of which as a matter of bargain, were intelligently and clearly understood by the contracting parties. The truth is the misnamed 'Liberty party' is under the control of as ambitious, unprincipled, and crafty leaders as is either the Whig or Democratic party; and no other proof of this assertion is needed than their unblushing denial of the great object of the national compact, namely, union at the sacrifice of the colored population of the United States. Their new interpretations of the Constitution are a bold rejection of the facts of history, and a gross insult to the intelligence of the age, and certainly never can be carried into effect without dissolving the Union by provoking a civil war." All the same, the pioneer to the contrary notwithstanding, many of these very Liberty party leaders were men of the most undoubted candor and honesty and of extraordinary intelligence.

Garrison was never able to see the Liberty party, and for that matter Wendell Phillips, Edmund Quincy, and others of the old organization leaders could not either, except through the darkened glass of personal antagonisms growing out of the schism of 1840. It was always, under all circumstances, to borrow a phrase of Phillips, "Our old enemy, Liberty party." And, as Quincy naïvely confesses in an article in the *Liberator* pointing out the reasons why Abolitionists should give to the Free-soil party incidenfal aid and comfort, which were forbidden to their "old enemy, Liberty party," the significant and amusing fact that the latter was "officered by deserters." Ay, there was indeed the rub! The military principle of the great leader forbade him to recognize deserters as allies. Discipline must be maintained, and so he proceeded to maintain the anti-slavery discipline of his army by keeping up a constant fusillade into the ranks of the deserter band, who, in turn, were every whit as blinded by the old quarrel and separation, and who slyly cherished the modest conviction that, when they seceded, the salt of old organization lost its savor, and was thenceforth fit only to be trampled under the Liberty party's feet. Without doubt, those old Abolitionists and Liberty party people belonged to the category of "humans."

The scales of the old grudge dropped from Garrison's eyes directly the Free-Soil party loomed upon the political horizon. He recognized at once that, if it was not against the slave, it was for the slave; apprehended clearly that, in so far as the new party, which, by the way, was only the second stage in the development of the central idea of his old enemy, Liberty party, as the then future Republican party was to be its third and final expression, apprehended clearly I say that, in so far as the new party resisted the aggressions and pretensions of the slave-power, it was fighting for Abolition—was an ally of Abolitionism.

In the summer of 1848, from Northampton, whither

he had gone to take the water cure, Garrison counseled Quincy, who was filling the editorial chair, in the interim, at the *Liberator* office, in this sage fashion: "As for the Free-Soil movement, I feel that great care is demanded of us disunionists, both in the *Standard* and the *Liberator*, in giving credit to whom credit is due, and yet in no case even seeming to be satisfied with it." In the winter of 1848 in a letter to Samuel May, Jr., he is more explicit on this head. "As for the Free-Soil movement," he observes, "I am for hailing it as a cheering sign of the times, and an unmistakble proof of the progress we have made, under God, in changing public sentiment. Those who have left the Whig and Democratic parties for conscience's sake, and joined the movement, deserve our commendation and sympathy; at the same time, it is our duty to show them, and all others, that there is a higher position to be attained by them or they will have the blood of the slave staining their garments. This can be done charitably yet faithfully. On the two old parties, especially the Whig-Taylor party, I would expend—*pro tempore*, at least—our heaviest ammunition." This is as it should be, the tone of wise and vigilant leadership, the application of the true test to the circumstances, viz., for freedom if against slavery; not to be satisfied, to be sure, with any thing less than the whole but disposed to give credit to whom it was due, whether much or little. Pity that the pioneer could not have placed himself in this just and discriminating point of view in respect of his old enemy, Liberty party, praising in it what he found praiseworthy, while blaming it for what he felt was blameworthy. But perfection weak human nature doth not attain to in this terrestrial garden of the passions, and so very likely the magnanimity which we have desired of Garrison is not for that garden to grow but another and a heavenly.

Garrison ill brooked opposition, came it from friends or foes. He was so confident in his own positions that he could not but distrust their opposites. Of course, if his were right, and of that doubt in his mind there was apparently none, then the positions of all others had to be wrong. This masterful quality of the man was constantly betrayed in the acts of his life and felt by his closest friends and associates in the anti-slavery movement. Quincy, writing to Richard Webb, narrates how, at the annual meeting of the American Anti-Slavery Society in 1843, Garrison was for removing it to Boston, but that he and Wendell Phillips were for keeping it where it then was in New York, giving at the same time sundry good and sufficient reasons for the faith that was in them, and how, thereupon, "Garrison dilated his nostrils like a war-horse, and snuffed indignation at us." "If the Boston friends were unwilling to take the trouble and responsibility," were the petulant, accusative words put by Quincy into his chief's mouth on the occasion, "then there was nothing more to be said; we must try to get along as well as we could in the old way." And how they disclaimed "any unwillingness to take trouble and responsibility," while affirming "the necessity of their acting on their own idea."

Another characteristic of the pioneer is touched upon by the same writer in a relation which he was making to Webb of Garrison's election to the presidency of the parent society. Says Quincy: "Garrison makes an excellent president at a public meeting where the order of speakers is in some measure arranged, as he has great felicity in introducing and interlocuting remarks; but at a meeting for debate he does not answer so well, as he is rather too apt, with all the innocence and simplicity in the world, to do all the talking himself."

The same friendly critic has left his judgment of other traits of the leader, traits not so much of the man as of the editor. It is delivered in a private letter of Quincy to Garrison on resigning the temporary editorship of the *Liberator* to "its legitimate possessor," who had been for several months health-hunting at Northampton in the beautiful Connecticut Valley. Quincy made bold to beard the Abolition lion in his lair, and twist his tail in an extremely lively manner. "Now, my dear friend," wrote the disciple to the master, "you must know that to the microscopic eyes of its friends, as well as to the telescopic eyes of its enemies, *the Liberator has faults;* these they keep to themselves as much as they honestly may, but they are not the less sensible of them, and are all the more desirous to see them immediately abolished. Luckily, they are not faults of principle—neither moral nor intellectual deficiencies—but faults the cure of which rests solely with yourself.

"I hardly know how to tell you what the faults are that we find with it, lest you should think them none at all, or else unavoidable. But no matter, of that you must be the judge; we only ask you to listen to our opinion. We think the paper often bears the mark of haste and carelessness in its getting up;

that the matter seems to be hastily selected and put in *higgledy-piggledy*, without any very apparent reason why it should be in at all, or why it should be in the place where it is. I suppose this is often caused by your selecting articles with a view to connect remarks of your own with them, which afterward in your haste you omit. Then we complain that each paper is not so nearly a complete work in itself as it might be made, but that things are often left at loose ends, and important matters broken off in the middle. I assure you, that Brother Harriman is not the only one of the friends of the *Liberator* who grieves over your 'more anon' and 'more next week'—which 'anon' and 'next week' never arrive. . . .

"Then we complain that your editorials are too often wanting, or else such, from apparent haste, as those who love your fame cannot wish to see; that important topics, which you feel to be such, are too often either entirely passed over or very cursorily treated, and important moments like the present neglected. . . .

"We have our suspicions, too, that good friends have been disaffected by the neglect of their communications; but of this we can only speak by conjecture. In short, it appears to those who are your warmest friends and the stanchest supporters of the paper, that you might make the *Liberator* a more powerful and useful instrumentality than it is, powerful and useful as it is, by additional exertions on your part. It is very unpleasant to hear invidious comparisons drawn between the *Liberator* and *Emancipator* with regard to the manner of getting it up, and to have not to deny but to excuse them—and we knowing all the time that you have all the tact and technical talent for getting up a good newspaper that Leavitt has, with as much more, intellectual ability as you have more moral honesty, and only wanting some of his (pardon me) industry, application, and method."

Garrison, to his honor, did not allow the exceeding candor of his mentor to disturb their friendship. The pioneer was not wholly without defence to the impeachment. He might have pleaded ill health, of which he had had *quantum suf.* since 1836 for himself and family. He might have pleaded also the dissipation of too much of his energies in consequence of more or less pecuniary embarrassments from which he was never wholly freed ; but, above all, he might have pleaded his increasing activity as an anti-slavery lecturer. His contributions to the movement against slavery were of a notable character in this direction, both in respect of quantity and quality. He was not alone the editor of the *Liberator*, he was unquestionably besides one of the most effective and interesting of the anti-slavery speakers—indeed in the judgment of so competent an authority as James Russell Lowell, he was regarded as the most effective of the anti-slavery speakers. Still, after all is placed to his credit that can possibly be, Quincy's complaints would be supported by an altogether too solid basis of fact. The pioneer was much given to procrastination. What was not urgent he was strongly tempted to put off for a more convenient time. His work accumulated. He labored hard and he accomplished much, but because of this habit of postponing for to-morrow what need not be done to-day, he was necessarily forced to leave undone many things which he ought to have done and which he might have accomplished had he been given to putting off for to-morrow nothing which might be finished to-day.

The pioneer was a man of sorrows and acquainted with grief, but never was he wholly cast down by his misfortunes. His cheerful and bouyant spirit kept him afloat above his sorrows, above his griefs. The organ of mirthfulness in him was very large. He was an optimist in the best sense of that word, viz., that all things work together for good to them that love goodness. In the darkest moments which the Abolition cause encountered his own countenance was full of light, his own heart pierced through the gloom and communicated its glow to those about him, his own voice rang bugle-like through reverse and disaster.

In his family the reformer was seen at his best. His wife was his friend and equal, his children his playfellows and companions. The dust of the great conflict he never carried with him into his home to choke the love which burned ever brightly on its hearth and in the hearts which it contained. What he professed in the *Liberator*, what he preached in the world, of non-resistance, woman's rights, perfectionism, he practiced in his home, he embodied as father, and husband, and host. Never lived reformer who more completely realized his own ideals to those nearest and dearest to him than William Lloyd Garrison.

He had seven children, five boys and two girls. The last, Francis Jackson, was born to him in the year 1848. Two of them died in childhood, a boy and a girl. The loss of the boy, whom the father had "named admiringly, gratefully, reverently," Charles Follen, was a terrible blow to the reformer, and a life-long grief to the mother. He seemed to have been a singularly beautiful, winning, and affectionate little man and to have inspired sweet hopes of future "usefulness and excellence" in the breasts of his parents. "He seemed born to take a century on his shoulders, without stooping; his eyes were large, lustrous, and charged with electric light; his voice was clear as a bugle, melodious, and ever ringing in our ears, from the dawn of day to the ushering in of night, so that since it has been stilled, our dwelling has seemed to be almost without an occupant," lamented the stricken father to Elizabeth Pease, of Darlington, England.

"Death itself to me is not terrible, is not repulsive," poured the heartbroken pioneer into the ears of his English friend, "is not to be deplored. I see in it as clear an evidence of Divine wisdom and beneficence as I do in the birth of a child, in the works of creation, in all the arrangements and operations of nature. I neither fear nor regret its power. I neither expect nor supplicate to be exempted from its legitimate action. It is not to be chronicled among calamities; it is not to be styled "a mysterious dispensation of Divine Providence"; it is scarcely rational to talk of being resigned to it. For what is more rational, what more universal, what more impartial, what more serviceable, what more desirable, in God's own time, hastened neither by our ignorance or folly? . . .

"When, therefore, my dear friend, I tell you that the loss of my dear boy has overwhelmed me with sadness, has affected my peace by day and my repose by night, has been a staggering blow, from the shock of which I find it very difficult to recover, you will not understand me as referring to anything pertaining to another state of existence, or as gloomily affected by a change inevitable to all; far from it. Where the cherished one who has been snatched from us is, what is his situation, or what his employment, I know not, of course; and it gives me no anxiety whatever. Until I join him at least my responsibility to him as his guardian and protector has ceased; he does not need my aid, he cannot be benefited by my counsel. That he will still be kindly cared for by Him who numbers the very hairs of our heads, and without whose notice a sparrow cannot fall to the ground; that he is still living, having thrown aside his mortal drapery, and occupying a higher sphere of existence, I do not entertain a doubt. My grief arises mainly from the conviction that his death was premature; that he was actually defrauded of his life through unskillful treatment; that he might have been saved, if we had not been so unfortunately situated at that time. This to be sure, is not certain; and not being certain, it is only an ingredient of consolation that we find in our cup of bitterness."

The pioneer was one of the most generous of givers. Poor indeed he was, much beyond the common allotment of men of his intelligence and abilities, but he was never too indigent to answer the appeals of poverty. If the asker's needs were greater than his own he divided with him the little which he had. To his home all sorts of people were attracted, Abolitionists, peace men, temperance reformers, perfectionists, homœopathists, hydropathists, mesmerists, spiritualists, Grahamites, clairvoyants, whom he received with unfailing hospitality, giving welcome and sympathy to the new ideas, food and shelter for the material sustenance of the fleshly vehicles of the new ideas. He evidently was strongly of the opinion that there are "more things in heaven and earth than are dreamt of" in the philosophy of any particular period in the intellectual development of man. No age knows it all. It was almost a lo, here, and a lo, there, with him, so large was his bump of wonder, so unlimited was his appetite for the incredible and the improbable in the domain of human knowledge and speculation. Great was the man's faith, great was his hope, great was his charity.

He was one of the most observant of men in all matters affecting the rights of others; he was one of the least observant in all matters appertaining to himself. With a decided taste for dress, yet his actual knowledge of the kind of clothes worn by him from day to day was amusingly inexact, as the following incident shows: Before wearing out an only pair of trousers, the pioneer had indulged in the unusual luxury of a new pair. But as there was still considerable service to be got out of the old pair, he, like a prudent man, laid aside the new ones for future use. His wife, however, who managed all this part of the domestic business, determined, without consulting him, the morning when the new trousers should be donned. She made the necessary changes when her lord was in bed, putting the new in the place of the old. Garrison wore for several days the new trousers, thinking all the time that they were his old ones until his illusions in this regard were dispelled by an incident which cost him the former. Some poor wretch of a tramp, knocking in an evil hour at the pioneer's door and asking for clothes, decided the magnificent possessor of two pairs of trousers, to don his new ones and to pass the old ones on to the tramp. But when he communicated the transaction to his wife, she hoped, with a good deal of emphasis, that he had not given away the pair of breeches which he was wearing, for if he had she would beg to inform him that he had given away his best ones! But the pioneer's splendid indifference to *meum* and *tuum* where his own possessions were concerned was equal to the occasion. He got his compensation in the thought that his loss was another's gain. That, indeed, was not to be accounted loss which had gone to a brother-man whose needs were greater than his own.

CHAPTER XVIII.

THE TURNING OF A LONG LANE.

GARRISON'S forecast of the future, directly after the annexation of Texas, proved singularly correct. Never, as at that moment, had the slave-power seemed so secure in its ascendency, yet never, at any previous period, was it so near its downfall. Freedom had reached that darkest hour just before dawn; and this, events were speedily to make clear. If the South could have trammeled up the consequences of annexation, secure, indeed, for a season, would it have held its political supremacy in America? But omnipotent as was the slave-power in the Government, it was not equal to this labor. In the great game, in which Texas was the stakes, Fate had, unawares, slipped into the seat between the gamesters with hands full of loaded dice. At the first throw the South got Texas, at the second the war with Mexico fell out, and at the third new national territory lay piled upon the boards.

Calhoun, the arch-annexationist, struggled desperately to avert the war. He saw as no other Southern leader saw its tremendous significance in the conflict between the two halves of the Union for the political balance. The admission of Texas had made an adjustment of this balance in favor of the South. Calhoun's plan was to conciliate Mexico, to sweep with our diplomatic broom the gathering war-clouds from the national firmament. War, he knew, would imperil the freshly fortified position of his section—war which meant at its close the acquisition of new national territory, with which the North would insist upon retrieving its reverse in the controversy over Texas. War, therefore, the great nullifier resolved against. He cried halt to his army, but the army heard not his voice, heeded not his orders, in the wild uproar and clamor which arose at the sight of helpless Mexico, and the temptation of adding fresh slave soil to the United States South, through her spoliation. Calhoun confessed that, with the breaking out of hostilities between the two republics an impenetrable curtain had shut from his eyes the future. The great plot for maintaining the political domination of the South had miscarried. New national territory had become inevitable with the firing of the first gun. Seeing this, Calhoun endeavored to postpone the evil day for the South by proposing a military policy of "masterly inactivity" whereby time might be gained for his side to prepare to meet the blow when it fell. But his "masterly inactivity" policy was swept aside by the momentum of the national passion which the war had aroused.

California and New Mexico became the strategic points of the slavery struggle at the close of the war. To open both to the immigration of slave-labor was thenceforth the grand design of the South. Over Oregon occurred a fierce preliminary trial of strength between the sections. The South was thrown in the contest, and the anti-slavery principle of the Ordinance of 1787 applied to the Territory. Calhoun, who was apparently of the mind that as Oregon went so would go California and New Mexico, was violently agitated by this reverse. "The great strife between the North and the South is ended," he passionately declared. Immediately the charge was made and widely circulated through the slave States that the stronger was oppressing the weaker section, wresting from it its just share in the common fruits of common victories. For had not California and New Mexico been won by the bravery and blood of the South as of the North, and how then was the North to deprive the South of its joint ownership of them without destroying the federal equality of the two halves of the Union? What was it but to subvert the Union existing among the States?

Disunion sentiment was thenceforth ladled out to the slave States in increasing quantities. The turning of the long lane in the domination of the slave-power was visibly near. With Garrison at one end and Calhoun at the other the work of dissolution advanced apace. The latter announced, in 1848, that the separation of the two sections was complete. Ten years before, Garrison had made proclamation that the Union, though not in form, was, nevertheless, in fact dissolved. And possibly they were right. The line of cleavage had at the date of Calhoun's announcement passed entirely through the grand strata of national life, industrial, moral, political, and religious. There remained indeed but a single bond of connection between the slave-holding and the non-slave-holding States, viz., fealty to party. But in 1848 not even this slender link was intact.

The anti-slavery uprising was a fast growing factor

in the politics of the free States. This was evinced by the aggressiveness of anti-slavery legislation, the repeal of slave sojournment laws, the enactment of personal liberty laws, the increasing preference manifested by Whig and by Democratic electors for anti-slavery Whig, and anti-slavery Democratic leaders. Seward and Chase, and Hale and Hamlin, Thaddeus Stevens and Joshua R. Giddings, were all in Congress in 1849. A revolution was working in the North; a revolution was working in the South. New and bolder spirits were rising to leadership in both sections. On the Southern stage were Jefferson Davis, Barnwell Rhett, David Atchison, Howell Cobb, Robert Toombs, and James M. Mason. The outlook was portentous, tempestuous.

The tide of excitement culuminated in the crisis of 1850. The extraordinary activity of the underground railroad system, and its failure to open the national Territories to slave immigration had transported the South to the verge of disunion. California, fought over by the two foes, was in the act of withdrawing herself from the field of contention to a position of independent Statehood. It was her rap for admission into the Union as a free State which precipitated upon the country the last of the compromises between freedom and slavery. It sounded the opening of the final act of Southern domination in the republic.

The compromise of 1850, a series of five acts, three of which it took to conciliate the South, while two were considered sufficient to satisfy the North, was, after prolonged and stormy debate, adopted to save Webster's glorious Union. These five acts were, in the agonized accents of Clay, to heal "the five fire-gaping wounds" of the country. But the wounds were immedicable, as events were soon to prove. Besides, two at least of the remedies failed to operate as emollients. They irritated and inflamed the national ulcers and provoked fresh paroxysms of the disease. The admission of California as a free State was a sort of perpetual *memento mori* to the slave-power. It hung forever over the South the Damoclean blade of Northern political ascendency in the Union. The fugitive slave law on the other hand produced results undreamt of by its authors. Who would have ventured to predict the spontaneous, irresistible insurrection of the humane forces and passions of the North which broke out on the passage of the infamous bill? Who could have foretold the moral and political consequences of its execution, for instance, in Boston, which fifteen years before had mobbed anti-slavery women and dragged Garrison through its streets? The moral indignation aroused by the law in Massachusetts swept Webster and the Whigs from power, carried Sumner to the Senate and crowned Liberty on Beacon Hill. It worked a revolution in Massachusetts, it wrought changes of the greatest magnitude in the free States.

From this time the reign of discord became universal. The conflict between the sections increased in virulence. At the door of every man sat the fierce figure of strife. It fulmined from the pulpit and frowned from the pews. The platforms of the free States resounded with the thunder of tongues. The press exploded with the hot passions of the hour. Parties warred against each other. Factions arose within parties and fought among themselves with no less bitterness. Wrath is infectious and the wrathful temper of the nation became epidemic. The Ishmaelitish impulse to strike something or someone, was irresistible. The bonds which had bound men to one another seemed everywhere loosening, and people in masses were slipping away from old to enter into new combinations of political activity. It was a period of tumultuous transition and confusion. The times were topsy-turvy and old Night and Chaos were the angels who sat by the bubbling abysses of the revolution.

In the midst of this universal and violent agitation of the public mind the old dread of disunion returned to torment the American *bourgeoisie*, who through their presses, especially those of the metropolis of the Union, turned fiercely upon the Abolitionists. While the compromise measures were the subject of excited debate before Congress, the anniversary meeting of the American Anti-Slavery Society fell due. But the New York journals, the *Herald* in particular, had no mind to allow the meeting to take place without renewing the reign of terror of fifteen years before. Garrison was depicted as worse than Robespierre, with an insatiable appetite for the destruction of established institutions, both human and divine. The dissolution of the Union, the "overthrow of the churches, the Sabbath, and the Bible," all were required to glut his malevolent passion. "Will the men of sense allow meetings to be held in this city which are calculated to make our country the arena of blood and murder," roared the *Herald*, "and render our city an object of horror to the whole South? . . . Public opinion should be regulated. These Abolitionists should not be allowed to misrepresent New York." In order to suppress the Abolitionists that paper did not blink at any means, however extreme or revolutionary, but declared boldly in favor of throttling free discussion. "When free discussion does not promote the public good," argued the editor, "it has no more right to exist than a bad government that is dangerous and oppressive to the common weal. It should be overthrown." The mob thus invoked came forward on the opening of the convention to overthrow free discussion.

The storm which the New York press was at so much labor to brew, Garrison did not doubt would break over the convention. He went to it in a truly apostolic spirit of self-sacrifice. "Not knowing the things that shall befall me there, saving that bonds and afflictions abide with me in every city," he wrote his wife an hour before the commencement of the convention. His prevision of violence was quickly fulfilled. He had called Francis Jackson to the chair during the delivery of the opening speech which fell to the pioneer to make as the president of the society. His subject was the Religion of the Country, to which he was paying his respects in genuine Garrisonian fashion. Belief in Jesus in the United States had no vital influence on conduct or character. The chief religious denominations were in practice pro-slavery, they had uttered no protest against the national sin. There was the Roman Catholic Church whose "priests and members held slaves without incurring the rebuke of the Church." At this point the orator was interrupted by one of those monstrous products of the

was finally quieted by the offer of Francis Jackson to give him a hearing as soon as Mr. Garrison had brought his address to an end.

Rev. W. H. Furness, of Philadelphia, who was a member of the convention and also one of the speakers, has preserved for us the contrasts of the occasion. "The close of Mr. Garrison's address," says he, "brought down Rynders again, who vociferated and harangued at one time on the platform, and then pushing down into the aisles, like a madman followed by his keepers. Through the whole, nothing could be more patient and serene than the bearing of Mr. Garrison. I have always revered Mr. Garrison for his devoted, uncompromising fidelity to his great cause. To-day I was touched to the heart by his calm and gentle manners. There was no agitation, no scorn, no heat, but the quietness of a man engaged in simple duties."

The madman and his keepers were quite vanquished on the first day of the convention by the wit, repartee, and eloquence of Frederick Douglass, Dr. Furness, and Rev. Samuel R. Ward, whom Wendell Phillips described as so black that "when he shut his eyes you could not see him." But it was otherwise on the second day when public opinion was "regulated," and free discussion overthrown by Captain Rynders and his villainous gang, who were resolved, with the authors of the compromise, that the Union as it was should be preserved.

But, notwithstanding the high authority and achievements of this noble band of patriots and brothers, Garrison's detestation of the Union but increased, and his cry for its dissolution grew deeper and louder. And no wonder. For never had the compact between freedom and slavery seemed more hateful than after the passage of the Fugitive Slave Bill. The state of panic which it created among the colored people in the free States will form, if ever written down, one of the most heartrending chapters in human history. Hundreds and thousands fled from their homes into the jaws of a Canadian winter to escape the jaws of the slave-hounds, whose fierce baying began presently to fill the land from Massachusetts to Ohio. It made no difference whether these miserable people had been always free or were fugitives from slavery, the terror spread among them all the same. The aged and the young turned their backs upon their homes and hurried precipitately into a strange country. Fathers with wives and children dependant upon them for their daily bread, were forced by the dread of being captured and returned to bondage to abandon their homes and loved ones, sometimes without so much as a touch of their hands or a tone of their voices in token of farewell. Perhaps on his way to work in the morning some husband or son has caught a glimpse among the faces on the street of one face, the remembrance of which to the day of death, he can never lose, a face he had known in some far away Southern town or plantation, and with which are connected in the poor fellow's brain the most frightful sufferings and associations. Crazed at the sight, with no thought of home, of the labors which are awaiting him, oblivious of everything but the abject terror which has suddenly taken possession of him, he hastens away to hide and fly, fly and hide, until he reaches a land where slave-hounds enter not, and panting fugitives find freedom. Wendell Phillips tells of an old woman of seventy who asked his advice about flying, though originally free, and fearful only of being caught up by mistake. The distress everywhere was awful, the excitement indescribable. From Boston alone in the brief space of three weeks after the rescue of Shadrach, nearly a hundred of these panic-stricken creatures had fled. The whole number escaping into Canada Charles Sumner placed as high as six thousand souls. But in addition to this large band of fugitives, others emigrated to the interior of New England away from the seaboard centers of trade and commerce where the men-hunters abounded.

The excitement and the perils of this period were not confined to the colored people. Their white friends shared both with them. We are indebted to Mr. Phillips for the following graphic account of these excitements and perils in Boston in March, 1851. He has been describing the situation in the city, in respect of the execution of the infamous law, to Elizabeth Pease, and goes on thus: "I need not enlarge on this; but the long evening sessions—debates about secret escapes—plans to evade where we can't resist—the door watched that no spy may enter—the whispering consultations of the morning—some putting property out of their hands, planning to incur penalties, and planning also that, in case of conviction, the Government may get nothing from them—the doing, and answering no questions—intimates forbearing to ask the knowledge which it may be dangerous to have—all remind one of those foreign scenes which have hitherto been known to us, transatlantic republicans, only in books."

On the passage of the Black Bill, as the Abolitionists stigmatised the law, it was not believed that the moral sentiment of Boston would execute it, so horrified did the community seem. But it was soon apparent to the venerable Josiah Quincy that "The Boston of 1851 is not the Boston of 1775. Boston," the sage goes on to remark, "has now become a mere shop—a place for buying and selling goods; and, I suppose, also of *buying and selling men.*" The great idol of her shopkeepers, Daniel Webster, having striven mightily for the enactment of the hateful bill while Senator of the United States, had gone into Millard Fillmore's Cabinet, to labor yet more mightily for its enforcement. The rescue of Shadrach, which Mr. Secretary of State characterized "as a case of treason," set him to thundering for the Union as it was, and against the "fanatics," who were stirring up the people of the free States to resist the execution of the Fugitive Slave Law. But he was no longer "the God-like" Webster, for he appeared to the editor of the *Liberator* as "an ordinary-looking, poor, decrepit old man, whose limbs could scarce support him; lank with age; whose sluggish legs were somewhat concealed by an overshadowing abdomen; with head downcast and arms shriveled, and dangling almost helpless by his side, and incapable of being magnetized for the use of the orator." The voice and the front of "the God-like" had preceded the "poor decrepit old man" to the grave. Garrison dealt no less roughly and irreverently with another of the authors of the wicked law and another of the superannuated divinities of a shopkeeping North, Henry Clay. "HENRY CLAY, with one foot in the grave," exclaimed the reformer, "and just ready to have both body and soul cast into hell, as if eager to make his damnation doubly sure, rises in the United States Senate and proposes an inquiry into the expediency of passing yet another law, by which every one who shall dare peep or mutter against the execution of the Fugitive Slave Bill shall have his life crushed out."

In those trial times words from the mouth or the pen of Abolitionists had the force of deadly missiles. Incapacitated as Garrison was to resort to physical resistance to the Fugitive Slave Law by his non-resistant doctrine, it seemed that all the energy and belligerency of the man went into the most tremendous verbal expressions. They were like adamantine projectiles flung with the savage strength of a catapult against the walls of slavery. The big sinners, like Webster and Clay, he singled out for condign punishment, were objects of his utmost severities of speech. It was thus that he essayed to breach the iron dungeon in which the national iniquity had shut the national conscience. Saturated was the reformer's mind with the thought of the Bible, its solemn and awful imagery, its fiery and prophetic abhorrence and denunciations of national sins, all of which furnished him an unfailing magazine whence were drawn the bolts which he launched against the giant sin and the giant sinners of his time. And so Clay had not only "one foot in the grave," but was "just ready to have both body and soul cast into hell."

While physical resistance of the Slave Law was

wholly out of the question with Garrison, he, nevertheless, refused to condemn the men with whom it was otherwise. Here he was anything but a fanatic. All that he required was that each should be consistent with his principles. If those principles bade him resist the enforcement of the Black Bill, the apostle of non-resistance was sorry enough, but in this emergency, though he possessed the gentleness of the dove, he also practised the wisdom of the serpent. That truth moves with men upon lower as well as higher planes he well knew. It is always partial and many-colored, refracted as it is through the prisms of human passion and prejudice. If it appear unto some minds in the red bar of strife and blood, so be it. Each must follow the light which it is given him to discern, whether the blue of love or the red of war. Great coadjutors, like Wendell Phillips, Theodore Parker, and Dr. Henry I. Bowditch, were for forcible resistance to the execution of the law. So were the colored people. Preparations to this end went on vigorously in Boston under the direction of the Vigilance Committee. The Crafts escaped the clutches of the slave-hunters, so did Shadrach escape them, but Sims and Burns fell into them and were returned to bondage.

From this time on Wendell Phillips became in Boston and in the North more distinctly the leader of the Abolition sentiment. The period of pure moral agitation ended with the passage of the Fugitive Slave Law. That act opened a new era in the movement, an era in which non-resistance had no place, an era in which a resort to physical force in settlement of sectional differences, the whole trend of things were making inevitable. Fighting, the Anglo-Saxon method, as Theodore Parker characterized it, of making a final settlement of just such controversies as was the slavery question, was in the air, had become without any general consciousness of it at the time appearing in the popular mind, a foregone conclusion, from the moment that the South wrested from the National Government the right to defy and override the moral sentiment of free State communities. With this advance of the anti-slavery agitation a stage nearer the end, when fighting would supersede all other methods, the fighters gravitated naturally to the front of the conflict, and the apostle of non-resistance fell somewhat into the background of the great movement started by him.

Garrison had begun, indeed, to recognize that there were other ways besides his way of abolishing slavery—had begun to see that these with his led to Rome, to the ultimate extinction of the evil, to which anti-slavery unionists and disunionists were alike devoted. His innate sagacity and strong sense of justice lifted the reformer to larger toleration of mind. At a dinner given in Boston in May, 1853, by the Free Democracy to John P. Hale, he was not only present to testify his appreciation of the courage aud services of Mr. Hale to the common cause, but while there was able to speak thus tolerantly—tolerantly for him certainly—of a Union dear to the company about the table yet hateful beyond measure to himself: "Sir, you will pardon me," spoke the arch anti-slavery disunionist, "for the reference. I have heard something here about our Union, about the value of the Union, and the importance of preserving the Union. Gentlemen, if you have been so fortunate as to find a Union worth preserving, I heartily congratulate you. Cling to it with all your souls!" For himself, he has not been so fortunate. With a price set on his head in one of the Southern States, and outlawed in all of them, he begs to be pardoned if found lacking in loyalty to the existing Union, which to him, alas, : "is but another name for the iron reign of the slave-power. We have no common country as yet. God grant we may have. We shall have it when the jubilee comes—and not till then," he declared, mindful of the convictions of others, yet bravely true to his own. The seeds of liberty, of hatred of the slave-power, planted by Garrison were springing up in a splendid crop through the North. Much of the political anti-slavery of the times were the fruit of his endeavor. Wendell Phillips has pointed out how the Liberty party was benefited by the meetings and speeches of Garrisonian Abolitionists. What was true of the Liberty party was equally true of Free Soil and Free Democracy. Although the little band remained small, it was potent in swelling, year after year, the anti-slavery membership of all the parties, Whig and Democratic, as well as of those already mentioned. "Uncle Tom's Cabin" might fairly be classed among the large indirect results produced by Garrison. "But" as Phillips justly remarked, "'Uncle Tom' would never have been written had not Garrison developed the facts; and never would have succeeded had he not created readers and purchasers." Garrisonism had become an influence, a power that made for liberty and against slavery in the United States. It had become such also in Great Britain. George Thompson, writing the pioneer of the marvelous sale of "Uncle Tom" in England, and of the unprecedented demand for anti-slavery literature, traced their source to his friend: "Behold the fruit of your labors," he exclaimed, "and rejoice."

Mr. Garrison's pungent characterization of the "Union" at the dinner of the Free Democracy as "but another name for the iron reign of the slave-power," found almost instant illustration of its truth in the startling demand of that power for the repeal of the Missouri Compromise. In 1850 the South lost California, but it received at the time an advantage of far-reaching consequence, viz., the admission of the principle of federal non-intervention upon the subject of slavery in the national Territories into the bill organizing Territorial Governments for New Mexico and Utah. The train which was to blow down the slave wall of 1820 and open to slave immigration the northern half of the Louisiana Territory, was laid in the compromise measures of 1850.

Calhoun, strongly dissatisfied as he was with the Missouri settlement, recoiled from countenancing any agitation on the part of the South looking to its repeal on the ground that such action was calculated to disturb "the peace and harmony of the Union." But four years after the death of the great nullifier, his disciples and followers dared to consummate a crime, the consequences of which he shrank from inviting. The political conditions four years had indeed modified in one important particular at least. In Calhoun's lifetime, there was no Northern leader bold enough to undertake to engineer an act of abrogation through Congress. If the North were willing, possessed sufficient magnanimity, to surrender, in the interest of brotherly love between the sections, the benefits which inured to it under the Missouri Compromise, neither Calhoun nor the South would have declined the proffered sacrifice. The selection of Stephen A. Douglas in 1854 as the leader of the movement for repeal put a new face on the business, which was thereby made to appear to proceed from the free, not from the slave States. This was adroit, the fixing upon the losing section the initiative and the responsibility of the act of abrogation.

Besides this element, there was another not less specious which lent to the scheme an air of fairness, and that was the application to the Territories of the American principle of local self-government, in other words, the leaving to the people of the Territories the right to vote slavery up or vote it down, as they might elect. The game was a deep one, worthy of the machinations of its Northern and Southern authors. But, like other elaborate schemes of mice and men, it went to pieces under the fatal stroke of an unexpected circumstance. The act which abrogated the Missouri Compromise broke the much-enduring back of Northern patience at the same time. In the struggle for the repeal Southern Whigs and Southern Democrats forgot their traditionary party differences in battling for Southern interests, which was not more or less than the extension to the national Territories of the peculiar institution. The final recognition of this ugly fact on the part of the free States, raised a popular flood in them big enough to whelm the Whig party and to float a great political organization, devoted to uncompromising opposition to the farther extension of slavery. The sectionalism of slavery was at last met by the sectionalism of freedom. From that moment the old Union, with its slave compromises, was doomed. In the conflict then impending its dissolution was merely a matter of time, unless indeed the North should prove strong enough to preserve it by the might of its arms, seeing that the North still clung passionately to the idea of national unity.

Not so, however, was it with Garrison. Sharper and sterner rose his voice against any union with slaveholders. On the Fourth of July following the repeal of the Missouri Compromise, the reformer at Framingham, Mass., gave a fresh and startling sign of his hatred of the Union by burning publicly the Constitution of the United States. Before doing so however, he consigned to the flames a copy of the *Fugitive Slave Law*, next the decision of Judge Loring remanding Anthony Burns to slavery, also the charge of Judge Benjamin R. Curtis to the Grand Jury touching the assault upon the court-house for the rescue of Burns. Then holding up the United States Constitution, he branded it as the source and parent of all the other atrocities—a covenant with death and an agreement with hell—and consumed it to ashes on the spot, exclaiming, "So perish all compromises with tyranny! And let all the people say, Amen!" This dramatic act and the "tremendous shout" which "went up to heaven in ratification of the deed" from the assembled multitude, what were they but the prophecy of a fiercer fire already burning in the land, soon to blaze about the pillars of the

Union, of a more tremendous shout soon to burst with the wrath of a divided people over that

> "perfidious bark
> Built i' th' eclipse, and rigged with curses dark."

CHAPTER XIX.

FACE TO FACE.

FACE to face at last were freedom and slavery. The final struggle between them for mastery had come. Narrow, indeed, was the issue that divided the combatants, slavery extension on the one side, and slavery restriction on the other, not total and immediate emancipation, but it was none the less vital and supreme to the two enemies. Back of the Southern demand for "More slave soil" stood a solid South, back of the Northern position, "No more slave soil" was rallying a fast uniting North. The political revolution, produced by the Kansas-Nebraska Bill, advanced apace through the free States from Maine to Michigan. A flood-tide of Northern resistance had suddenly risen against the slave-power.

Higher than anywhere else rose this flood-tide in Massachusetts. The judge who remanded Anthony Burns to slavery was removed from office, and a Personal Liberty Law, with provisions as bold as they were thorough, enacted for the protection of fugitive slaves. Mr. Garrison sat beside the President of the State Senate when that body voted to remove Judge Loring from his office. Such was Massachusetts's answer to the abrogation of the Missouri Compromise, and a triumphant slave-power. Its instant effect was to accelerate in the South the action of the disunion working forces there, to hurry the inevitable moment when the two sections would rush together in a death-grapple within or without Webster's once glorious Union.

Indeed the foes had already closed in a frightful wrestle for the possession of Kansas. When the National Government adopted the popular sovereignty doctrine in solution of the Territorial problem between the two halves of the Union, freedom and slavery thereupon precipitated their forces upon the debatable land, and, for the first time, the men of the North and the men of the South came into actual physical collision in defence of their respective ideas and institutions. The possession of land is nine points of the law among Anglo-Saxons, and for this immense advantage both sides flung themselves into Kansas—the North by means of emigrant aid societies, the South by means of bands of Border ruffians under the direction of a United States Senator. It was distinctly understood and ordained in connection with the repeal of the compromise of 1820, that final possession of the Territories then thrown open to slave labor should be determined by the people inhabiting the same. In the contest for peopling Kansas the superior colonizing resources of the free States was presently made manifest. They, in any fair contest with ballots, had a majority of the polls, and were, therefore, able to vote slavery down. Worsted as the South clearly was in a show of heads, it threw itself back upon fraud and force to decide the issue in its favor. The cartridge-box took the place of the ballot-box in bleeding Kansas, and violence and anarchy, as a consequence, reigned therein for the space of several years.

This is no place to depict those scenes of slave-holding outrages, supported as they were by a Northern President with Southern principles. The sight of them rapidly changed the pacific character of the free States. Many a peace man dropped his peace principles before this bloody duel between the civilization of the South and that of the North. Ministers and churches took up collections to send, not Bibles, but Sharp's rifles to their brethren in Kansas. The South had appealed to the sword, and the North had sternly accepted the challenge. War was in the air, and the Northern temper, without there being any general consciousness of it, was fast mounting to the war point in the thermometer of the passions, thanks to the perfidy and ruffianism of the slave-power in Congress and Kansas.

This trend and strong undertow of the nation toward a civil outbreak and commotion, though unnoted by the multitude, was yet, nevertheless, seen and felt by many thoughtful and far-seeing minds; and by no one more clearly than by T. W. Higginson, who at the twentieth anniversary of the Boston mob, discoursed thus on this head: "Mr Phillips told us that on this day, twenty years ago, the military could not protect the meeting, because the guns were outside in the mob—or the men who should have carried them! There has been a time since when the men were on the outside and the guns too; and as surely as this earth turns on its axis, that time will come again! And it is for you, men, who hear me, to think what you will do when that time comes; and it is for you, women, who hear me, to think what you will do, and what you are willing—I will not say, to *consent* that those you love should do, but what you are willing to *urge* them to do, and to send them from your homes, knowing that they will do it, whether they live or die." The murderous assault upon Charles Sumner in the Senate Chamber at Washington by Preston S. Brooks, served to intensify the increasing belligerancy of the Northern temper, to deepen the spreading conviction that the irrepressible conflict would be settled not with the pen through any more fruitless compromises, but in Anglo-Saxon fashion by blood and iron.

Amid this general access of the fighting propensity, Garrison preserved the integrity of his non-resistant principles, his aversion to the use of physical force as an anti-slavery weapon. Men like Charles Stearns talked of shouldering their Sharp's rifles against the Border ruffians as they would against wild beasts. For himself, he could not class any of his fellow-creatures, however vicious and wicked, on the same level with wild beasts. Those wretches were, he granted, as bad and brutal as they were represented by the free State men of Kansas, but to him they were less blameworthy than were their employers and indorsers, the pro-slavery President and his Cabinet, pro-slavery Congressmen, and judges, and doctors of divinity, and editors. Incomparably guilty as these "colossal conspirators against the liberty, peace, happiness, and safety of the republic" were; and, though his moral indignation "against their treasonable course" burned like fire, he, nevertheless, wished them no harm. He shrank from the idea of the physical collision of man with a brother man, and with him all mankind were brothers. No one is able to draw a sword or point a rifle at any member of the human family, "in a Christian state of mind." He held to Jesus, who condemned violence, forbade the entertainment by his disciples of retaliatory feelings and the use of retaliatory weapons. When Jesus said "Love your enemies," he did not mean, "Kill them if they go too far."

Garrison's moral radicalism and political sagacity were never exhibited to better advantage than during these tremendous years of the crisis. He saw the sudden rise of a great political organization opposed to the farther extension of slavery to national territory. It was by no means a party after his heart, and for total and immediate emancipation, and the dissolution of the Union, yet he perceived that while this was true, it was, nevertheless, in its narrow purpose, battling against the slave-power, fighting the slave system, and to this extent was worthy of the commendation of Abolitionists. "It helps to disseminate no small amount of light and knowledge," the reformer acutely observed, "in regard to the nature and workings of the slave system, being necessitated to do this to maintain its position ; and thus, for the time being, it is moulding public sentiment in the right direction, though with no purpose to aid us in the specific work we are striving to accomplish, namely, the dissolution of the Union, and the abolition of slavery throughout the land." While bating no jot of his anti-slavery principles, he all the same put in practice the apostolic injunction to give credit to whom credit is due, by cordially commending what he found worthy of commendation in the purpose and policy of the Republican party, and by urging a like conduct upon his followers. In the Presidential canvass of 1856 his sympathies went strongly with Frémont as against Buchanan and Fillmore, although his Abolition principles precluded him from voting for the Republican candidate or from urging his disciples to vote for him. But, barring this moral barrier, had he "a million votes to bestow" he "would cast them all for Frémont . . . not because he is an Abolitionist or a Disunionist . . . but because he is for the non-extension of slavery, in common with the great body of the people of the North, whose attachment to the Union amounts to idolatry."

When the election was over the motto of the *Liberator* was still "No union with slaveholders," and would have remained the same though Frémont instead of Buchanan had triumphed at the polls, until indeed the domination of the slave-power had ended, and the North and the National Constitution had been divorced from all criminal connection with slavery. The anti-slavery agitation for the dissolution of the Union went on with increased zeal. A State convention, called by T. W. Higginson and others, "to consider the practicability, probability, and expediency of a separation between the free and slave States, and to take such other measures as the condition of the times may require," met at Worcester, Mass., January 15, 1857, with Frank W. Bird in the chair, and William Lloyd Garrison among the vice-presidents. The pioneer's speech on the occasion was a characteristic and noteworthy utterance. Its tone throughout was grave and argumentative. Here is a specimen of it, and of the way in which he met the most serious objection to the Abolition movement for disunion: "The air is filled with objections to a movement of this kind. I am neither surprised nor disquieted at this. One of these is of a very singular nature, and it is gravely urged that it is conclusive against disunion. It is to this effect: We must remain in the Union because it would be inhuman in us to turn our backs upon millions of slaves in the Southern States, and to leave them to their fate! Men who have never been heard of in the anti-slavery ranks, or who are ever submitting to a compromise of principle, have their bowels wonderfully moved all at once with sympathy for the suffering slave! Even our esteemed friend, Theodore Parker (who deals in no cant) says, in his letter, that he cannot consent to cut himself off from the slave population. Now, we who are engaged in this movement claim to be equally concerned for the liberation of the slave. If we have not yet proved our willingness to suffer the loss of all things, rather than turn and flee, God knows that we are prepared to bear any new cross that He, in His Providence, may be disposed to lay upon us. For one, I make no parade of my anxiety for the deliverance of those in bondage; but I do say that it strikes me as remarkable that those who, for a quarter of a century, have borne the heat and burden of the day, should have the imputation cast upon them of intending to leave four millions of slaves in their chains, by seeking the overthrow of this Union! . . .

" . . . I declare that this talk of leaving the slave to his fate is not a true representation of the case; and it indicates a strange dullness of comprehension with regard to our position and purpose. What! Is it to forsake the slave when I cease to be the aider and abettor of his master? What! When the North is pressing down upon four millions of slaves like an avalanche, and we say to her, 'Take off that pressure—stand aside—give the slave a chance to regain his feet and assert his freedom!' is that turning our backs upon him? Here, for example, is a man engaged in highway robbery, and another man is acting as an accessory, without whose aid the robber cannot succeed. In saying to the accomplice. 'Hands off! Don't aid the villain!' shall I be told that this is enabling the highwayman to rob with impunity? What an absurdity! Are we not trying to save the pockets of all travelers from being picked in seeking to break up all connection with highway robbery?"

The convention projected a general convention of the free States to consider the subject, and "*Resolved*, That the sooner the separation takes place, the more peaceful it will be; but that peace or war is *a secondary consideration* in view of our present perils. Slavery must be conquered, peaceably if we can, forcibly if we must." The projected general convention, owing to the monetary crisis of 1857, did not take place; but the extraordinary public excitement on the slavery question increased rather than diminished during the year. The increasing menace to the domination of the slave-power from this source had become so great that it was deemed prudent on the part of the upholders of that power to allay it by means of an authoritative utterance upon the vexed question of slavery in the national Territories from the highest judicial tribunal in the land. The Northern respect for the opinion of the Supreme Court, the South and her allies in the free States counted upon as the vehicle of the quieting medicament. For, if the Missouri Compromise were pronounced by that Court unconstitutional and, therefore, *ab initio*, null and void, no wrong was done the North through its formal repeal by Congress. The act of abrogation, in this view, added nothing to the South which did not belong to it as well before as after its passage, detracted nothing from the North which was justly its due in the premises. In pursuance of this cunningly devised scheme the Supreme Court delivered itself of an opinion in the famous "Dred Scott Case." So abhorrent it was to the intelligence and moral sense of the free States, that it produced results altogether opposed to those designed by the men who invoked it. Instead of checking, the execrated judgment augmented enormously the existing excitement. Garrison's bitter taunt that "the Union is but another name for the iron reign of the slave-power," was driven home to the North, by the Dred Scott decision, with the logic of another unanswerable fact. Confidence in the independence and impartiality of the Supreme Court was seriously shaken, and widespread suspicion struck root at the North touching the subserviency of that tribunal to the interests and designs of the slave-power.

The popular agitation at this fresh and alarming evidence of the purpose and power of the South upset the machinations of the schemers, swelled the numerical strength of the new Northern party opposed to the Territorial aggressions and pretensions of the slave section. So rapid was the growth of the Republican party that the slave leaders anticipated its accession to power at the then next Presidential election. So certain were they in their forebodings of defeat that they set about in dead earnest to put their side of the divided house in order for the impending struggle for Southern independence. Military preparations went forward with a vengeance, arms and munitions of war which were the property of the General Government began to move southward, to Southern military depots and posts for the defence of the United States South, when at last the word "DISUNION" should be pronounced over the Republic. The Lincoln-Douglass dèbate augmented everywhere the excitement, fed the already mighty numbers of the new party. More and more the public consciousness and conviction were squaring with Mr. Lincoln's oracular words in respect that the Union could not "endure permanently half slave and half free."

The darkness and tumult of the rising tempest were advancing apace, when suddenly there burst from the national firmanent the first warning peal of thunder, and over Virginia there sped the first bolt of the storm. John Brown with his brave little band, at Harper's Ferry, had struck for the freedom of the slave. Tired of words, the believer in blood and iron as a deliverer, had crossed from Pennsylvania into Virginia on the evening of October 16, 1859, and seized the United States Armory at Harper's Ferry. Although soon overpowered, captured, tried, and hanged for his pains by the slave-power, the martyr had builded better than he knew. For the blow struck by him then and there ended almost abruptly the period of argument and ushered in the period of arms. The jar from that battle-ax at the roots of the slave system hurled together in a death struggle right and wrong, freedom and slavery, in the republic.

This attempt on the part of John Brown to liberate the slaves seemed to Garrison "misguided, wild, and apparently insane, though disinterested and well-intended." On non-resistant grounds he deplored this use of the sword to effect emancipation, and condemned the leader. But, judging him according to the standard of Bunker Hill and the men of 1776, he did not doubt that Brown deserved "to be held in grateful and honorable remembrance to the latest posterity, by all those who glory in the deeds of a Wallace or Tell, a Washington or Warren."

The raid of Brown and his subsequent execution, and their reception at the North revealed how vast was the revolution in public sentiment on the slavery question which had taken place there, since the murder of Lovejoy, eighteen years before. Lovejoy died defending the right of free speech and the liberty of the press, yet the Attorney-General of Massachusetts declared that "he died as the fool dieth." Brown died in an invasion of a slave State, and in an effort to emancipate the slaves with a band of eighteen followers, and he was acclaimed, from one end of the free States to the other, hero and martyr. Mr. Garrison commenting on this immensely significant fact, acutely and justly observed that: "The sympathy and admiration now so widely felt for him, prove how marvelous has been the change affected in public opinion during the thirty years of moral agitation—a change so great indeed, that whereas, ten years since, there were thousands who could not endure my lightest word of rebuke of the South, they can now easily swallow John Brown whole and his rifle into the bargain. In firing his gun, he has merely told us what time of day it is. It is high noon, thank God!"

But there is another circumstance hardly less significant of another change at the North even more momentous than the one just noted.

On December 2d, the day on which Brown was hung, solemn funeral observances were held throughout the North by Abolitionists. At the great meeting in Boston, held in Tremont Temple, and presided over by Samuel E. Sewall, Garrison inquired as to the number of non-resistants who were present. To this question there came a solitary reply. There was but one non-resistant beside himself in the hall. Where were his followers? Why had they forsaken their principles? The tide of Northern belligerency, which was everywhere rising to its flood, everywhere rushing and mounting to the tops of those dams which separate war and peace had swept away his followers, had caused them to forsake their principles. True to their Anglo-Saxon instinct, they had reverted to the more human, if less Christian method of cutting the Gordian knot of the republic with the sword.

The irresistible drift of the North toward the point where peace ends and war begins, which that solitary "I" at the John Brown meeting denoted, was still further indicated by what appeared not wholly unlike a change in Mr. Garrison's attitude on the same subject His non-resistant position was the same, but somehow his face seemed to turn warward too, with the rest of the nation, in the following passage taken from his address at that John Brown meeting:

"Nevertheless, I am a non-resistant," said he, speaking to that solitary confession of non-resistance principles, "and I not only desire, but have labored unremittingly to effect the peaceful abolition of slavery, by an appeal to the reason and conscience of the slaveholder; yet, as a peace man, an ultra peace man, I am prepared to say: Success to every slave insurrection at the South, and in every slave country. And I do not see how I compromise or stain my peace profession in making that declaration. Whenever there is a contest between the oppressed and the oppressor, the weapons being equal between the parties, God knows that my heart must be with the oppressed, and always against the oppressor. Therefore, whenever commenced, I cannot but wish success to all slave insurrections. . . . Rather than see men wearing their chains, in a cowardly and servile spirit, I would as an advocate of peace, much rather see them breaking the head of the tyrant with their chains. Give me, as a non-resistant, Bunker Hill, and Lexington, and Concord, rather than the cowardice and servility of a Southern slave plantation."

The unmistakable signs of disintegration, the swift action of the national tragedy, the Charleston Convention, the disruption of the Democratic party, the last bond between the North and the South, filled the heart of the pioneer with solemn joy. "Only think of it!" he exulted at the anniversary of the American Anti-Slavery Society in New York, May 8, 1860; "only think of it! the party which has for so many years cried out, 'There must be no agitation on this subject' is now the most agitated of all the parties in the country. The party which declares that there ought not to be any sectionalism as against slavery, has now been sundered geographically, and on this very question! The party which had said, 'Let discussions cease forever,' is busily engaged in the discussion, so that, possibly, the American Anti-Slavery Society might adjourn *sine die*, after we get through with our present meetings, and leave its work to be carried on in the other direction!" This was all true enough. The sections were at last sundered, and a day of wrath was rising dark and dreadful over "States dissevered, discordant, belligerent."

CHAPTER XX.

THE DEATH-GRAPPLE.

THE triumph of the Republican party at the polls was the signal for the work of dissolution to begin. Webster's terrific vision of "a land rent with civil feuds" became reality in the short space of six weeks after Lincoln's election, by the secession of South Carolina from the Union. Quickly other Southern States followed, until a United States South was organized, the chief stone in the corner of the new political edifice being Negro slavery. It was not six weeks after the inauguration of Abraham Lincoln, when the roar of cannon in Charleston Harbor announced to the startled country that war between the States had begun. The first call of the new President for troops to put down the rebellion and to save the Union, and the patriotic uprising which it evoked made it plain that the struggle thus opened was to be nothing less than a death-grapple between the two sections.

Before the attack on Fort Sumter, Garrison was opposed to coercing the rebel States back into the Union. He admitted the Constitutional power of the National Government to employ force in maintaining the integrity of the Republic. "The Federal Government must not pretend to be in actual operation, embracing thirty-four States," the editor of the

Liberator commented, "and then allow the seceding States to trample upon its flag, steal its property, and defy its authority with impunity; for it would then be (as it is at this moment) a mockery and a laughing-stock. Nevertheless to think of whipping the South (for she will be a unit on the question of slavery) into subjection, and extorting allegiance from millions of people at the cannon's mouth, is utterly chimerical. True, it is in the power of the North to deluge her soil with blood, and inflict upon her the most terrible sufferings; but not to conquer her spirit, or change her determination."

He, therefore, proposed that "the people of the North should recognize the fact that THE UNION IS DISSOLVED, and act accordingly. They should see, in the madness of the South, the hand of God, liberating them from 'a covenant with death' and an 'agreement with hell,' made in a time of terrible peril, and without a conception of its inevitable consequences, and which has corrupted their morals, poisoned their religion, petrified their humanity as towards the millions in bondage, tarnished their character, harassed their peace, burdened them with taxation, shackled their prosperity, and brought them into abject vassalage."

It is not to be wondered at that Garrison, under the circumstances, was for speeding the South rather than obstructing her way out of the Union. For hardly ever had the anti-slavery cause seen greater peril than that which hung over it during the months which elapsed between Lincoln's election and the attack on Sumter, owing to the paralyzing apprehensions to which the free States fell a prey in view of the then impending disruption of their glorious Union. Indeed no sacrifice of anti-slavery accomplishments, policy, and purpose of those States were esteemed too important or sacred to make, if thereby the dissolution of the Union might be averted. Many, Republicans as well as Democrats, were for repealing the Personal Liberty Laws, and for the admission of New Mexico as a State, with or without slavery, for the enforcement of the Fugitive Slave Law, for suppressing the right of free speech and the freedom of the press on the subject of slavery, and for surrendering the Northern position in opposition to the extension of slavery to national Territories, in order to placate the South and keep it in the Union. Nothing could have possibly been more disastrous to the anti-slavery movement in America than a Union saved on the terms proposed by such Republican leaders as Willian H. Seward, Charles Francis Adams, Thomas Corwin, and Andrew G. Curtin. The Union, under the circumstances, was sure death to the slave, in disunion lay his great life-giving hope. Therefore his tried and sagacious friend was for sacrificing the Union to win for him freedom.

As the friends of the Union were disposed to haggle at no price to preserve it, so was Garrison disposed to barter the Union itself in exchange for the abolition of slavery. "Now, then, let there be a CONVENTION OF THE FREE STATES," he suggested, "called to organize an independent government on free and just principles; and let them say to the slave States: Though you are without excuse for your treasonable conduct, depart in peace! Though you have laid piratical hands on property not your own, we surrender it all in the spirit of magnanimity! And if nothing but the possession of the Capitol will appease you, take even that without a struggle! Let the line be drawn between us where free institutions end and slave institutions begin!"

But the thunder of the rebel guns in Charleston Harbor wrought in the reformer a complete revolution in this regard. In the tremendous popular uprising which followed that insult to the national flag he perceived that the old order with its compromises and dispositions to agree to anything, to do anything for the sake of preserving the Union had passed away forever. When it was suggested as an objection to his change of base that the "Administration is endeavoring to uphold the Union, the Constitution, and the Laws, even as from the formation of the Government," he was not for a moment deceived by its apparent force, but replied sagely that "this is a verbal and technical view of the case." "Facts are more potential than words," he remarked with philosophic composure, "and events greater than parchment arrangements. The truth is, the old Union is *non est inventus*, and its restoration, with its pro-slavery compromises, well-nigh impossible. The conflict is really between the civilization of freedom and the barbarism of slavery—between the principles of democracy and the doctrines of absolutism—between the free North and the man-imbruting South; therefore, to this extent hopeful for the cause of impartial liberty."

With the instinct of wise leadership, he adjusted himself and his little band of Abolitionists, as far as he was able, to the exigencies of the revolution. In his madness there was always remarkable method. When the nation was apathetic, dead on the subject of slavery, he used every power which he possessed or could invent to galvanize it into life. But with the prodigious excitement which swept over the free States at the outbreak of the war, Garrison saw that the crisis demanded different treatment. Abolitionists and their moral machinery he felt should be withdrawn, for a season at least, from their conspicuous place before the public gaze, lest it happen that they should divert the current of public opinion from the South to themselves, and thus injure the cause of the slave. He accordingly deemed it highly expedient that the usual anniversary of the American Anti-Slavery Society, held in New York, ought, under the circumstances, to be postponed, coming as it would but a few weeks after the attack on Sumter, and in the midst of the tremendous loyal uprising against the rebels. This he did, adding, by way of caution, this timely counsel: "Let nothing be done at this solemn crisis needlessly to check or divert the mighty current of popular feeling which is now sweeping southward with the strength and impetuosity of a thousand Niagaras, in direct conflict with that haughty and perfidious slave-power which has so long ruled the republic with a rod of iron, for its own base and satanic purposes."

The singular tact and sagacity of the pioneer in this emergency may be again seen in a letter to Oliver Johnson, who was at the time editing the *Anti-Slavery Standard*. Says the pioneer: "Now that civil war has begun, and a whirlwind of violence and excitement is to sweep through the country, every day increasing in interest until its bloodiest culmination, it is for the Abolitionists to 'stand still and see the salvation of God,' rather than to attempt to add anything to the general commotion. It is no time for minute criticism of Lincoln, Republicanism, or even the other parties, now that they are fusing, for a death-grapple with the Southern slave oligarchy; for they are instruments in the hands of God to carry forward and help achieve the great object of emancipation for which we have so long been striving. . . We need great circumspection and consummate wisdom in regard to what we may say and do under these unparalleled circumstances. We are rather, for the time being, to note the events transpiring than seek to control them. There must be no needless turning of popular violence upon ourselves by any false step of our own."

The circumspection, the tact, and sagacity which marked his conduct at the beginning of the rebellion characterized it to the close of the war, albeit at no time doing or saying aught to compromise his anti-slavery principle of total and immediate emancipation. On the contrary, he urged, early and late, upon Congress and the President the exercise of the war power to put an end for ever to slavery. Radical Abolitionists like Stephen S. Foster were for denying to the Administration anti-slavery support and countenance, and for continuing to heap upon the Government their denunciations until it placed itself "openly and unequivocally on the side of freedom," by issuing the edict of emancipation. Against this zeal without discretion Garrison warmly protested. "I cannot say that I do not sympathize with the Government," said he, "as against Jefferson Davis and his piratical associates. There is not a drop of blood in my veins, both as an Abolitionist and a peace man, that does not flow with the Northern tide of sentiment; for I see, in this grand uprising of the manhood of the North, which has been so long groveling in the dust, a growing appreciation of the value of liberty and free institutions, and a willingness to make any sacrifice in their defence against the barbaric and tyrannical power which avows its purpose, if it can, to crush them entirely out of existence. When the Government shall succeed (if it shall succeed) in conquering a peace, in subjugating the South, and shall undertake to carry out the Constitution as of old, with all its pro-slavery compromises, then will be my time to criticise, reprove, and condemn; then will be the time for me to open all the guns that I can bring to bear upon it. But blessed be God that 'covenant with death' has been annulled, and that 'agreement with hell' no longer stands. I joyfully accept the fact, and leave all verbal criticism until a more suitable opportunity."

But it must be confessed that at times during the struggle, Lincoln's timidity and apparent indifference as to the fate of slavery, in his anxiety to save the Union, weakened Garrison's confidence in him, and excited his keenest apprehensions "at the possibility of the war terminating without the utter extinction of slavery, by a new and more atrocious compromise on the part of the North than any that has yet been made." The pioneer therefore adjudged it prudent to get his battery into position and to visit upon the President for particular acts, such as the revocation of anti-slavery orders by sundry of his generals in the field, and upon particular members of his Cabinet who were understood to be responsible for the shuffling, hesitating action of the Government in its relation to slavery, an effective fire of criticism and rebuke.

Nevertheless Mr. Garrison maintained toward the Government a uniform tone of sympathy and moderation. "I hold," said he, in reply to strictures of Mr. Phillips upon the President at the annual meeting of the Massachusetts Society in 1862; "I hold that it is not wise for us to be too microscopic in endeavoring to find disagreeable and annoying things, still less to assume that everything is waxing worse and worse, and that there is little or no hope." He himself was full of hope which no shortcomings of the Government was able to quench. He was besides beginning to understand the perplexities which beset the administration, to appreciate the problem which confronted the great statesman who was at the head of the nation. He was getting a clear insight into the workings of Lincoln's mind, and into the causes which gave to his political pilotage an air of timidity and indecision.

"Supposing Mr. Lincoln could answer to-night," continued the pioneer in reply to his less patient and hopeful coadjutors, "and we should say to him: 'Sir, with the power in your hands, slavery being the cause of the rebellion beyond all controversy, why don't you put the trump of jubilee to your lips, and proclaim universal freedom?'—possibly he might answer: 'Gentlemen, I understand this matter quite as well as you do. I do not know that I differ in opinion from you; but will you insure me the support of a united North if I do as you bid me? Are all parties and all sects at the North so convinced and so united on this point that they will stand by the Government? If so, give me the evidence of it, and I will strike the blow. But, gentlemen, looking over the entire North, and seeing in all your towns and cities papers representing a considerable, if not a formidable portion of the people, menacing and bullying the Government in case it dared to liberate the slaves, even as a matter of self-preservation, I do not feel that the hour has yet come that will render it safe for the Government to take that step.' I am willing to believe that something of this kind weighs in the mind of the President and the Cabinet, and that there is some ground for hesitancy as a mere matter of political expediency." This admirable and discriminating support of the President finds another capital illustration in weighty words of his in answer to animadversions of Prof. Francis W. Newman, of England, directed against Mr. Lincoln. Says Garrison: "In no instance, however, have I censured him (Lincoln) for not acting upon the highest abstract principles of justice and humanity, and disregarding his Constitutional obligations. His freedom to follow his convictions of duty as an individual is one thing—as the President of the United States, it is limited by the functions of his office, for the people do not elect a President to play the part of reformer or philanthropist, nor to enforce upon the nation his own peculiar ethical or humanitary ideas without regard to his oath or their will."

Great indeed was the joy of the pioneer when President Lincoln on January 1, 1863, issued his Emancipation Proclamation. The same sagacious and statesmanlike handling of men and things distinguished his conduct after the edict of freedom was made as before. When the question of Reconstruction was broached in an administrative initiative in Louisiana, the President gave great offence to the more radical members of his party, and to many Abolitionists by his proposal to readmit Louisiana to Statehood in the Union with no provision for the extension of the suffrage to the negro. This exhibition of the habitual caution and conservatism of Mr. Lincoln brought upon him a storm of criticism and remonstrances, but not from Garrison. There was that in him which appreciated and approved the evident disposition of the President to make haste slowly in departing from the American principle of local self-government even in the interest of liberty. Then, too, he had his misgivings in relation to the virtue of the fiat method of transforming chattels into citizens. "Chattels personal may be instantly translated from the auction-block into freemen," he remarked in defence of the administrative policy in the reconstruction of Louisiana, "but when were they ever taken at the same time to the ballot-box, and invested with all political rights and immunities? According to the laws of development and progress it is not practicable. . . . Besides, I doubt whether he has the Constitutional right to decide this matter. Ever since the Government was organized, the right of suffrage has been determined by each State in the Union for itself, so that there is no uniformity in regard to it. . . . In honestly seeking to preserve the Union, it is not for President Lincoln to seek, by a special edict applied to a particular State or locality, to do violence to a universal rule, accepted and acted upon from the beginning till now by the States in their individual sovereignty. . . . Nor, if the freed blacks were admitted to the polls by Presidential fiat do I see any permanent advantage likely to be secured by it; for, submitted to as a necessity at the outset, as soon as the State was organized and left to manage its own affairs, the white population with their superior intelligence, wealth, and power, would unquestionably alter the franchise in accordance with their prejudices, and exclude those thus summarily brought to the polls. Coercion would gain nothing." A very remarkable prophecy, which has since been exactly fulfilled in the Southern States. Garrison, however, in the subsequent struggle between Congress and Mr. Lincoln's successor over this selfsame point in its wider relation to all of the Southern States, took sides against Andrew Johnson and in favor of the Congressional fiat method of transforming chattels personal into citizens. The elimination of Abraham Lincoln from, and the introduction of Andrew Johnson upon the National stage at this juncture, did undoubtedly effect such a change of circumstances, as to make the Congressional fiat method a political necessity. It was distinctly the less of two evils which at the moment was thrust upon the choice of the Northern people.

The same breadth and liberality of view, which marked his treatment of Mr. Lincoln upon the subject of emancipation and of that of reconstruction, marked his treatment also of other questions which the suppression of the rebellion presented to his consideration. Although a radical peace man, how just was his attitude toward the men and the measures of the War for the Union. Nothing that he did evinced on his part greater tact or toleration than his admirable behavior iu this respect. To his eldest son, George Thompson, who was no adherent of the doctrine of non-resistance, and who was commissioned by Governor Andrew, a second lieutenant in the Fifty-fifth Massachusetts Regiment, the pioneer wrote expressing his regret that the young lieutenant had not been able "to adopt those principles of peace which are so sacred and divine to my soul, yet you will bear me witness that I have not laid a straw in your way to prevent your acting up to your own highest convictions of duty." Such was precisely his attitude toward the North who, he believed, in waging war against the South for the maintenance of the Union, was acting up to her own highest convictions of duty. And not a straw would he place across her path, under those circumstances, though every step bore witness to one of the most gigantic and destructive wars in history.

Garrison did not have to wait for posthumous appreciation from his countrymen. His steady and discriminating support of the Government, and his ardent sympathy with the arms of the North won him appreciation in his lifetime. Indeed, there came to him, if not popularity, something closely akin to it during the war. His visit to the capital in June, 1864, well illustrates the marvelous changes which had taken place in the Union touching himself and his cause. On his way to Washington the pioneer stopped over at Baltimore, which he had not revisited for thirty-four years, and where the Republican Convention, which renominated Lincoln was in session. He watched the proceedings from the gallery, and witnessed with indescribable emotions the enthusiastic demonstrations of joy with which the whole body of delegates greeted the radical anti-slavery resolution of the Convention. To the reformer it was "a full indorsement of all the Abolition fanaticism and incendiarism" with which he had been branded for years. The jail where he had been held a prisoner for seven weeks, like the evil which he had denounced, was gone, and a new one stood in its place, which knew not Garrison. In the court-house where he was tried and sentenced he was received by a United States judge as an illustrious visitor. Judge Bond hunted up the old indictment against the junior editor of the *Genius of Universal Emancipation*, where it had lain for a generation, during which that guiltless prisoner had started a movement which had shaken the nation by its mighty power, and slavery out of it. "Eight or nine of the original jurymen who gave the verdict against Mr. Garrison are still living," wrote Theodore Tilton, at the time, to the *Independent*, "and Judge Bond jocosely threatened to summon them all into Court, that Mr. Garrison might forgive them in public."

At Washington the pioneer's reception seemed to him like a dream. And no wonder. He was heartily received by President Lincoln and Secretary Stanton. He was accorded the most marked attentions on the floor of both branches of Congress. On every side there rose up witnesses to the vastness of the revolution which had taken place, and to the fact that the great Abolitionist was no longer esteemed an enemy of the Republic but one of its illustrious citizens. This was evinced in a signal and memorable manner a little later when the National Government extended to him an invitation to visit Fort Sumter as its guest on the occasion of the re-raising over it of the Stars and Stripes. He went, and so also went George Thompson, his lifelong friend and coadjutor, who was the recipient of a similar invitation from the Secretary of War.

This visit of Mr. Garrison, taken in all its dramatic features, is more like a chapter of fiction, with its strange and improbable incidents and situations, than a story of real life. The pioneer entered Georgia and trod the streets of Savannah, whose legislature thirty-three years before had set a price upon his head. In Charleston he witnessed the vast ruin which the war had wrought, realized how tremendous had been the death-struggle between Freedom and Slavery, and saw everywhere he turned that slavery was beaten, was dead in its proud, rebellious center. Thousands upon thousands of the people whose wrongs he had made his own, whose woes he had carried in his soul for thirty-five years, greeted him, their deliverer, in all stages of joy and thanksgiving. They poured out at his feet their overflowing love and gratitude. They covered him with flowers, bunches of jessamines, and honeysuckles and roses in the streets of Charleston, hard by the grave where Calhoun lay buried. "'Only listen to that in Charleston streets!' exclaimed Garrison, on hearing the band of one of the black regiments playing the air of 'Old

John Brown, and we both broke into tears," relates Rev. Theodore L. Cuyler, who stood by the side of the pioneer that April morning under the spire of St. Michael's church.

"The Government has its hold upon the throat of the monster, slavery," Mr. Garrison assured an audience of nearly four thousand freedmen, "and is strangling the life out of it." It was even so. Richmond had fallen, and Lee had surrendered. The early and total collapse of the rebellion was impending. The Government was, indeed, strangling the life out of it and out of slavery, its cause and mainspring. The monster had, however, a crowning horror to add to a long list of horrors before fetching its last gasp. The assassination of President Lincoln was the dying blow of slavery, aimed through him at the Union which he had maintained. Appalling as was the deed, it was vain, for the Union was saved, and liberty forever secured to the new-born nation. As Garrison remarked at the tomb of Calhoun, on the morning that Lincoln died, "Down into a deeper grave than this slavery has gone, and for it there is no resurrection."

CHAPTER XXI

THE LAST.

"GARRISON," said George Thompson on the steamer which was conveying the Government party out of Charleston Harbor on their return trip; "Garrison you began your warfare at the North in the face of rotten eggs and brickbats. Behold you end it at Charleston on a bed of roses!" The period of persecution had indeed ended, the reign of missiles had ceased, but with the roses there came to the pioneer not a few thorns. Bitter was the sorrow which visited him in the winter of 1863. Without warning his wife was on the night of December 29th, stricken with paralysis, which crippled her for the rest of her life. No words can adequately express all that she had been to the reformer in his struggle with slavery. She was a providential woman raised up to be the wife and helpmate of her husband, the strenuous man of God. "As a wife for a period of more than twenty-six years," he wrote her on the completion of her fiftieth year, "you have left nothing undone to smooth the rugged pathway of my public career—to render home the all-powerful magnet of attraction, and the focal point of domestic enjoyment—to make my welfare and happiness at all times a matter of tender solicitude—and to demonstrate the depth and fixedness of that love which you so long ago plighted to me. . . . Whatever of human infirmity we may have seen in each other, I believe few have enjoyed more unalloyed bliss in wedded life than ourselves." For twelve years after that sad December night the lovely invalid was the object of her husband's most tender and assiduous care. And when at last she left him in January, 1876, the loneliness which fell upon his heart seemed more than he could bear.

Differences with old associates was a grievous thorn which came to the pioneer during the progress of the war. The first marked disagreement between him and them occurred at the annual meeting of the Massachusetts Anti-Slavery Society not a month after his wife's prostration. The clash came between the leader and his great coadjutor Wendell Phillips over a resolution introduced by the latter, condemning the Government and declaring its readiness "to sacrifice the interest and honor of the North to secure a sham peace." Garrison objected to the severity of this charge. He believed that there was but one party at the North of which it was true, and that was the party of Copperheads. He endeavored, therefore, to modify the harshness of the resolution by giving it a more moderate tone. But the anti-Lincoln feeling of the Convention proved too strong for his resistance, and Mr. Phillips's resolution was finally adopted as the sentiment of the society.

The discordant note thus struck grew sharper and louder during the year. The divergence of views in the ranks of the Abolitionists touching the Southern policy of the Administration grew wider, until the subject of Mr. Lincoln's renomination sundered the little band into two wings—one for renomination, headed by Garrison, the other against renomination, and led by Phillips. These differences presently developed into, if not positive antagonism, then something closely akin to it between the two wings and the two leaders. No little heat was generated from the strong, sharp things said on both sides. Garrison was wiser than Phillips in his unwillingness to have the country, in the homely speech of the President, "swap horses while crossing a stream."

Serious differences of opinion sprang up also between the two leaders and the two wings in relation to the proper time for dissolving the anti-slavery organizations. Garrison held on one side that this time had come with the adoption of the thirteenth amendment abolishing slavery, while Phillips held on the other that the societies should continue their operations until the negro was invested with the right to vote. And here it seems that Phillips was wiser than Garrison in his purpose not to abandon in 1865 the old machinery for influencing public sentiment in the negro's interest.

At the anniversary of the American Anti-Slavery Society, in May, 1865, Garrison contended for its dissolution, declaring that "Nothing is more clear in my own mind, nothing has ever been more clear, than that this is the fitting time to dissolve our organization, and to mingle with the millions of our fellow-countrymen in one common effort to establish justice and liberty throughout the land." For two days the debate upon this question raged in the convention, but when the vote was taken it was found that a large majority of the delegates agreed with Mr. Phillips.

Mr. Garrison was, nevertheless, reëlected President, but declined and withdrew from the society. The controversy was renewed at the annual meeting of the Massachusetts Anti-Slavery Society in January, 1866. But here again a large majority voted against dissolution. Warm words fell from both Garrison and Phillips and their respective supporters, which tried sorely the friendship of the two leaders.

In accordance with his views touching the discontinuance of the anti-slavery societies, Garrison discontinued the publication of the *Liberator* after the completion of its thirty-fifth volume in December, 1865. He did not mean by this act to cease his labors for the negro. Far from it. For he, like Phillips, stood for his absolute equality before the law. But he perceived that old things had passed away, and with them the need of the old instruments, and that what remained to be done for the black man required to be done with new means. "The object," said he in his valedictory, "for which the *Liberator* was commenced, the extermination of chattel slavery, having been gloriously consummated, it seems to me specially appropriate to let its existence cover the historic period of the great struggle; leaving what remains to be done to complete the work of emancipation to other instrumentalites (of which I hope to avail myself), under new auspices, with more abundant means, and with millions instead of hundreds for allies."

With the discontinuance of the *Liberator* Garrison's occupation, from which he had derived a regular though somewhat uncertain income for the support of his family, was gone. He was not in destitute circumstances, however, thanks to the generosity of friends, who had already secured him the home in Roxbury, where he spent the remaining years of his life. He had also been one of the legatees under the will of Charles F. Hovey, who left about forty thousand dollars to the anti-slavery cause. But the age of the reformer, he was then sixty, and the state of his health, which was much impaired, together with the helplessness of his wife, made some provision for his and her support, other than the little which he possessed, a matter of anxious thought on the part of himself and his friends. He had given thirty-five years of his life to the public good. His services to his country and to the world were above all price, all money considerations. It was felt that to him who had given so much to the world, the world should in his need make some substantial acknowledgement in return.

Some of his countrymen, accordingly, conceived the plan of a national testimonial to the philanthropist, which should ensure to him during the rest of his life a competence.

A committee having this end in view was organized March 28, 1866, at the house of Dr. Henry I. Bowditch. John A. Andrew, who was its chairman, wrote the address to the public, to which were appended the chief names in the politics and literature of the land. Nearly two years afterward, on March 10, 1868, the committee were able to place in Mr. Garrison's hands the handsome sum of thirty-one thousand dollars with a promise of possibly one or two thousand more a little later. To the energy and devotedness of one man, the Rev. Samuel May, Jr., more than to any other, and perhaps than all others put together, this noble achievement was due. The pioneer was deeply moved at the high and generous character of the recognition accorded his labors. "Little, indeed, did I know or anticipate how prolonged or how virulent would be the struggle," said he in his reply to the committee, "when I lifted up the standard of immediate emancipation, and essayed to rouse the nation to a sense of its guilt and danger. But having put my hands to the plow, how could I look back? For, in a cause so righteous, I could not doubt that, having turned the furrows, if I sowed in tears I should one day reap in joy. But, whether permitted to live to witness the abolition of slavery or not, I felt assured that, as I demanded nothing that was not clearly in accordance with justice and humanity, sometime or other, if remembered at all, I should stand vindicated in the eyes of my countrymen." The names of John Bright, John Stuart Mill, William E. Foster, and Samuel Morley, among the contributors to the fund, lent to the testimonial an international character.

In May, 1867, Garrison went abroad the fourth time, and traveled in Great Britain and on the Continent. Everywhere that he went he was received as an illustrious visitor and as a benefactor of mankind. At a breakfast in London which "was intended to commemorate one of the greatest of the great triumphs of freedom, and to do honor to a most eminent instrument in the achievement of that freedom," and at which were gathered the genius, the wealth, and aristocracy of England and Scotland, John Bright, who presided, welcomed the illustrious guest "with a cordiality which knows no stint and no limit for him and for his noble associates, both men and women," and ventured to speak a verdict which he believed would be sanctioned by all mankind, viz., that "William Lloyd Garrison and his fellow-laborers in that world's work—are they not

"On Fame's eternal bead-roll worthy to be filed?"

With the discontinuance of the *Liberator* Garrison's active career came to a close. But his sympathetic interest in the freedmen, temperance, the cause of women, and in other reformatory enterprises continued unabated. He watched with stern and vigilant eye, and bleeding heart the new rebellion at the South whose purpose was the nullification of the civil and political rights of the blacks, and the overthrow of the military rule of the National Government in the Southern States. He did not see what time has since made clear that a genuine reconstruction of the South, and the ultimate solution of the Southern problem had, in accordance with social laws, to proceed from within, from the South itself, not from without and from Washington. The old fire again burned in his speech as tidings of the violence of the whites and the sufferings of the blacks reached him from the former slave section. Indeed, the last written words of his, addressed to the public, were words in defence of the race to whose freedom he had devoted his life—words which, trumpet-tongued raised anew the rallying-cry of "Liberty and equal rights for each, for all, and for ever, wherever the lot of man is cast within our broad domains!"

True to his grand motto "My country is the world! my countrymen are all mankind," he espoused the cause of the Chinese, and denounced the National policy of excluding them on the ground of race from the republic but a few months before his death. The anti-Chinese movement appeared to him "narrow, conceited, selfish, anti-human, anti-Christian." "Against this hateful spirit of caste," wrote the dying philanthropist, "I have earnestly protested for the last fifty years, wherever it has developed itself, especially in the case of another class, for many generations still more contemned, degraded, and oppressed; and the time has fully come to deal with it as an offence to God, and a curse to the world wherever it seeks to bear sway."

On the same grand principle of human fraternity Mr. Garrison dealt with the questions of trade and tariffs also. He believed in liberty, civil, religious, and commercial. He was in fact a radical free trader on moral and humanitary grounds. "He is the most sagacious political economist," was a remark of his, "who contends for the highest justice, the most far-reaching equality, a close adherence to natural laws, and the removal of all those restrictions which foster national pride and selfishness." And here is another like unto it: "Believing that the interests of the American people in no wise materially differ from those of the people of any other country, and denying the rectitude or feasibility of building ourselves up at their expense by an exclusive policy, obstructing the natural flow of material exchanges, I avow myself to be a radical free trader, even to the extent of desiring the abolition of all custom-houses, as now constituted, throughout the world. That event is far distant, undoubtedly, but I believe it will come with the freedom and enlightenment of mankind. My faith is absolute that it will prove advantageous to every branch of industry, whether at home or abroad."

The closing years of the reformer's life were years of great bodily suffering. A disease of the kidneys and a chronic catarrh of the head made steady inroads upon the resources of his constitution, made life at times a wheel on which he was racked with physical tortures, all of which he bore with the utmost fortitude and serenity of spirit. "The longer I live, the longer I desire to live," he wrote Samuel J. May, "and the more I see the desirableness of living; yet certainly not in this frail body, but just as it shall please the dear Father of us all." One by one he saw the little band of which he was leader dwindle as now one and now another dropped by the way. And it was he or Mr. Phillips, or both, who spoke the last loving words over their coffins. As the little band passed on to the unseen country, a new joy awoke in the soul of the leader left behind, the joy of anticipation, of glad reunion beyond the grave. "How unspeakably pleasant it will be to greet them, and to be greeted by them on the other side of the line," it seemed to him as he, too, began to descend toward the shore of the swift, silent river. The deep, sweet love for his mother returned with youthful freshness and force to him, the man of seventy-three years, at the thought of coming again into her presence. A strange yearning was tugging at his heart for all the dear ones gone before. The fond mother, who had watched over his childhood, and the fond wife, who had been the stay of his manhood, were the first two whom he yearned to meet after crossing the river

The joyous thought of his approaching meeting with those white-souled women cheered and comforted the reformer amid excruciating physical sufferings. Worn out by heroic and Herculean labors for mankind and by a complication of diseases, he more and more longed for rest, to go home to beloved ones as he expressed it. To the question, "What do you want, Mr. Garrison?" asked by the attending physician on the day before his death, he replied, weariedly, "To finish it up!" And this he did at the home of his daughter, Mrs. Henry Villard, in New York, in the midst of children and grandchildren, near midnight, on May 24, 1879.

"While that ear could listen," said Wendell Phillips over the illustrious champion of liberty as he lay dead in the old church in Roxbury; "While that ear could listen, God gave what he has rarely given to man, the plaudits and prayers of four millions of victims." But as he lay there he had, besides, the plaudits and praise of an emancipated nation. The plaudits and praise of an emancipated race, mingling melodiously with those of an emancipated nation made noble music about his bier. In the city, where forty-three years before he was mobbed, the flags floated at half-mast in his honor; and on Beacon Hill, where the Government once desired his destruction, the voice of appreciation was heard and tokens of the State's sorrow met the eye. Great in life great also in death was William Lloyd Garrison.

"Men of a thousand shifts and wiles, look here!
See one straightforward conscience put in pawn
To win a world; see the obedient sphere
By bravery's simple gravitation drawn!

Shall we not heed the lesson taught of old,
And by the present's lips repeated still,
In our own single manhood to be bold,
Fortressed in conscience and impregnable will?"

INDEX.